W9-CFY-980

The American Wine Cookbook

TED
HATCH

DOVER PUBLICATIONS, INC.
NEW YORK

Published in Canada by General Publishing Company, Ltd., 30 Lesmill Road, Don Mills, Toronto, Ontario.

Published in the United Kingdom by Constable and Company, Ltd., 10 Orange Street, London WC 2.

This Dover edition, first published in 1971, is an unabridged and unaltered republication of the work originally published by G. P. Putnam's Sons in 1941.

International Standard Book Number: 0-486-22796-0
Library of Congress Catalog Card Number: 76-166428

Manufactured in the United States of America
Dover Publications, Inc.
180 Varick Street
New York, N.Y. 10014

CONTENTS

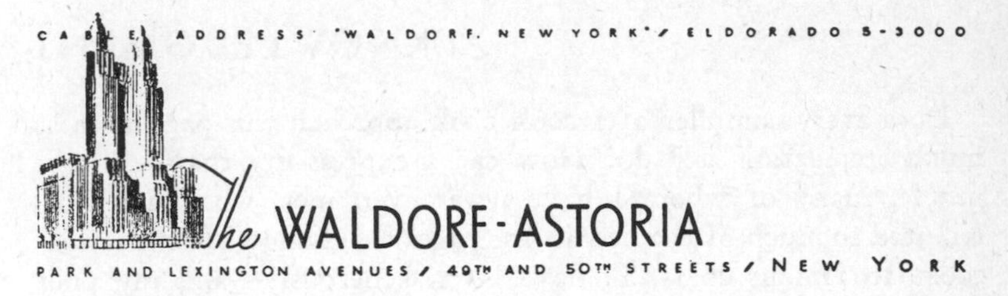

CABLE ADDRESS 'WALDORF. NEW YORK' / ELDORADO 5-3000
The WALDORF-ASTORIA
PARK AND LEXINGTON AVENUES / 49TH AND 50TH STREETS / NEW YORK

Oscar's Office

I have come to divide all cook books into two classes - those which enable you to cook well and those which enable you to cook better. Members of the first class are legion, those of the second class are rare indeed.

"The American Wine Cook Book" is more than a collection of wine recipes, although that alone would more than justify its existence. The author has ambitiously attempted to tell the home cook how to put the professional touch of the cordon bleu into her everyday cookery with no more than average equipment and with easily obtainable materials, and, in my opinion, has made a memorable success of the job.

His use of American wines exclusively is, of course, timely. But professional chefs had come to realize their quality even before Prohibition. In the kitchens of the most famous establishments, they are today used almost exclusively.

Here is an outstanding book.

Oscar of the Waldorf

New York, N.Y.
October, 1941

ACKNOWLEDGMENT

Does every compiler of a cook book approach this page with as much trepidation as I do? How can I express my thanks to the people, many of whom I have never even met, who have contributed so much of the best in the pages that follow! From family cooks to famous chefs, all have given generously—and my poor best is a collective but tremendously sincere "thank you."

Special credit must be given to the following organizations: American Spice Trade Association, New York City; The Angostura-Wupperman Corporation, New York City; Beaulieu Vineyard, Rutherford, California; Brothers of the Christian Schools, Napa, California; B. Cribari & Sons, Madrone, California; Fishery Council, New York City; Gambarelli & Davitto (Italian-Swiss Colony), New York City; Park & Tilford Import Corporation (W. R. Keevers), New York City; The Smithfield Ham Products Company, Smithfield, Virginia; the U. S. Department of Agriculture, Bureau of Home Economics, and the U. S. Department of the Interior, Fish and Wild Life Service, Washington, D. C.; Vischer Products Company, Chicago, Illinois; The Waring Corporation, New York City; Widmer's Wine Cellar, Inc., Naples, New York; the Wine Institute and the Wine Advisory Board, San Francisco, California. Glassware shown herein was supplied by Saks, Fifth Avenue and The Waldorf-Astoria.

The Taylor Wine Company of Hammondsport, New York, deserves special mention. At the commencement of this book Mr. Greyton Taylor offered me the full facilities of his organization, and he meant it. Frances M. Page, head of their wine-testing kitchens, has co-operated untiringly, and many of the following recipes were developed or perfected in their kitchens.

CHAPTER ONE

Cooking With Wine

If, by some miracle, a painter should discover a whole new spectrum of colors for his palette, what new worlds would open up to him!

And yet, if you are one of those who have never used wine in cooking, exactly that kind of experience awaits you. Volumes have been written on wines as beverages. The following pages are devoted almost entirely to wines as *flavors.*

You know, of course, that all great chefs find wines indispensable in their creations. Without their subtle touch many of their most famous successes would be commonplace and ordinary. Has this knowledge given you the impression that wine cookery is too difficult for the ordinary homemaker? Or too expensive? Then please get ready to replace those misconceptions with a more pleasant set of facts.

The truth is that it is easier to cook with wine than without it. You will be amazed to find out how many of your favorite recipes can be raised to new heights with a touch—just a touch—of wine. Leftovers become an opportunity instead of a problem; indeed, the greatest fascination of wine cookery is the endless opportunity and temptation to experiment.

Now, how about the question of cost?

Traditionally, we Americans are apt to look on wine as a luxury, and yet the humblest European peasant, than whom there are no thriftier people in the world, uses wine as matter-of-factly as we use sugar or butter. How can they afford it? Because they use what they term "the wine of the country"—and so can you. We have so long considered imported wines as unapproachable in quality that we may take some time to recognize the facts. The great reputation of foreign wines rests largely upon their "vintage" and "Chateau" bottlings, which constitute about ten per cent of their entire production. These are the result of unusually favorable soil or climatic conditions or years of ageing or both. And it is an established fact that, with a few exceptions, the best American wines equal or surpass the best of the other ninety per cent, and at a fraction of their cost.

The first thing to learn about wine cookery is that the most expensive wines are not by any means always the most desirable. The very qualities that make them expensive—delicate bouquets and flavors—are usually completely lost at the first touch of heat. As you progress in wine cookery you will find, all too often, recipes in which special bottlings or even vintage wines are "musts." Such advice stems from snobbery, ignorance, or both. In the following pages when Chablis is to be preferred to Riesling, for instance, we will say so. But when we say "dry white wine," use what you have.

Now we come to a point that, so far as we can learn, has never been touched upon in print before. And it is vitally important. It is this:

Every wine, from a culinary standpoint, has *three* flavors—its *natural* flavor, its *simmered* flavor, and its *cooked* flavor. The best way to understand this is by experiment.

Take a glassful of the wine you intend to use. Pour it in a small saucepan and hold it over the flame until it just simmers. Allow it to cool, taste it, and compare it with the wine in the bottle. Quite a different flavor, isn't it? And that's what you are going to get when your recipe says, "Add wine and bring just to the simmering point." Then take another glassful. This time let it really boil for two or three minutes at least. And again it has changed, this time more decidedly. And that flavor is what you get when you use it for basting or subject it to prolonged high heat in any recipe. You will notice, too, that it is not nearly so masterful now, which, of course, means that you can use it more liberally. If you will do this with each wine before using, it may avoid disappointment and will certainly make you a better wine cook right from the start.

To those who are "dry" by principle, this is as good a time as any to point out that alcohol boils at a temperature of 172.4° F. This means that any possible alcoholic content of your wine has completely disappeared long before the boiling point of water (212° F.) has been reached. And if you are still concerned with "dat ol' debbil" alcohol, remember that your old friends, vanilla and lemon extract, run from 80 to 100 proof. Don't take our word—look at the label!

CLASSIFICATION OF WINES

This book is not intended in any sense to be a manual on beverage wines. Your dealer can supply you with booklets prepared by importers and vintners which cover this subject quite adequately. But for our present purposes all wines can be broadly classified as:

red or white
sweet or dry
fortified or unfortified
still or sparkling
aromatized (Vermouth, Dubonnet)

Red wines may be the deepest ruby or the lightest rose. White ones are never really white but range from amber to straw-colored. It is an interesting fact that white wines may be, and frequently are, made from red, blue, or black grapes. It is only when the skins and pulp are fermented together before pressing that the color of the skin is imparted to the finished product.

Sweet wines are just that—sweet. "Dry" does not mean sour—merely that the original grape sugar has been chemically changed by fermentation. There are degrees of sweetness, of course, and there are degrees of dryness ranging from a palate-cleansing freshness to a definite tartness.

Fortified wines are those to which distilled spirits, usually brandy, have been added. The purpose of this is not merely to increase the alcoholic content, as is commonly supposed, but to stop fermentation when a certain definite flavor has been reached. Unfortified or "light" wines range from seven per cent to twelve per cent in alcoholic content—fortified wines from eighteen per cent to twenty-two per cent. Fortified wines will keep indefinitely after being opened. Unfortified wines will turn to vinegar (a very delicious one, by the way) in a comparatively short time. This can be prevented by adding a few drops of cooking oil and refrigerating. The protective film of the oil keeps the air away and, combined with the low temperature of your refrigerator, will keep them in good condition for several weeks.

RED WINES. Of the red wines, perhaps the best known is *Port*. It may be very sweet or not very sweet, but it is always a sweet wine, never really dry, although Tawny Ports may approach that grading. It is fortified. Its heavy, rich, altogether distinctive flavor is, in itself, a caution to use it sparingly. Then there are white Ports, which are more on the order of Angelicas and Tokays and are more or less interchangeable with them.

Burgundy and *Claret* are the two chiefs of the clan of dry red wines. Claret—which technically is a red Bordeaux—is usually somewhat lighter in body than Burgundy, but, except when used in recipes which do not require cooking, is, for your purpose, interchangeable with it. This will be heresy to the purist, but it is absolutely true, so use whichever you have and let the critics, if they can, tell you the difference. Both Burgundy and Claret are unfortified wines.

Cabernet is one of the finest American wines. Neither a Burgundy nor a Claret, yet more nearly resembling the latter, it has a splendid bouquet and flavor all its own.

Zinfandel, Barbera, and *Barberona* are less well known than they should be. Made from grapes of the same name, the two latter particularly are most used for blending. A really good Zinfandel will hold its own in any company.

Chianti, for which we were formerly dependent on Italy, is now being duplicated here. It is quite light and dry. Both red and white types are available.

Sherry is commonly classified as a sweet red wine, but this is misleading—very. In color, it ranges from a rich brown to pale amber. It is fortified and may be quite sweet or fairly dry, but it never goes to extremes either way. Its versatility in the kitchen is inexhaustible—you will find yourself reaching for the Sherry bottle perhaps oftener than any other. No use trying to describe its bouquet and flavor—it has been tried for ages but never successfully. But both are very assertive, and it is the easiest of all wines to overdo. The change in both under the influence of heat is very marked, and it is especially advisable that you do a few minutes' experimenting with it before you start to use it. It can be your slave or your master depending entirely upon how well you understand what to expect from it.

Madeira is a fortified wine ranging from very sweet to quite dry. No one seems to understand why it has declined in popularity in America, but American vintners are not yet producing it except in small quantities. In recipes calling for Madeira an approximate result may be obtained by substituting Sherry.

WHITE WINES. Of all the white wines, the outstanding sweet types are *Tokay, Muscatel, Malaga, Angelica,* and *Catawba.* All are fortified, and each is characterized by a distinctive flavor of the grape from which it is made. Heat makes a considerable change, not always for the better, so that they find their principal uses in desserts, where they are invaluable. Recipe writers, incidentally, are apt to take a bit too much for granted and simply say "white wine" when they mean "dry white wine." The result of using a sweet wine when a dry one is required is apt to be disastrous, to say the least, and yet is frequently done.

Of all the dry white wines, all of which are unfortified, you need only to remember *Sauterne*, *Chablis* (pronounced "Sha-blee"), and *Riesling* or *Rhine Wine*, also commonly called *Hock*. These are nearly, but not quite, interchangeable, as they differ considerably in dryness. This, again, is heresy, but experience will teach you that it is the absolute truth. Domestic Sauterne vies with Sherry in all-around usefulness. It is never really sweet, but it may approach sweetness. Foreign Sauternes (spelled with the final "s," which is silent) is always sweet. Domestic Sauterne may be quite dry but never quite so dry as Chablis, which is next in scale. Dryest of all is Riesling or Rhine wine.

Of the sparkling wines, *Sparkling Burgundy* is just what its name implies. Abroad it is not highly considered. All too frequently it is merely an inferior wine which has been artificially carbonated. Indeed, domestic sparkling Burgundy is usually decidedly superior to the imported product.

True *Champagne*, which may be either sweet or dry, owes its sparkle to natural fermentation, much of which takes place in the bottle, and its production is a long and complicated process. Imitation Champagne is white wine artificially carbonated.

Neither has any place whatever in actual cookery although both have very interesting possibilities in connection with desserts, etc. when they are to be added after all the other ingredients are cold. Heating them, of course, destroys their effervescence immediately by driving off the carbonic-acid gas, while a vintage Champagne, no matter what fabulous sum it may have cost, may, when boiled, be actually less desirable than a good dry white wine.

AROMATIZED WINES. *Vermouth* is the most familiar type. It is made by adding certain herbs and flavoring elements to blended wines. It is both dry and sweet and usually has only a small place in cooking but is capable of very interesting results and well repays experiment. Use it with restraint as its flavor is pronounced. *Dubonnet* has not yet been successfully duplicated in America.

BUYING WINES

Perhaps you feel a bit helpless at the thought of selecting the right kinds of wines. This may help: First, don't look for bargains—at least, until you know pretty well what to look for in the way of quality. In wines, as in everything else, you get pretty nearly what you pay for, and too cheap wines, like too cheap eggs, are expensive at any price. Second, choose a really good dealer and follow his advice. The chances are that he won't know anything about wine cookery—you are undoubtedly much better informed than the average dealer by this time. But if he knows his business he will be able to tell you about relative qualities, and that's what you really want to know.

Some American wine men have abandoned the use of European names and instead are labeling their products according to the variety of grapes used, the region in which they were grown, or both. Should you be offered a bottle of wine whose label is unfamiliar to you, ask the dealer with what European type it corresponds.

Just one final admonition—*don't use too much wine*. It's much better to hear, "U'mm, what makes these beans so good?" than "Oh, you used Sherry in the beans, didn't you?"

SPECIAL COOKERY SUGGESTIONS

Every effort has been made to select recipes which are within the scope of the average cook and the average kitchen. However, there are some ingredients which are unobtainable in certain sections.

Shallots, which are simply a small and delicate member of the onion family, are an example. If you haven't them or can't get them, simply substitute onions, white for choice, instead. The result will be almost identical.

No parsley? Use tender carrot tops instead and cut down the quantity by about one fourth.

In place of chives, in a pinch use the minced green tops of young onions, or scallions as they are called in the eastern states.

Herbs may seem like a problem. We in America are just becoming herb-conscious again. (In grandmother's day everyone used herbs, fresh in summer, dry in winter.) But, except for those who live in large cities or who have their own gardens, fresh herbs are usually out of the question. Fortunately, dried herbs give exactly the same results and have the additional advantage of keeping almost indefinitely when tightly covered. Every dealer has dried thyme, marjoram, sage, savory, and bay (laurel) leaves. (This last is not an herb, of course, but is usually classed with them.) Tarragon, rosemary, chervil, basil, and borage are less easy to find, but if your grocer doesn't carry them he can easily get them for you, and they are not expensive. Don't try to get along without them. Then, when your recipe says "a few sprigs of chervil," add a pinch of dried chervil instead. If any are unfamiliar to you, taste them "as is"; then you will know what to expect when you use them. Remember that any herb develops its flavor on cooking, so when you use one that is new to you be very sparing. This is especially true of tarragon, which is capable of delightful things if kept in restraint but which is a genuine bully if allowed to get out of hand.

The term, "fines herbes," seems to have a different meaning to every user. So, when you encounter it, mix up parsley, thyme, marjoram, chervil, tarragon, and what have you until you have a combination you like. There's your "fines herbes," and nobody can deny you.

So with "herb bouquet" or "bouquet garni." The simplest would be two or three sprigs of parsley, a three- or four-inch piece of celery, and about the same amount of the white part of a stalk of leek, all tied together with white thread. For vegetable soups you might add a bit of thyme, basil, or a bay leaf; for consommés or meat soups, add instead, to your basic combination, marjoram, chervil, and bay leaf. Keep tarragon and fennel in mind but use with restraint. Don't forget that there is a kinship between dill and fish. In a word, match your bouquet garni to your dish as you would a hat to a costume. Dried or powdered herbs should be enclosed in a small cheesecloth bag—old tea bags are perfect. Be careful not to allow the bouquet garni to remain too long, particularly in soups and sauces, or it will impart a bitter flavor.

How many recipes there are that call for stock! And yet, did you ever see a stock kettle? They are almost as extinct as the auk except in restaurant kitchens. But don't let that stop you. A can of bouillon or a few beef cubes dissolved in water is the perfect answer. Does the recipe call for chicken broth? Canned chicken soup pinch hits here, but you will probably want to strain out the rice or okra unless you buy the madrilene type. Some esoteric writers are fond of calling for the use of "glacé viande." Your dealer probably doesn't know what it is either—by that name—but, if you ask for beef extract, he reaches for it at once, and it's exactly the same thing. Incidentally, bouillon cubes are interchangeable with it.

Parmesan cheese, especially in grated form, is expensive and almost unobtainable. Use instead a very old, sharp, dry cheese; grate it and keep it in a cool place, tightly covered.

Truffles, always expensive, are now literally almost worth their weight in gold. Try using pickled walnuts instead. A few trained palates may notice the difference, but they'll like them.

CHAPTER TWO

Soups

Undoubtedly the commonest culinary use of wine is the addition of Sherry to soup. Unfortunately, in many cases, it ends there.

There is a natural affinity between wine and soup; in fact, many are not complete without wine—green turtle soup without Sherry, for example. Yet, there are many soups to which the robust flavor of Sherry is decidedly not adapted but which respond gloriously to the subtler red and white wines, both dry and sweet.

A generation or so ago, soup was almost entirely homemade. Today, by far the greater proportion comes from cans. There are several reasons for this, but the principal one is that the commercial soup is made by specialists. Their formulas are unvarying and are the result of very long experience, and their ingredients are almost invariably of a higher grade than are available to the average housewife. Incidentally, it is interesting to know that, even in the largest plants, soup is always made in small batches, seldom over fifty gallons at a time.

For this reason you will find no recipes in the following pages for the commoner varieties because those you can buy are actually better than those you can make, no matter how expert you are, and infinitely cheaper.

And how interesting they are to experiment with! Try combining two kinds—chicken and cream of mushroom with Sauterne; cream of pea and bouillon with dry white wine; cream of tomato and pea with Sherry; the variety is almost endless. And don't be afraid to add to them when you have the inspiration. Canned pea soup with two teaspoons of Sherry to each portion and a sprinkling of chopped mint on top is a brand-new taste sensation.

Fruit soups, both hot and cold, served either as a first or a last course, have long been favorites in Europe but are just coming into vogue here. Practically all of them require wine, and a few recipes are given here as patterns. Nearly all of them demand the more delicately flavored white wines. Again, experiments are more apt than not to result in delicious surprises.

An innovation is to serve the wine separately in a decanter and let each guest add the amount he or she desires.

But if you add it yourself always remember that too much is more than enough. A tablespoon per portion is usually plenty.

CREAM OF BEAN SOUP

2 cups marrow beans
2 medium-sized onions
1 cup sour cream
1 cup Sauterne
1 cup milk (approximately)
½ pound fat salt pork
salt and pepper

Look over beans and soak overnight in cold water. Boil beans and onions together until beans are very tender, 2 to 3 hours, and pureé. Add wine, sour cream, and sufficient milk for desired consistency. Cut salt pork in cubes, try out, drain, and add. Reheat. Serves 4 to 6.

RED KIDNEY BEAN SOUP

2 cups red kidney beans
3 cans condensed beef consommé
3 cans water
2 slices bacon, chopped and fried
1 onion, chopped
1 carrot, chopped
1 teaspoon dried sweet herbs
6 tablespoons Sherry

Soak beans in water overnight and simmer in consommé, together with bacon, onion, carrot, and herbs, for 1 hour. Strain or not as preferred. Add Sherry just before serving. If too thick add hot water. Serves 6.

MOCK TURTLE SOUP DE LUXE

2 cans condensed mock turtle soup
1½ cans water
½ cup Sherry
1 hard-cooked egg, sliced
chopped parsley

Simmer the soup and water for 15 minutes, and put through colander or strainer. Add Sherry and serve with a slice of hard-cooked egg and a topping of parsley. Serves 4.

MOCK TURTLE SOUP FAMILY STYLE

1 cup red kidney beans
water
1 tablespoon butter
1 medium-sized onion, chopped
½ small clove garlic, crushed and minced
1 tablespoon flour
grated peel of 1 lemon
salt
dash of Tabasco
sprinkle of cayenne
2 hard-cooked eggs, chopped
1 cup Sherry

Soak beans overnight in cold water; drain and cook, covered, in large amount of boiling salted water until tender, 2 to 3 hours. Drain and measure water. There should be 3 pints. If too much, reduce by boiling. If not enough, add boiling water to make up quantity. Mash beans through sieve. Brown onion, garlic, and flour in butter, gradually stir in water, add beans and grated lemon peel, and season quite highly. Simmer gently 1 hour. Add Sherry and chopped hard-cooked eggs just before serving. Serves 6.

WINE SAGO SOUP

1 pound sago
6 cups water
½ lemon, sliced very thin
salt
3½ cups dry wine, either white or red

Wash sago well, drop into boiling water, add lemon, and boil until sago is completely tender, stirring frequently. Add wine, season to taste, bring to a very gentle simmer, and serve. Serves 6.

CONSOMMÉ MADRILÈNE WITH WINE

2 tablespoons gelatin
1 cup cold water
2 cans condensed consommé or bouillon
2 tablespoons Sherry
1 bay leaf, crushed
salt and pepper

Soften gelatin in water. Heat soup and add gelatin with wine and bay leaf. Simmer 3 minutes and chill. Serve diced in bouillon cups. Serves 4 to 6.

PORTUGUESE LIVER SOUP

1 pound liver, sliced
4 cups cold water
¼ teaspoon grated lemon peel
½ cup seeded raisins
⅛ teaspoon nutmeg
¼ teaspoon cinnamon
1 small bay leaf
2 cups dry white wine
salt and paprika
dash of cayenne
2 egg yolks, beaten

Put liver in cold water, bring to a boil, and simmer 5 minutes. Take out and, when cool enough to handle, remove outer skin and larger veins. Put twice through food chopper, using finest blade. Return to broth, add lemon peel, raisins, cinnamon, bay leaf, and wine, and season to taste. Simmer 20 minutes, remove from heat, and stir in egg yolks. Serves 6.

CHICKEN CORDIALE

4 cups chicken broth
4 eggs
3 tablespoons lemon juice
salt and pepper
2 tablespoons Sherry

Bring broth to a gentle boil. Beat eggs very thoroughly and add lemon juice and seasonings. Stir gradually into broth. Add Sherry just before serving. Serves 4.

CHICKEN SOUP WITH AVOCADO

1 cup avocado, cubed
2 hard-cooked eggs, chopped
5 cups chicken consommé *and*
1 cup clam broth, *or*
6 cups chicken consommé
3 tablespoons Sherry
salt and pepper
dash of cayenne
1 tablespoon chopped parsley

Mix together avocado and chopped egg and put in heated tureen. Mix broth and wine, season, and bring just to a boil. Pour over avocado and egg, and sprinkle with chopped parsley. Serves 6.

GIBLET SOUP

Giblets from 2 chickens, or 1 goose or turkey
3 cans condensed beef bouillon
2 medium-sized onions, chopped fine
½ cup chopped celery
½ cup chopped carrots
⅓ cup cooked rice
½ cup dry red wine

Cover giblets with cold salted water and boil until very tender, about 45 minutes to 1 hour. Cool and chop giblets fine. Add consommé, vegetables, and rice to giblet stock and simmer until vegetables are tender, about 30 minutes. Season, add giblets and wine, and reheat. Serves 6.

ONION SOUP AU GRATIN

8 medium-sized onions, sliced
6 tablespoons butter
2 tablespoons flour
1 cup Claret
3 cups beef stock or consommé
6 slices toast
Parmesan cheese, grated

Brown sliced onions in butter until golden brown, add flour, and stir until smooth. Add wine and consommé, and simmer 25 minutes. Pour into individual soup casseroles. Place slice of toast sprinkled with grated cheese on top of each. Place casserole in hot oven (400°) until the cheese melts and is a golden brown. Serves 6.

ONION SOUP FRENCH

4 medium-sized white onions, sliced
2 tablespoons butter
4 cups soup stock or canned consommé
1 cup dry red wine
1 tablespoon Sherry
salt and pepper
3 cups grated Parmesan cheese
8 half-slices toast

Sauté onions in butter slowly until lightly browned. Add stock or consommé, wine and seasonings, and simmer 20 minutes. Place 2 half-slices of toast in each soup plate, add soup, sprinkle generously with cheese, and place under broiler until cheese is slightly browned. Serve rest of cheese separately. Serves 4.

TURTLE SOUP THICK

4 cups (1 can) green turtle soup
2 cans condensed beef bouillon
6 tablespoons Sherry
3 tablespoons flour
6 slices lemon

Cut turtle meat into cubes, add, together with broth, to bouillon, and simmer 20 minutes. Cool. Mix Sherry and flour to a paste and add. Bring to a boil and simmer, stirring constantly, about 3 minutes. Serve with 1 lemon slice in each portion. Serves 6.

NEW ORLEANS TURTLE SOUP

½ medium-sized onion, sliced
3 tablespoons butter
1 tablespoon flour
1 pound green turtle meat, fresh or canned
1 small can tomatoes
2 cups bouillon
½ small bay leaf
⅛ teaspoon thyme
1 teaspoon chopped parsley
dash of Worcestershire sauce
dash of Angostura bitters
salt and pepper
¼ cup Sherry

Sauté onion in butter, add flour, and brown. Cut turtle meat in one inch pieces and sauté until slightly brown. Add tomatoes, bouillon, bay leaf, thyme, parsley, Worcestershire, and Angostura, and season to taste. Simmer gently 15 to 20 minutes. Add Sherry just before serving. Serves 4.

TURTLE SOUP WITH CHABLIS

2 cups cooked turtle meat, fresh or canned
1 small clove garlic, crushed and minced
½ green pepper, chopped fine
1 teaspoon chopped mint
2 teaspoons chopped parsley
1 quart water
2 hard-cooked eggs, coarsely chopped
1 cup Chablis
salt and pepper

Cut meat in small pieces. Put in water with garlic, green pepper, mint, and parsley, bring to a boil, and simmer 15 minutes. Season, add wine and egg, and bring just to a simmer. Serves 6 to 8.

OYSTER BISQUE

2 cups oysters
water
½ cup minced celery
1 medium-sized onion, minced
2 tablespoons butter
2 tablespoons flour
3 cups milk
salt and pepper
2 egg yolks, beaten
⅓ cup Sherry

Drain oysters and chop very fine. Add enough water to oyster liquor to make 2 cups. Add chopped oysters, celery, and onion and simmer slowly 30 minutes, stirring frequently. Make a roux of butter and flour, and add milk gradually. Bring to a boil while stirring and add oyster mixture. Mix beaten egg yolks with Sherry and add. Season to taste. Reheat but do not allow to boil after egg yolks have been added. Serves 6.

OYSTER GUMBO I

3 tablespoons diced salt pork
3 tablespoons butter
3 tablespoons chopped onion
2 green peppers, chopped
2 tablespoons flour
1 cup dry white wine
3 cups condensed chicken broth
4 cups water
12 small okra pods, *or*
1 cup canned okra, drained
2 leeks, white part only, sliced
½ cup chopped celery
1 tablespoon chopped parsley
1 teaspoon mace or nutmeg
3 dozen oysters
salt

Try out salt pork until dry but not brown. Add butter and sauté onion and peppers until tender. Add all other ingredients except oysters and simmer gently 45 minutes. Strain. Season to taste. Add oysters and oyster liquor, and cook only until they are plump and edges curled. Serves 6 to 8.

OYSTER GUMBO II

4 tablespoons butter
½ onion, diced
2 tablespoons flour
2 cups Sauterne
1 quart water
2 bouillon cubes
½ green pepper, minced
2 sprigs parsley
2 cloves garlic, minced
4 celery stalks
½-cup canned diced mushrooms
1 quart oysters
1 cup canned okra
salt

Melt butter in saucepan. Add diced onions and brown. Stir in flour, then add wine, water, and bouillon cubes. Add salt, green pepper, parsley, garlic, and celery stalks. Cook slowly 40 to 50 minutes. Then add mushrooms and oysters with their liquor and boil 4 minutes. Remove celery stalks and parsley. Skim and stir in okra. Serve with plain boiled rice. Serves 6.

OYSTER AND SHRIMP GUMBO FILÉ

2 slices chopped bacon
1 medium-sized onion, chopped
1 clove garlic, crushed and minced
1 tablespoon parsley, minced
1 tablespoon flour
1 can condensed tomato soup
2 cups water
1 cup dry white wine
1 cup shrimp, cut in quarters
12 oysters
salt and pepper
1 tablespoon filé powder

Fry bacon, onions, and garlic and parsley until bacon is crisp. Add flour and stir in well. Gradually add tomato soup, wine, and water. Bring to a simmer; add cut-up shrimp. Simmer until shrimp are pink. Add oysters and their liquor, and simmer until oysters are plump and edges curled. Remove from heat, season to taste, and stir in filé powder. Do not heat again after filé is added. Serves 4.

BISQUE OF SHRIMP, BRETON STYLE

1 tablespoon minced onion
1 tablespoon minced celery
½ tablespoon minced carrot
4 tablespoons minced mushrooms
2 tablespoons butter
2 cups chicken stock
½ teaspoon salt
dash of cayenne
1 pound cooked shrimp, chopped fine
½ cup light cream
½ cup very dry white wine

Sauté the onion, celery, carrot, and mushrooms gently in butter for two minutes. Add stock, season, and simmer 15 minutes. Add shrimp and simmer 5 minutes more. Put through sieve or fine colander. Add cream and wine. Heat, but do not allow to boil after cream has been added. Serves 4.

CRAB BISQUE

1 can crab meat
1 can cream of pea soup
1 can cream of tomato soup
1 cup cream
⅓ cup Sherry

Heat above ingredients together. Serve topped with 1 teaspoon whipped cream for each serving. Serves 6.

COLONIAL CRAB SOUP

2 hard-cooked eggs
1 tablespoon butter
1 tablespoon flour
1 quart milk
1½ cups crab meat
½ teaspoon A1 sauce
1 teaspoon mushroom sauce
⅛ teaspoon mace
½ cup cream
salt and pepper
¾ cup Sherry

Put hard-cooked eggs several times through food chopper using finest knife. Blend in butter and flour. Heat milk just to boiling and add slowly to egg paste. Mix thoroughly. Add crab meat, A1 and mushroom sauces and mace, and simmer gently 5 minutes. Add cream, season, and reheat. Add wine just before serving. Serves 6.

CRAB SOUP

2 cups crab meat
2 tablespoons butter
2 cups hot milk
1 small onion or shallot, chopped
1 cup heavy cream
2 dashes Worcestershire sauce
1 teaspoon flour
salt and pepper
¼ cup Sherry

Put the crab meat (and its eggs, if any), onion, and butter in double boiler, and simmer for 10 minutes. Add hot milk, then the cream and Worcestershire sauce. Thicken with flour and season to taste. Simmer very gently (do not allow to boil) for 30 minutes. Add Sherry just before serving. Serves 4.

CREAM OF CRAB SOUP

1 pound crab meat
2 hard-cooked eggs, chopped
1 tablespoon butter
1 quart milk
salt
white pepper
½ cup Sherry

Bring milk to a simmer and stir in all the other ingredients except the Sherry. Do not allow to boil but keep at simmering point for 15 minutes. Add wine just before serving. Serve with slice of lemon dusted with paprika in each portion and croutons. Serves 6.

CLAM CHOWDER

2 cans clam chowder
1 can wet shrimp
1 small onion
salt
celery salt
dash of cayenne
½ teaspoon marjoram
⅓ cup dry white wine

Clean shrimp, break into small pieces, and put in soup kettle with chowder, using shrimp liquor also. Add onion, pricked with fork, while it is heating. Remove onion before serving. Add seasonings, bring to a boil, and add wine. Serves 4.

SHELLFISH CHOWDER

3 tablespoons butter
4 tablespoons minced onion
1 small can shrimp, chopped
1 small can clams, minced
1 can condensed vegetable soup
2 cups Medium White Sauce (p. 27)
salt and pepper
½ cup Chablis or Riesling

Sauté onion, shrimp, and clams for 5 minutes. Blend together vegetable soup and White Sauce, combining both with mixture in pan. Bring just to a simmer. Remove from heat, season to taste, and add wine just before serving. Serves 4.

FISH CHOWDER I

1 pound carp or pike
1 pound eel
1 pound perch
1 medium-sized onion, chopped
1 medium-sized carrot, chopped
1 parsley root, chopped
1 leek, chopped
1 stalk celery, chopped
¼ teaspoon powdered thyme
3 tablespoons butter
6 sprigs parsley
1 bay leaf
4 peppercorns, crushed
1 teaspoon salt
4½ cups water
1½ cups dry white wine
2 tablespoons butter
4 slices lemon
8 slices toast, buttered

Skin eel, clean and scale fish, and cut in 2-inch pieces. Melt butter, put in fish together with vegetables and seasonings, and cook over very low heat, stirring frequently, until brown, about 15-20 minutes. Add water and wine, and simmer gently until fish is done. Place fish on hot platter, strain sauce, add butter and lemon slices. Simmer 2-3 minutes. Put one slice toast in each soup plate and fill with soup, reserving a little to pour over fish on platter. Serves 8.

FISH CHOWDER II

¼ pound salt pork, diced
3 medium-sized onions, chopped
2 pounds fish filets
4 pilot biscuits
¼ teaspoon allspice
¼ teaspoon nutmeg
dash of cayenne
salt
3 tablespoons catsup
½ cup Sherry

Try out salt pork until it is very crispy, and brown the onions lightly in the fat. Cut fish in small pieces and put in soup kettle with a little more than sufficient water to cover (about 6 cups). Add the pilot biscuit, broken up, season, and simmer 1 hour. A few minutes before serving, add the catsup and wine, and bring just to a simmer. Serves 4.

FISH BROTH

(A very old French recipe

2 medium-sized beets, chopped fine
2 medium-sized onions, chopped fine
¼ cup olive oil or vegetable oil
2 medium-sized tomatoes, chopped
2 cloves garlic, crushed and minced
1 small head dill, chopped
1 bay leaf
peel of ¼ orange, sliced thin
2 cups dry white wine
2 cups water
salt and pepper
2 pounds any kind of fish, cut up
A few crabs, shrimp, or a small eel
1 pound vermicelli
½ teaspoon saffron

Sauté beets and onion in oil until tender but not brown. Add tomatoes, garlic, dill, and bay leaf, orange peel, wine, and water. Add fish and shellfish, and boil briskly for 20 minutes. Strain through colander and press fish with wooden spoon until as dry as possible. The longer this step the better the result. Strain through cloth, bring to a boil, add vermicelli and saffron, and cook until vermicelli is tender. Check seasoning and serve with croutons. Serves 6 to 8.

FISH SOUP

(Adapted from an old Czechoslovakian recipe)

1 tablespoon butter
1 tablespoon chopped carrot
1 tablespoon chopped cauliflower
1 tablespoon chopped celery
4 tablespoons brown roux (p. 28)
1 quart fish fumet (p. 56)
salt
pepper
2 pounds fish, fileted
¼ cup dry white wine

Sauté the vegetables in butter until a delicate brown. Add fumet and fish, and simmer slowly until fish flakes of its own accord. Thicken with the roux and simmer 5 minutes more. Add wine, season to taste, and serve. Serves 4.

FLORENTINE FISH SOUP

3 tablespoons olive oil or vegetable oil
⅓ cup chopped celery
¼ cup chopped onion
2 cups canned tomatoes
3 cups water
2 medium-sized potatoes, sliced
2 tablespoons minced parsley
1 bay leaf
½ teaspoon thyme
1½ cups codfish, flaked
¼ cup dry white wine
salt and pepper
croutons
grated cheese

Sauté celery and onion in oil until tender. Add tomatoes, water, potatoes, parsley, bay leaf, and thyme and simmer gently 30 minutes. Add flaked codfish and simmer 10 minutes more. Remove from heat, add wine, and season to taste. Serve with croutons and grated cheese. Serves 6.

BOUILLABAISSE

There is no standard recipe for this famous dish. Although it originated in Italy, its name is most closely associated with Marseilles, which is usually accepted as its home. Even there, each restaurant and each family varies the formula according to the market and personal taste. It is impossible to duplicate any Marseilles recipe in this country as so many of the ingredients are unobtainable here. Essentially, it is more of a stew than a soup, with fish and shellfish in as great a variety as conditions permit.

Here is a recipe which will cheer up any homesick Frenchman. But, remember, you can vary it just as much as circumstances require.

BOUILLABAISE

1 quart boiling water
1 cup butter
1 pound fish filet (flounder, halibut, or any firm white-meated fish)
1½ cups shrimp, cut in pieces
12 oysters
2 cups lobster meat, cut in large pieces
12 small clams
2 medium-sized onions, chopped fine
1 small clove garlic, crushed and minced
1 large bay leaf
2 tablespoons chopped parsley
1 teaspoon saffron
juice of 1 lemon
salt and pepper
1 cup Sherry

Simmer all ingredients except Sherry for 20 minutes, covered. Season and add Sherry. Pour into soup plates over slices of toast or serve with French bread. Serves 6.

AVOCADO BOUILLON

1 can clear chicken broth
1 can clam broth
1 large avocado pear, sieved
salt and pepper
dash of cayenne
¼ cup Sherry
½ cup whipped cream
3 tablespoons pistachio nuts, chopped

Bring broth and avocado meat just to simmering. Season and add Sherry. Serve topped with whipped cream sprinkled with pistachio nuts. Serves 4.

WINE ZWIEBACK SOUP

8 zwiebacks
4 cups boiling water
grated peel of ½ lemon
4 cups white wine, dry or sweet

Roll the zwiebacks to crumbs, put in boiling water with grated lemon peel, and continue boiling for 15 minutes. Strain, add wine, and sugar to taste if desired. Serve ice-cold with a bowl of broken-up zwieback. Serves 6.

APPLE SOUP

2 pounds apples
8-10 cups water
¼ teaspoon salt
grated rind of 1 lemon
1 1-inch stick cinnamon
1 cup sugar (approximately)
2 tablespoons potato flour
¼ cup water
¼ cup currants, washed and soaked
½ cup white wine, sweet or dry
2 tablespoons lemon juice

Cook apples as for apple sauce with salt, grated lemon rind, cinnamon, and sugar, and put through colander or strainer. Return to stove and stir in potato flour mixed with ¼ cup water, add currants, and cook gently, stirring constantly, 10-12 minutes. Stir in lemon juice and wine, and serve as a dessert. Serves 6.

ICED APPLE SOUP

6 tart apples, pared, cored, and sliced
3 cups water
grated rind of ½ lemon
⅛ teaspoon cinnamon
2 tablespoons bread crumbs
1 tablespoon sugar
juice of 1 lemon
2 cups dry red wine
1 tablespoon currant jelly, melted

Cover apples with boiling water, add lemon rind, cinnamon, bread crumbs, and sugar and cook until apples are very tender, stirring frequently. Put through sieve and chill. Add lemon juice, wine, and melted jelly and stir well. Serve very cold. Serves 4.

ICED FRUIT SOUP

2 tablespoons quick cooking tapioca
1 cup boiling water
1 cup pineapple juice
1 cup grape juice
1 cup grapefruit juice
rind of 1 lemon, grated
1 1½-inch stick cinnamon
1½ cups red or black raspberries (fresh or frosted)
⅓ cup Sherry

Stir tapioca into boiling water, cook until perfectly clear, about 5 minutes, stirring frequently. Add fruit juices, lemon peel, cinnamon, and sugar and simmer 10 minutes. Cool slightly, add berries, and chill. Add Sherry when very cold. Serve extremely cold. Serves 4.

QUINCE SOUP

4 medium-sized quinces, peeled, cored, and quartered
1 quart water
1 ½-inch stick cinnamon
6 cloves
¼ teaspoon salt
2 cups dry white wine
sugar

Cook quinces with spices until transparent and tender. Put through colander. Return to juice, add wine and salt, and sweeten to taste. Reheat and serve. Excellent either hot or iced. Serves 4 to 6.

COLD RED RASPBERRY SOUP

1 quart red raspberries
⅓ cup sugar
⅓ tablespoon cornstarch
1½ tablespoons water
⅓ cup Sherry

Mash berries and sugar together, let stand 1 hour, and put through sieve fine enough to remove seeds. Bring to a simmer in double boiler, add cornstarch mixed with water, and cook until clear, about 5 minutes. Chill and stir in Sherry. Serve over finely cracked ice in tall glasses. Serves 4.

WINE CREAM SOUP

6 eggs
juice of 1 lemon
grated rind of 1 lemon
4 tablespoons sugar
1 tablespoon cornstarch
4 cups water
4 cups dry white wine

Separate eggs, beat yolks, add juice and grated rind of lemon, sugar and cornstarch mixed. Stir well and put in double boiler together with wine and water. Beat constantly and remove immediately it begins to simmer. Beat whites very dry, form them in balls with teaspoon, and put them in soup after it has cooled. Sprinkle with sugar and put in refrigerator. Serve very cold. Serves 6.

VICHYSOISSE

4 stalks leeks (white part only), chopped
½ cup butter
4 medium-sized potatoes (not new ones) sliced wafer-thin
1 stalk celery, coarsely chopped
2 tablespoons parsley, coarsely chopped
1 pint heavy cream
2 quarts chicken broth
2 tablespoons Madeira or Sherry (not too dry)
salt
white pepper
pinch of mace
dash of Worcestershire sauce
2 tablespoons sour heavy cream
2 tablespoons chopped chives

Sauté leeks gently in butter for 10 minutes or until tender but not brown. Add potatoes, celery, parsley, and broth. Boil 30 minutes. Force through a coarse sieve and allow to cool. Add all other ingredients except chives and chill almost to freezing. Whip vigorously. Serve topped with chives. Warning: to prevent discoloration, cool in enamel, china, or stainless steel dish. Serves 6 to 8.

CHAPTER THREE

Sauces

Anyone who can bake, roast, boil, and fry really well is a good cook. And anyone who will pay strict attention to mixing directions and exact measurements, not only of ingredients, but of time and temperature, can, with the aid of any good cook book, achieve that distinction.

But the one who has a repertoire of really fine sauces deserves a master's degree. In fact, in the sharply drawn class lines of professional chefs, the "*saucier*" heads the aristocracy.

There is a French saying that while anyone can become proficient in other branches of cookery, one must be born a sauce maker. This is only partially true. None of the sauces in the following pages requires any particular skill to prepare. The most important thing is the choice of exactly the right sauce for the dish with which it is to be served. Remember, it should enhance, not disguise, the flavor of the food with which it is used. For example, a robust sauce which is perfect for steak would be ruinous to the delicate flavor of brook trout. If you have any doubt as to which of two sauces to use, choose the less aggressive one and you will almost invariably be right.

The three foundation sauces are White Sauce, Brown Sauce, and Velouté. Probably you know these recipes by heart, but they are added for the sake of completeness.

MEDIUM WHITE SAUCE

2 tablespoons butter
2 tablespoons flour
½ teaspoon salt
dash of white pepper (if desired)
1 cup milk

Melt butter in top of double boiler, add flour, and blend very thoroughly, stirring until this mixture or *roux* begins to bubble. Then add milk slowly, stirring constantly. Season and let simmer 5 minutes.

For *Thin White Sauce* cut amount of flour and butter in half.

For *Heavy White Sauce* double amount of flour and butter.

For *Cream Sauce* use cream instead of milk.

Velouté Sauce is a variation of white sauce but made with a white stock or chicken consommé instead of milk.

BROWN SAUCE

2 tablespoons butter
3 tablespoons flour
1 cup beef bouillon *or*
1 cup water and 2 bouillon cubes *or*
1 cup water and 2 teaspoons beef extract
salt and pepper

Make a roux of the butter and flour, and stir constantly until well browned. Add the bouillon gradually and stir until thickened. Season to taste.

A roux is simply a fat and a starch, most commonly butter and flour, cooked together. For "brown roux" either the butter or the flour or both are allowed to brown slightly.

"*Beurre manié*" is a kneaded mixture of butter and flour, usually in the proportion of five to three. It is added in small lumps or balls to sauces and soups to thicken them. A professional touch which the home cook may profitably remember as it is the perfect and easy way to avoid lumpiness. Make up a cupful or two and keep it in the refrigerator.

If you are unable to use any of these sauces at once, a bit of butter allowed to melt on top will prevent the formation of "skin."

It is perfectly correct, and in many cases preferable, to serve the sauce in a separate dish, from which it may be ladled according to individual preferences. Never make the mistake of pouring sauce *over* broiled steaks, chops, fish, or fowl. The crisp brown surface must last until it gets on the plate. Here, separate service is decidedly best. And don't skimp on quantities. Requests for second helpings are embarrassing when answered by an empty dish.

Here you run into a problem. The French have a saying, "little sauce is good sauce." Almost invariably, the liquid or juices remaining in the cooking dish are reduced by simmering to a third or a quarter of their original volume. When you feel, on reading a recipe, that the quantity of sauce will not be sufficient,

see if you can't use trimmings and more liquid to stretch it out. With poultry dishes, condensed chicken consommé is one answer; with most meat dishes, condensed bouillon. There is no single rule, but ingenuity pays.

You will undoubtedly notice that some of the recipes in this chapter do not call for wine in their preparation. They are, however, necessary to complete many of the dishes in other chapters and are included to save the trouble of looking them up in reference works.

RED WINE SAUCE NO. I

(For mutton, venison, and game)

1 2-inch stick, or 1 teaspoon, cinnamon
12 whole cloves
3 tablespoons sugar
grated peel of 1 lemon
¼ cup Port
1 6-ounce glass red currant jelly

Bruise or grind the cinnamon and cloves together. Put them in small saucepan with sugar, lemon peel, and wine. Simmer for 15 minutes. Just before serving, melt in the currant jelly. Approximately 1 cup sauce.

Modifications: use 6 cloves; Burgundy instead of Port; black currant jelly instead of red.

RED WINE SAUCE WITH MINT

(for lamb and mutton)

Add 1 tablespoon fresh mint, minced, to each cup of Red Wine Sauce No. I.

RED WINE SAUCE NO. II

1 cup currant jelly
1 cup mutton broth from which grease has been skimmed *or*
1 cup beef bouillon
¾ cup brown sugar
1 cup catsup
½ tablespoon flour
1 cup Claret or Burgundy
¼ cup brandy

Melt the jelly in the broth. Add brown sugar and catsup. Thicken with flour. When cool, stir in wine and brandy. Heat before serving just to simmering. Approximately 4 cups sauce.

RED WINE SAUCE NO. III

1 tablespoon butter
½ medium-sized onion, chopped
1 tablespoon flour
1 tablespoon prepared mustard
1 teaspoon Worcestershire sauce
1 teaspoon Angostura bitters
½ cup bouillon
½ cup Claret

Sauté the onion in butter until tender but do not brown. Add flour, mustard, Worcestershire, and Angostura. Stir over low heat until smooth and thick. Add bouillon and Claret, and simmer until well blended. Approximately 1 cup sauce.

OLIVE RED SAUCE
(for red meats)

Add 2 tablespoons sliced stuffed olives to 1 cup Red Wine Sauce (p. 29).

PORT SAUCE
(for mutton or venison)

2 tablespoons butter
2 tablespoons flour
1 cup water
¼ cup currant jelly
2 teaspoons lemon juice
½ teaspoon salt
¼ cup Port
4 maraschino or preserved cherries, chopped

Make a roux of butter and flour. Add water slowly, stirring constantly, until sauce begins to simmer. Cook 3 to 4 minutes. Add currant jelly, lemon juice, wine, and salt. Simmer 2 minutes, stirring constantly. Stir in cherries and serve. Approximately 1½ cups sauce.

BROWN WINE SAUCE
(for red meats, tongue, etc.)

2 tablespoons butter
2 tablespoons flour
¾ cup condensed beef bouillon
¼ cup dry red wine
salt and pepper

Make a roux of butter and flour, and stir until well browned. Add bouillon and wine gradually, and stir until thickened. Season to taste. Approximately 1 cup sauce.

WHITE WINE SAUCE NO. I

3 tablespoons butter
3 tablespoons flour
1/4 cup dry white wine
3/4 cup water
1 cup milk
1/4 teaspoon salt
1 tablespoon Sherry (preferably dry)

Make a roux of the butter and flour; add water, wine, and milk gradually. Add salt and simmer 5 minutes, stirring constantly. Add Sherry just before serving. Approximately 2 cups sauce.

WHITE WINE SAUCE NO. II

2 medium-sized onions, minced
2 tablespoons butter
3/4 cup dry white wine
2 cups condensed tomato soup
1/2 teaspoon chili powder
1/2 teaspoon salt
1/8 teaspoon white pepper

Sauté the onions in butter until they are a light golden brown. Add wine and simmer slowly until the wine is reduced by half. Add all the other ingredients and stir well. Simmer ten minutes. Approximately 2 1/2 cups sauce.

WHITE WINE SAUCE NO. III
(For sea foods and white meats)

3 tablespoons butter
2 tablespoons flour
1 cup hot cream
1/4 cup dry white wine

Make a roux of butter and flour. Add wine to hot cream and add slowly to roux, stirring constantly. Whip vigorously with a wire whisk or fork. Simmer 5 minutes. Approximately 1 1/4 cups sauce.

WINE BUTTER SAUCE
(for vegetables)

4 tablespoons butter
1/4 cup dry red, or white, wine or Sherry
salt and pepper

Melt butter, mix in wine thoroughly. Season. Serve hot, poured over vegetables. Approximately 1/2 cup.

WINE CHEESE SAUCE

(for vegetables, fish, etc.)

¼ pound cheese
1 tablespoon butter
2 tablespoons flour
1 cup dry white wine
1 bouillon cube
½ teaspoon Angostura bitters (optional)
salt and pepper

The cheese should be rich and well flavored, preferably of the cheddar type. Melt it, together with butter, in double boiler. Add flour and mix thoroughly. Gradually add wine, in which bouillon cube has been dissolved, and Angostura. Cook until creamy. Season to taste. Approximately 1½ cups sauce.

OLIVE WHITE SAUCE
(for white meats or fish)

Add 2 tablespoons sliced stuffed olives to 1 cup White Wine Sauce (p. 31).

BARBECUE SAUCE NO. I

1 cup olive oil or vegetable oil
1 cup dry white wine
1 cup vinegar
1 small clove garlic, crushed and minced
2 medium-sized onions, chopped or grated
salt and pepper
dash of cayenne

Shake all together in glass fruit jar until well mixed. Let stand at least 8 hours. Keeps indefinitely. Approximately 3 cups sauce.

BARBECUE SAUCE NO. II

½ pound butter *or*
1 cup vegetable oil
2 tablespoons Worcestershire sauce
⅓ cup catsup
1 tablespoon ground mustard
juice of 1 lemon
½ cup dry white wine
salt, pepper, and paprika

Melt butter and stir in all other ingredients, mixing thoroughly. Approximately 1¾ cups sauce.

BARBECUE SAUCE NO III

(Especially good for lamb, mutton, or venison)

1½ cups vinegar
2 cups olive oil or vegetable oil
½ cup dry red wine
2 tablespoons Worcestershire sauce
4 tablespoons chopped parsley
¼ teaspoon powdered *or*
1 teaspoon fresh, each of
  marjoram
  thyme
  rosemary
salt and pepper

Mix all ingredients thoroughly and let stand overnight. Approximately 4 cups sauce.

THE OLD MASTER'S BARBECUE SAUCE

1 cup butter
1 cup dry red wine
2 cups water
2 medium-sized onions, chopped or grated
1 clove garlic, minced and crushed
½ cup Chili sauce
¼ teaspoon Tabasco sauce
½ teaspoon ground mustard
2 tablespoons vinegar
½ to 1 teaspoon Chili powder
¼ teaspoon ground mace
1 tablespoon grated horseradish
¼ teaspoon powdered thyme
¼ teaspoon powdered marjoram
1 tablespoon chopped parsley
1 tablespoon Worcestershire sauce
salt and pepper

Simmer all together for ¾ hour, stirring occasionally. Approximately 4½ cups sauce.

CHESTNUT SAUCE

(for poultry and game)

Put ¾ cup boiled chestnuts through food chopper, using coarsest blade, and add to 1 cup Brown Wine Sauce (p. 30). Approximately 1¾ cups sauce.

ROUENNAISE CHESTNUT SAUCE

(for any dark poultry or birds)

(From Gabriel Lugot, Executive Chef,
The Waldorf-Astoria, New York City)

In the pan or saucepan which has been used for the preparation of the bird—using the same fat—cook a few chopped shallots, adding one glass of excellent California Claret. Reduce. Off the fire, add the same quantity of raw strained bird liver, just warm. Add also the same quantity of fresh mashed chestnuts. Put at the right consistency with a little excellent American Brandy. Rectify seasoning. Strain and finish with the juice of the bird—already cooked. Serve as an accompaniment.

CHESTNUT PURÉE WITH SHERRY

1½ pounds chestnuts
boiling water
¼ cup butter, melted
1 cup cream
1 can condensed cream of mushroom soup
4 bouillon cubes
4 tablespoons hot water
1 cup Sherry
1 teaspoon celery salt
salt and pepper

Cover chestnuts with boiling water and cook rapidly until tender enough to be pierced easily with fork, about 20 to 30 minutes. When just cool enough to handle, remove shells and brown skin and put through ricer; add melted butter and put through ricer again. Mix cream, soup, bouillon cubes dissolved in hot water, wine, and seasonings. Add mashed chestnuts and simmer over very low heat, stirring constantly, until very thick and begins to separate from pan. Approximately 5 cups sauce.

Note: It is essential that chestnuts be not allowed to get cold before being peeled and put through ricer the first time. The best way is to allow them to cool slightly in the water in which they were cooked, take them out one at a time, and replace after shelling.

BEURRE NOIR (BLACK BUTTER)

3 parts butter
1 part wine vinegar

Heat butter to a light brown, being careful not to burn or it will be bitter. Dash in vinegar and remove from heat.

SAUCE ESPAGNOLE

Butter
⅔ cup chopped carrots
⅔ cup chopped onions
¼ cup chopped turnip
2 cloves garlic, minced
1 tablespoon chopped parsley
1 teaspoon chopped marjoram
1 teaspoon chopped thyme
¼ cup chopped celery
2 bay leaves
½ pound chopped ham
½ pound chopped lean veal
2 cups chopped tomatoes
⅛ teaspoon ground white pepper
½ teaspoon ground allspice
⅛ teaspoon ground cloves
8 cans condensed beef bouillon
6 cups water
1 cup Sherry
¾ cup flour
salt

Sauté carrots, onions, turnip, herbs, celery, and meat in 4 tablespoons butter until lightly browned. Drain butter and reserve. Add to saucepan, tomatoes, seasonings, bouillon, and water. Simmer 30 minutes. Strain. Measure reserved butter and add enough melted butter to make ¾ cup. Add flour and make a light brown roux. Make sauce by adding strained broth gradually. Let boil and simmer until reduced to desired consistency. Stir in Sherry and season.

This is a basic sauce, perhaps the most extensively used of all. It not only is frequently specified alone but is the principal ingredient of many other sauces. It can be made up in large quantity and kept under refrigeration for use as desired.

SAUCE MADÈRE À LA CREOLE

2 cups Sauce Espagnole
½ cup condensed tomato soup
½ cup chopped mushrooms
4 tablespoons Madeira (or Sherry)
dash of cayenne

Heat sauce and soup to simmering, add mushrooms, and simmer 10 minutes. Add wine. Approximately 2½ cups sauce.

SAUCE MADÈRE NO. I

¼ cup butter
½ cup onion, grated
6 tablespoons flour
1½ cups Sauterne
1 tablespoon minced gherkins
1 cup finely chopped mushrooms
1 cup Madeira (or Sherry)
salt and pepper

Lightly brown onions in butter and blend flour. Stir in Sauterne slowly and simmer 3 minutes. Strain, add gherkins and mushrooms, and simmer 10 minutes. Add Madeira or Sherry after removing from heat, season, and reheat not quite to simmering point. Approximately 2½ cups sauce.

SAUCE MADÈRE NO. II
(for beef, veal, poultry, and game)

2 cups Sauce Espagnole (p. 35)
½ cup condensed tomato soup
4 tablespoons Madeira
dash of cayenne

Heat sauce and soup to simmering, and add wine. Approximately 2½ cups sauce.

SAUCE MADÈRE WITH SCALLIONS
(for veal or fish)

3 tablespoons butter
12 scallions, chopped
2 tablespoons flour
¾ cup hot water
¼ teaspoon salt
dash of white pepper
2 teaspoons catsup
1 teaspoon minced parsley
3 tablespoons Madeira (or Sherry)

Sauté the scallions in butter until tender, add flour, and cook until slightly brown, stirring constantly. Add water gradually and cook until thickened, stirring constantly. Add rest of ingredients, blend, and serve over meat or fish. 1 cup sauce.

ANCHOVY SAUCE NO. I

1½ cups White Wine Sauce (p. 31)
2½ tablespoons anchovy paste

(For chicken, fish, veal or pork chops)

Heat and stir until the anchovy paste is thoroughly blended. Approximately 1½ cups sauce.

ANCHOVY SAUCE NO. II

1 cup butter
2 teaspoons anchovy paste
⅓ cup dry Sherry

Melt butter, blend in anchovy paste, add Sherry gradually, and simmer 5 minutes, stirring briskly. Approximately 1⅓ cups sauce.

ANCHOVY SAUCE

(for spaghetti)

3 tablespoons olive oil or vegetable oil
¼ cup finely chopped onion
¼ cup minced parsley
2 cups canned tomatoes
4 tablespoons anchovy paste
¼ cup dry red or white wine
⅛ teaspoon white pepper

Sauté onion and parsley in oil until golden. Put tomatoes through colander or coarse sieve and add together with all other ingredients. Stir and simmer for 5 minutes. Approximately 2 cups sauce.

BÉARNAISE SAUCE NO. I

6 tablespoons tarragon vinegar
2 tablespoons chopped shallots or onion
4 egg yolks, well beaten
½ pound butter, melted
1 tablespoon Sherry
1 tablespoon chopped chervil or parsley
1 tablespoon chopped tarragon (optional)
dash of salt
dash of cayenne

Put vinegar and onion or shallot in small saucepan and boil until vinegar is reduced to about 4 tablespoons. Cool and stir in beaten egg yolks thoroughly. Place in double boiler over water that is only simmering and add the melted butter, a very little at a time, stirring constantly. If it shows any tendency to curdle, add hot water, a teaspoon at a time, stirring rapidly. Remove from heat just as soon as all the butter has been added, strain, add wine and chopped herbs, and season. Approximately 1¼ cups sauce.

BÉARNAISE SAUCE NO. II

1 tablespoon chopped shallots
1 teaspoon chopped tarragon
1 teaspoon chopped chervil
12 peppercorns, crushed
2 tablespoons dry white wine
1 tablespoon white wine vinegar
1½ cups butter
5 egg yolks
1 tablespoon cream
salt
cayenne

Place shallots, ½ teaspoon tarragon, ½ teaspoon chervil, peppercorns, wine, and vinegar in high small saucepan and simmer very slowly until nearly dry. Remove and cool. Clarify butter by melting and removing scum. Put egg yolks and cream in small double boiler and beat with egg whisk until they begin to get creamy. Then add clarified butter and continue whisking. Stir in first mixture and if too thick add a little more cream. Strain and add ½ teaspoon each chopped tarragon and chervil. Approximately 1½ cups sauce.

SAUCE CHARON

Follow directions for Béarnaise Sauce (p. 37), omitting last addition of tarragon and chervil and adding 2 tablespoons tomato purée.

SAUCE FOYOT OR VALOIS

Follow directions for Béarnaise Sauce (p. 37) and add 1 tablespoon beef extract.

TOKAY SAUCE

1 cup Brown Sauce (p. 28)
1 tablespoon chopped celery
1 tablespoon chopped pimiento
4 tablespoons white Tokay

Simmer celery and pimiento in Brown Sauce until celery is tender, about 20 minutes. Remove from heat and stir in wine just before serving. Serve with broiled steaks, chops, or hamburger. Serve around, not over, meat. Approximately 1¼ cups sauce.

BORDELAISE SAUCE NO. I

(for roasts, steaks, and chops)

4 shallots, minced
1 bay leaf, crushed
1 sprig parsley, minced
2 cups dry red wine
2 cups Brown Sauce (p. 28)
salt and pepper

Simmer together shallots, bay leaf, and parsley in wine over very low heat until reduced to a sirupy consistency. Stir constantly after it begins to thicken. Add Brown Sauce and cook in double boiler for 30 minutes. Strain and serve hot. 4½ cups sauce.

BORDELAISE SAUCE NO. II

1 cup Brown Sauce (p. 28)
½ cup Tomato Sauce (p. 49)
6 tablespoons beef or veal marrow
1½ tablespoons Sherry

Mix all ingredients and heat. Approximately 2 cups sauce.

SAUCE À LA BONNE FEMME

(for dark-meated fish and red meat)

3 tablespoons butter
1 medium-sized onion, chopped
1 clove garlic, crushed and minced
⅔ cup dry red wine
1 teaspoon flour
½ sprig parsley, minced
½ teaspoon paprika
1 hard-cooked egg, finely chopped

Sauté onion and garlic in butter to a golden brown. Add flour. Add wine, stirring constantly, and simmer about 5 minutes, then add parsley, paprika, and egg. Approximately 1 cup sauce.

TIREAU SAUCE

(for very dark-meated fish, lamb, mutton, or venison)

1 teaspoon ground cinnamon
10 almonds, blanched and pounded to a paste
6 whole cloves
¼ cup brown sugar, firmly packed
grated rind of 1 lemon
1 cup red currant jelly
1 cup dry red wine
salt and pepper

Combine all ingredients, bring to a boil, and simmer 25 minutes. Season. Strain and serve. Approximately 2 cups sauce.

SAUCE BERCY

1/4 cup butter
1/4 pound shallots, chopped very fine
1 cup dry white wine, Chablis preferably
2 tablespoons finely chopped parsley
1/2 teaspoon lemon juice
salt and pepper

Sauté shallots in butter over very low heat until they are soft but not brown. Add wine and simmer until quite thick. Just before serving add parsley, lemon juice, and seasonings. Serve separately with steak or chops. Approximately 3/4 cup sauce.

SAUCE D'ÉPICE

(for red meats)

3 tablespoons chopped onion
1 clove garlic, crushed and minced
1 tablespoon butter
1 1/2 cups dry red wine
2 tablespoons grated Roquefort
1/8 teaspoon nutmeg
1/4 teaspoon cloves
1/2 teaspoon paprika
1/2 teaspoon Angostura bitters
1 teaspoon Maggi's seasoning
1/2 teaspoon anchovy paste
1 teaspoon minced parsley
3 beef cubes
salt and cayenne

Sauté onion and garlic slowly in butter until very soft but not brown. Add all other ingredients except salt and cayenne, and reduce by approximately one half. Season to taste. Serve very hot. Approximately 1 cup sauce.

WINE SAUCE FROM GRAVY

(for lamb, mutton, or venison)

1/2 cup gravy
1 tablespoon flour
1/2 cup currant jelly
1/2 cup catsup
1/2 cup dry red wine
1/4 cup brandy

Use gravy left in pan after roasting meat. Skim off all fat and reserve 2 tablespoons. Blend in flour. Stir in gravy. When perfectly smooth add jelly, catsup, and wine and let it boil up well. Remove from heat and stir in brandy. 2 1/4 cups sauce.

SAUCE GENOISE

for fish, shellfish, meats, and vegetables)

3 tablespoons chopped celery
2 tablespoons chopped onion
2 tablespoons chopped parsley
2 tablespoons olive oil
salt and pepper
1 can tomatoes
½ cup dry white wine

Sauté celery, onion, and parsley in olive oil until tender but not brown. Season, add tomatoes and wine, and cook over very low heat until very thick, stirring every few minutes and constantly during last part of cooking. Approximately 3 cups sauce.

CREOLE SAUCE

4 tablespoons chopped green pepper
2 tablespoons chopped onion
¼ cup sliced mushrooms
1 clove garlic, crushed and minced
2 tablespoons butter
2 tablespoons flour
½ cup condensed tomato soup
1 cup Sauce Espagnole (p. 35)
½ cup dry white wine
salt and cayenne

Sauté pepper, onion, mushrooms, and garlic in butter until tender but not brown. Stir in flour; add soup, Sauce Espagnole, wine, and seasonings. Simmer 5 minutes, stirring constantly. Approximately 2 cups sauce.

CUMBERLAND SAUCE

(for any meats, especially ham, and game)

½ cup currant jelly
6 tablespoons finely shredded orange peel, white part removed
5 tablespoons orange juice
2 tablespoons lemon juice
2 teaspoons dry mustard
2 teaspoons paprika
1 teaspoon ground ginger
5 tablespoons Port
salt and cayenne

Melt jelly in double boiler. Cover orange peel with cold water, boil 5 minutes, drain, and add to jelly. Add all other ingredients and season to taste. Serve cool but not chilled. 1¼ cups sauce.

SAUCE PÉRIGUEUX

(for meat)

6 mushrooms, minced
½ clove garlic, crushed and minced
1 tablespoon chopped parsley
2 tablespoons chopped scallions
2 tablespoons olive oil or vegetable oil
2 tablespoons flour
½ cup dry white wine
½ cup stock or bouillon
salt and pepper

Sauté mushrooms, garlic, scallions, and parsley in oil until slightly browned. Blend in flour. Add wine and stock, salt and pepper. Simmer 10 minutes. Approximately 1 cup sauce.

POLSCI SAUCE

(for boiled tongue, roasts, or game)

1 tablespoon butter
1 tablespoon minced onion
1 tablespoon minced celery
1 tablespoon minced carrot
1 tablespoon minced raw ham
1 tablespoon flour
1 cup beef bouillon
1 teaspoon Worcestershire sauce
⅓ cup seedless raisins
½ cup almonds, ground
½ teaspoon sugar
¾ cup Sauterne (not too dry)

Sauté vegetables and ham in butter until vegetables are soft. Stir in flour and cook 3 minutes while stirring. Stir in bouillon slowly, cook 10 minutes, and strain. Add all other ingredients in order given and simmer slowly 10 minutes, or until raisins are plump. Approximately 2½ cups sauce.

COCKTAIL SAUCE

(an unusual recipe)

1 cup mayonnaise
2 tablespoons chili sauce
2 tablespoons catsup
1 tablespoon tarragon vinegar
1 tablespoon Burgundy or Claret
1 teaspoon lemon juice
salt and pepper

Mix all ingredients thoroughly and season to taste. Approximately 1¼ cups sauce.

SAUCE AUX FINES HERBES

2 tablespoons butter
¾ cup chopped mushrooms
1 tablespoon flour
¾ cup stock or bouillon
⅓ cup chopped tomatoes
⅛ teaspoon rosemary
½ teaspoon chervil
dash of white pepper
¼ teaspoon salt
2 tablespoons dry white wine

Sauté mushrooms in butter until tender. Add flour and stir until brown. Add stock and simmer until thickened. Add tomatoes, rosemary, chervil, pepper, salt, and wine. Simmer for 5 minutes and serve. Approximately 1½ cups sauce.

SAUCE COLBERT

1 cup hot water
1 tablespoon beef extract
2 tablespoons melted butter
juice of 1 lemon
1 teaspoon minced tarragon or parsley
2 tablespoons Sherry
salt and pepper

Dissolve beef extract in hot water in double boiler. Add butter gradually, beating constantly with wire whisk. Add lemon juice, Sherry, and minced tarragon or parsley. Approximately 1¼ cups sauce.

SAUCE ITALIENNE

3 tablespoons butter
5 shallots, chopped fine, *or*
2 tablespoons chopped onion
1 cup mushrooms, sliced thin
¼ cup dry white wine
1 cup Tomato Sauce (p. 49)
1 cup Brown Sauce (p. 28)
1 tablespoon chopped parsley

Sauté shallots or onion and mushrooms gently in 2 tablespoons butter for 5 minutes; add wine, and simmer 5 minutes longer; add Tomato Sauce and Brown Sauce, and simmer 3 minutes longer. Add remaining tablespoon butter and parsley. Approximately 2¼ cups sauce.

SPAGHETTI SAUCE

1 pound ground beef
3 tablespoons butter
1 can condensed tomato soup
½ cup chili sauce
1 large onion sliced
1 teaspoon powdered garlic
1 teaspoon poultry dressing
¼ cup vinegar
⅛ teaspoon cayenne
salt
1 cup water
1 cup Sherry

Brown ground beef in butter. Add all other ingredients and simmer, covered, 3 to 4 hours, adding more water if necessary. Approximately 4 cups sauce.

SAUCE BIGARADE

(for duck)

1 teaspoon butter
1 teaspoon flour
½ cup orange juice
½ tablespoon lemon juice
½ tablespoon orange rind, sliced very thin
1 tablespoon Port jelly (p. 274)
pinch of salt

Make a roux of butter and flour. Gradually add orange and lemon juice, and simmer, stirring constantly, 3 minutes. Add jelly and salt, and stir until jelly is melted. Approximately ¾ cup sauce.

RAISIN AND WINE SAUCE

(for ham)

½ cup small currants
1 cup dry red wine
1 tablespoon cornstarch
½ cup sugar
½ tablespoon dry mustard
½ teaspoon powdered cloves
½ teaspoon powdered cinnamon
¼ cup mild vinegar

Soak currants in wine overnight. Drain off wine. Use same wine for sauce. Mix dry ingredients together. Add wine and vinegar, and cook until thickened. Add currants and heat. Approximately 1½ cups sauce.

WINE SAUCE FOR HAM

2 tablespoons butter
½ teaspoon salt
½ teaspoon dry mustard
dash of cayenne and paprika
1 teaspoon Worcestershire sauce
½ cup currant jelly
¼ cup dry white wine
¼ cup Sherry
4 thin strips lemon rind
2 tablespoons lemon juice

Melt butter, add seasonings, and mix well. Add jelly, wines, lemon rind and juice. Cook gently, stirring occasionally, until jelly is melted and sauce slightly thickened, 10-15 minutes. Serve hot. Approximately 1 cup sauce.

MUSTARD SAUCE

1 cup Medium White Sauce (p. 28)
½ teaspoon dry mustard
2 tablespoons dry white wine

Add mustard and wine to White Sauce and simmer, stirring constantly. Do not allow to boil. Approximately 1 cup sauce.

SAUCE TROUVILLAISE

(for fish)

4 tablespoons butter
1 thick slice onion
¼ cup chopped mushrooms
¼ cup chopped shrimp
¼ cup chopped oysters
¼ teaspoon salt
⅛ teaspoon paprika
2 tablespoons flour
1 tablespoon grated Swiss cheese
1 cup milk
¼ cup dry white wine
1 egg yolk, lightly beaten

Sauté thick slice of onion in butter until tender but not brown. Remove onion and discard. Sauté mushrooms in butter until tender. Place in double boiler, add chopped shrimp, oysters, and seasonings, and blend in flour and cheese. Add milk gradually and cook, stirring constantly, until smooth, about 5 minutes. Add wine and egg yolk and bring to a simmer but do not boil. Beat with rotary egg beater for 3 minutes. Approximately 2 cups sauce.

BÉCHAMEL SAUCE

1 cup condensed chicken consommé
2 tablespoons chopped onion
1 teaspoon chopped carrot
1 teaspoon chopped celery
1 teaspoon chopped parsley
1 small bay leaf
2 tablespoons butter
2 tablespoons flour
½ cup cream
salt and pepper

Bring consommé, onion, carrot, celery, and parsley to a boil and simmer 25 minutes. Strain and measure. Add enough boiling water to make ½ cup. Make a roux of butter and flour. Add stock and cream slowly, and simmer until thick, stirring constantly—about 5 minutes. Approximately 1 cup sauce.

SAUCE MORNAY

(for fish)

1½ cups Béchamel Sauce
2 egg yolks, beaten
1 teaspoon grated Parmesan cheese
1 teaspoon grated Swiss cheese
3 tablespoons cooking liquor of fish with which sauce is to be used, much reduced
¼ cup cream
2 tablespoons butter
salt and pepper

While Béchamel Sauce is still hot but not boiling, stir in beaten egg yolks, cheese, and fish liquor. Add cream and butter, season and reheat, but do not boil. Approximately 2 cups sauce.

SAUCE À LA NORMANDE

(for fish)

1 cup Velouté Sauce (p. 28)
¼ cup strong fish stock (p. 56)
¼ cup dry white wine
2 egg yolks, beaten
1 tablespoon butter
juice of ½ lemon
salt and pepper

Add fish stock and wine to Velouté Sauce, bring just to a simmer, stir in egg yolks, butter, and lemon juice and stir constantly over low heat until thickened. Do not allow to boil after egg yolks are added. Approximately 1½ cups sauce.

CRAWFISH BUTTER

2 tablespoons butter
claws, heads, and shells only of 3 cooked crawfish

Pound together to a paste and pass through a sieve.

SAUCE PORTUGUESE

(for fish)

1 cup sliced mushrooms
1 medium-sized green pepper, chopped
1 medium-sized onion, sliced
12 green olives, pimiento stuffed
2 cups canned tomatoes
2 tablespoons butter
2 tablespoons flour
salt and pepper

Simmer mushrooms, pepper, and onion, in enough water to cover, until tender. Add tomatoes and olives, and bring to a boil. Make a roux of butter and flour and add. Simmer, stirring constantly, for 2 or 3 minutes. Approximately 2½ cups sauce.

CAPER SAUCE

1 cup chicken broth
½ cup very dry white wine
1 tablespoon butter
2 tablespoons capers
1 tablespoon caper liquid
½ teaspoon salt
⅛ teaspoon pepper
4 tablespoons sour cream

Mix broth and wine, and simmer until reduced about one third. Add butter and flour, and stir until thick over low heat. Add capers and juice. Remove from heat and add cream. 2 cups sauce.

SAUCE SIERRA

(for shellfish, chicken, or white meats)

3 tablespoons melted butter
1 tablespoon beef extract
½ cup dry white wine
¼ cup mushroom catsup
1 tablespoon lemon juice
1 tablespoon sugar
salt and cayenne

Mix ingredients, bring just to simmering point, stirring occasionally, and serve hot. Approximately 1 cup sauce.

HOLLANDAISE SAUCE

1 ½ cups butter
6 egg yolks
1 tablespoon boiling water
3 tablespoons lemon juice
salt

Fill lower part of double boiler with water to within about an inch of bottom of top part. Melt butter, beat in egg yolks, add boiling water and lemon juice, and continue beating rapidly until very thick. If it begins to curdle, add a little more boiling water and continue beating. Approximately 2 cups sauce.

HOLLANDAISE SAUCE WITH SAUTERNE

1 ½ cups butter
6 egg yolks, lightly beaten
1 tablespoon boiling water
¼ cup Sauterne
salt

Put just enough water in lower part of double boiler so that it is about an inch below bottom of top part. Melt butter in top of double boiler, beat in egg yolks until thoroughly mixed, add boiling water, then add wine a little at a time, beating constantly. When all wine is added, remove from heat and season. Approximately 2 cups sauce.

MOCK HOLLANDAISE SAUCE WITH WINE

6 hard-cooked egg yolks, mashed
1 ½ cups melted butter
¼ cup dry white wine
salt
cayenne

Test butter with finger—it should be almost body temperature. Blend a tablespoon at a time with egg yolks. Season to taste, using cayenne very sparingly. Add wine and beat until very smooth. Approximately 2 cups sauce.

SAUCE AURORE

1 ½ cups White Wine Sauce (p. 31)
4 tablespoons tomato paste
4 tablespoons butter

Bring the Wine Sauce to a simmer, and blend in tomato paste and butter. Approximately 2 cups sauce.

TOMATO-SHERRY SAUCE

2 cups tomato soup
½ teaspoon salt
⅛ teaspoon pepper
1 medium-sized onion, sliced thin
2 tablespoons butter
2 tablespoons flour
¼ cup Sherry

If condensed soup is used, use 1 cup soup and dilute with 1 cup water. Boil onions, soup, and seasonings until onions are tender. Put through sieve or colander. If necessary, add water to make 1 cup. Make a roux of butter and flour and gradually add purée and wine. Simmer gently for 2 or 3 minutes. Approximately 1¼ cups sauce.

For plain Tomato Sauce, omit Sherry.

TARTAR SAUCE

1 cup mayonnaise
2 tablespoons dry white wine
1 tablespoon chopped sour pickles
1 tablespoon chopped capers
1 tablespoon chopped olives
1 tablespoon chopped parsley

Mix all ingredients just before using. Approximately 1¼ cups sauce.

POULETTE SAUCE

(for poultry, sweetbreads, vegetables, etc.)

2 tablespoons butter
2 tablespoons flour
2 cups condensed consommé
2 tablespoons chopped parsley
1 medium-sized onion, minced very fine
juice of 1 lemon
¼ cup Sherry
4 egg yolks, beaten
salt
white pepper

Make a roux of butter and flour, blend in consommé, add parsley and onion, which should be chopped to a paste, and lemon juice. Simmer 20 minutes. Add Sherry. Remove from heat, stir in well-beaten egg yolks, and season to taste. Serve at once. Approximately 2½ cups sauce.

SPRING SAUCE

(Best for quail, squab, young grouse, young pheasant, etc.)

3 tablespoons butter
4 tablespoons diced bacon
2 shallots, chopped
12 mushrooms, sliced
2 tablespoons brandy
1 cup Claret
1 cup strong chicken broth
1 tablespoon chopped parsley
1 tablespoon chopped chervil
1 tablespoon chopped celery
½ tablespoon chopped chives
few grains cayenne
4 crushed peppercorns
salt

Fry butter, bacon, shallots, and mushrooms together in earthenware saucepan. When a rich brown, pour in brandy. Light it and allow to burn out. Add all other ingredients and simmer 15 minutes. Strain. (If desired, blood from birds on which sauce is to be used may be added. A little vinegar should be added to the blood to prevent congealing. Simmer 4 minutes more.) Approximately 2 cups sauce.

CHAPTER FOUR

Fish

Fish deserves much better treatment than it gets in the average kitchen. The commonest, almost the universal, fault is overcooking. Nine out of ten otherwise good cooks, and professional chefs are not excluded, cook fish actually twice as long as necessary. It is one of the most delicate of foods, both in flavor and texture, but too much heat over too long a period invariably results in loss of flavor and hardening of fiber.

All forms of fish cookery are easy, but there are a few essential points to bear in mind.

First, when frying, remember the adage of the Southern Mammies (and can they fry fish!), "Feesh lak's to swim, chile," and less than a quarter of an inch of fat in the frying pan is never enough. Rolling in egg or milk and corn meal or dry bread crumbs is usually, although not always, another "must" for frying. Whatever fat you use, and suit yourself about that, try adding half as much butter. The rich golden-brown color and delicate nutlike flavor is worth this small extra extravagance.

Be sure to have the fat hot—just this side of smoking: 350-375° F. if you have a deep-fat thermometer. Turn the fish only once, and three to six minutes is enough for any fish or filet small enough to fry, half of that if not rolled in corn meal or crumbs. If you have to fry more than one panful, strain the fat you have used and wipe out the pan (paper towels are great for this). Then you won't have any burned crumbs to spoil the taste and looks of the next batch. In deep-fat frying, be sure to have the cooking vessel not more than half filled so as to avoid unnecessary splattering or the possible chance of the fat's catching fire.

And don't think there isn't a wrong way to broil fish. Unless the broiler is first heated thoroughly and then greased, nothing in the world can keep the fish from sticking to it. Start with the skin side down and the fish about two inches away from the heating unit. When it is gently browned, turn the skin side up.

If the fish is large, two pounds or more, you may have to reduce the flame or lower the broiler rack to finish the cooking, but ten minutes to the pound is plenty.

Have you ever heard of the guide's method of baking fish in an overcoat of mud? Primitive as it is, it is one of the best methods known. He takes the cleaned but unscaled fish, covers it with a thick layer of black mud, and buries it in a bed of glowing embers. Half an hour or so later he digs it out, and the gray, hard envelope breaks off easily, taking skin and scales with it, leaving just about the best fish you have ever tasted. Would you like to try it in your own kitchen? No, you don't need mud! Just make the thickest paste you can of flour and water, nothing else—but do get it thick. Clean the fish but don't bother to scale it. Wipe it dry, season, wet your hands, and cover it thickly with the flour paste. Don't leave the smallest spot exposed. After it has been in the oven ten or fifteen minutes, take it out and examine it. You will probably find that the dough has run in two or three places, leaving the fish surface exposed. Cover these spots with more dough and put it back. You will want your oven just as hot as you can possibly get it, but the cooking time is not critical as all the natural juices are sealed in. Half an hour is about right for a medium-sized fish while a fairly large one, say three or four pounds, will take an hour. If you want it stuffed, use your favorite recipe but use a light hand with the seasonings as the dough envelope seals in every bit of flavor.

A few taps with the handle of a knife will crack the hard cover. Peel it off gently and there, all white and gleaming, lies the fish you will remember for a long, long time. Not the least advantage of this method is that there won't be the slightest trace of cooking odor. Of course, you will want to put a tablespoon of dry white wine inside it before you seal it up; or, if you have a strongly flavored fish—mackerel, redfish, or herring, for example—use a dry red wine instead.

There is another method of accomplishing a similar result which also has the advantage of being odorless and is a bit easier. Over a generation ago, an ingenious Frenchman discovered that fish could be cooked in a greased paper bag. *Poisson en papillot* appeared on the menus of famous restaurants all over the world. The technique was a bit tricky—the bag had a tendency to char and even burn away unless the oven temperature was just right, and, of course, even greasing the bag didn't make it entirely waterproof.

A few years ago, an American manufacturer developed a different kind of paper, waterproof and almost unbelievably tough. Butter makers adopted it for wrapping with whoops of joy because it kept wanted flavors in and unwanted flavors out. Then, some inspired genius thought of using it for cooking, and the first really new culinary method in centuries was introduced.

Parchment-paper cookery of fish is not only simple—it is practically fool-proof. Simply clean and scale your fish, wet the paper, and lay the fish on it. Add the wine and seasonings, gather the corners together to make a bag, and tie it tightly. Remember to use a bowknot, of course. Bake it, if you choose, in a greased pan in a medium oven, 350-375° F., allowing twenty minutes for a two-pound fish. Add five minutes extra for each additional pound. Or, if you want to use the oven for something else, drop your parchment bag in a large kettle of boiling water and cover. Cooking time is surprisingly little longer, and the chances are in favor of somewhat better results as you don't have to worry about regulating the temperature.

You'd expect the experts of the National Fisheries Association to have top-hole ideas about their specialty. The "hot oven" method they regard as one of their best for small fish, fish steaks, and fish filets. And when they say "hot oven," they mean exactly that. 500° F. by your oven thermometer if you have one—if not, preheat for about half an hour.

Dip your fish in milk, fresh or diluted evaporated, to which you have added salt in the proportion of one teaspoon to a cup. Then roll in hard, dry bread crumbs (you can buy them in cartons now) until it is thoroughly covered. Dot both sides generously with butter. Put in a well-greased pan *without water* and place it in the red-hot oven for about ten minutes. Don't turn it. Remove it carefully with a pancake turner or spatula to a hot platter and serve with the sauce you have selected.

Simple as this method is, two things must be carefully observed: first, be sure you do a thorough job of crumbing. You need a perfect blanket to retain the natural juices of the fish; second, the oven must be hot, hotter, hottest. Do this, and you'll have the crisp tan crust and perfect flavor of perfectly fried fish with much less bother; and the whole job is done so quickly that the cooking odors simply don't have time to get out and penetrate the house. The only limitation to the "hot oven" method is that it is not adapted to fish much over two pounds. The bigger fellows must be baked, boiled, or steamed.

Very fat fish take kindly to baking. Little or no basting is necessary. Lean fish should be gashed quite deeply, strips of salt pork inserted, and basted occasionally with melted butter. Have the oven fairly hot, 375-400° F., and allow ten minutes per pound up to four pounds and five minutes per pound for every additional one. A greased rack in the bottom of the pan is almost a necessity. It makes certain that your fish will go on the platter whole—otherwise, it is almost certain that it will not.

Boiling or, more correctly, poaching is much commoner in Europe than it is here. Americans in general have the idea that "boiled" fish is tasteless. So it is when actually boiled in plain water as most of us do. The lowliest French family would never think of using anything but court bouillon, which sounds formidable but is really absurdly simple. There are almost as many recipes for it as there are cooks, but the fundamental idea of all is the same. You see, the vegetables, herbs, and other ingredients whose flavor you want to impart to the fish take comparatively long cooking to extract their flavor. So they are cooked first, that's all, and the resulting liquid is court bouillon. Madame Prunier, head of Prunier's—the most famous sea-food restaurants in the world—pretty well covers the subject when she says it should have "an interesting taste." A basic recipe is given on page 55, but you'll probably modify it every time you use it.

Fish should never be actually boiled unless you intend to make soup. The court bouillon should be barely at the simmering point, "trembling" (again to quote Madame Prunier), and kept there until the fish is done. That's all there is to poaching, but it is all the difference between success and failure in cooking fish in liquid.

Lean fish are best for poaching because they keep their shape better, but here is a trick that will enable you to serve a really attractive platter instead of something that looks like fish hash. Simply wrap the fish in a piece of cheesecloth long enough so that the ends can hang over the edges of the cooking dish. Timetables are not so important. Just watch it carefully, and the first moment you see that the flesh shows signs of separating from the bones, lift it out.

Steaming is a satisfactory method for preparing thick pieces cut from large fish or fish steaks. Simply place a few slices of lemon and a bay leaf or two on top of the fish in the steamer. But, remember, it is just as easy to overcook by steaming as by any other method. Thirty to thirty-five minutes should be ample for the largest fish you are apt to cook in this way.

Smaller fish should have the backbone broken in several places, especially when you intend to fry or broil them, to prevent curling. Larger fish should be gashed slantwise quite deeply, no matter what method of cooking you use, to enable them to keep their shape.

When you have fish prepared by the dealer, be sure to tell him to include the roe, if any. Shad roe is, of course, the choicest, but all roe is excellent except that of pike, pickerel, and muskallonge which are inedible.

No attempt has been made to include recipes for every type of fish. This would not only make a book of encyclopedic proportions but would be a needless duplication of effort. Varieties that are plentiful and cheap in some sections are either prohibitively expensive or actually unobtainable in others. To mention just one out of many examples, Lake Superior whitefish—an expensive delicacy in most of the United States, unknown in Europe—is a commonplace in the Middle West.

Then there are the so-called "pan fish": blue gills, bullheads, catfish, sunfish, etc., many of them ranking in flavor with the aristocratic brook trout and pompano.

Use your own good judgment in adapting these recipes to the fish you have or can easily get. A recipe for one light, delicately flavored fish will almost invariably give good results with other fish of the same type.

COURT BOUILLON

3 ½ quarts water
4 tablespoons salt
½ cup vinegar
1 cup very dry white wine
1 small carrot, sliced
1 small onion, sliced
1 tablespoon parsley, chopped
½ small bay leaf
1 sprig thyme, *or*
¼ teaspoon ground thyme
½ teaspoon white pepper

Simmer all together for 45 minutes. Strain and keep cold until ready for use. Approximately 3 quarts.

FISH STOCK HOTEL LAFAYETTE

Place some fish bones and fish heads (preferably sole) in a pan and cover with water (3/4 quart). Add some parsley, some thyme, and a few laurel leaves. Boil for 30 minutes and pass through a strainer.

FISH FUMET

(fish stock)

- 1 pound fish trimmings and bones, chopped
- 2 1/2 cups water
- 2 tablespoons minced onion
- 6 stalks parsley
- 6 peppercorns
- 2 cups dry white wine
- salt

Simmer fish trimmings, onion, parsley, and peppercorns for 20 minutes. Add wine, salt to taste, and boil gently 30 minutes longer. Strain. Approximately 4 cups.

FISH JELLY—WHITE WINE

- 3 1/2 cups fish fumet
- 1/2 pound cooked meat of any white fish, finely chopped or pounded
- 1 leek, finely chopped (white part only)
- 1 tablespoon chopped parsley
- 1 egg white
- 1 1/2 tablespoons gelatin

Add the fish meat, leek, and parsley to the fumet and simmer 45 minutes. Cool until lukewarm. Soften gelatin in a little cold water. Add together with lightly beaten egg white and stir until thoroughly mixed. Strain through coarse cloth or fine sieve.

FISH JELLY—RED WINE

Follow directions for fish fumet, using dry red wine instead of white wine. Then proceed as for Fish Jelly—White Wine.

FISH GLAZE

Reduce fish fumet by slow simmering until it is of the consistency of thick sirup. Pour over fish and put in very hot oven or under broiler for 3 minutes. (Glazing must be done very quickly or the sauce may curdle.)

VELOUTÉ DE POISSON HOTEL LAFAYETTE

Melt two ounces of butter in a pan, add a little flour (1 ounce) and keep stirring over a slow fire until the mixture begins to brown. Slowly add one pint of "fish stock" (p. 56) and keep stirring until brought to a boil. This sauce should be cooked for an hour and then forced through a strainer.

BAKED STRIPED BASS

1 (3-4 pound) bass
12 green onions, white part only, cut up
2 tablespoons chopped parsley
2 tablespoons butter
2 cups dry white wine (approximately)
salt and pepper

Select a baking dish as nearly the length of the fish as possible, grease it, and line with parchment paper. Put in fish, onions, parsley, and butter. Add sufficient wine to cover, season, and bake, uncovered, in moderately hot oven (375-400°), basting every 10 minutes. Allow 10 minutes per pound if under 4 pounds; add 5 minutes to total cooking time for each pound over 4 pounds. If necessary, place under broiler for last few minutes to brown thoroughly. Lift out parchment paper and slide contents on serving dish. Serves 6 to 8.

BASS PORTUGUESE STYLE

1 (3-4 pound) bass (or similar textured fish)
1 clove garlic, crushed
olive oil
salt and pepper
¼ cup dry white wine
2 tablespoons minced onion
2 cups Portuguese Sauce (p. 47)
½ cup bread crumbs
2 tablespoons butter

Clean and scale fish but do not remove head or tail. Rub with olive oil, salt, and pepper. Rub baking dish with crushed clove of garlic and grease well. Place fish in pan, add wine, and sprinkle minced onion on top of fish. Bake in moderate oven (350-375°) 30-45 minutes, basting frequently. Pour Portuguese Sauce over, cover with bread crumbs, and dot with butter. Place under broiler until crumbs are browned. Serves 6-8.

BAKED BASS

(Adapted from a very old French recipe)

¼ pound butter
3 medium-sized onions, chopped, *or*
2 onions and 2 shallots, chopped
1 (3-3½ pound) bass
salt
white pepper
¼ cup Burgundy or Claret
3 teaspoons chopped almonds or pecans
1 cup coarsely chopped mushrooms
1 cup buttered bread crumbs

Sauté onions (and shallots) in a little butter until tender but not brown. Grease a piece of parchment paper large enough to come up over the ends and sides of a long and narrow pan or baking dish. Spread on onions and lay in fish, which has been rubbed on both sides with the seasonings. Add wine and sprinkle over with nuts. Add butter in which onions were sautéed and dot with rest of butter. Put mushrooms around the sides. Bake in a very hot oven (450-500°) for 35 minutes, basting frequently. There should be very little liquid left when fish is done, but, if necessary to prevent burning, add a very small amount more of wine. Ten minutes before it is done, sprinkle on buttered bread crumbs and let them brown. Take the paper by the sides and slide the fish onto a platter. Garnish with parsley. Serves 6.

Any other fish of similar size and texture may be substituted for bass.

BAKED BASS À LA WELLINGTON

1 (4-5 pound) bass
2 cups dry bread crumbs
¼ cup Sherry
4 tablespoons butter
1 teaspoon chopped parsley
2 teaspoons chopped capers
salt and pepper
paprika

Scale and clean fish but do not remove head, tail, or fins. Moisten bread crumbs with ¼ cup Sherry, melt butter, and mix in together with parsley and capers. Season to taste. Stuff bass with mixture and sew up. Bake in moderately hot oven (375-400°), basting frequently with remaining Sherry, 30-45 minutes. Serves 6-8.

BAKED BASS, GENEVA STYLE

1 (3-4 pound) bass
2 carrots, sliced
1 small onion, sliced
3 tablespoons chopped celery
6 tablespoons butter
1½ cups very dry white wine
4 tablespoons cream
4 tablespoons Hollandaise Sauce (p. 48)
salt and pepper

Butter a baking dish well, put in fish, surround with vegetables, and dot with rest of butter. Bake in a moderate oven (350-375°) 40 to 50 minutes. Place on serving dish and keep hot. Add wine to the cooking liquor and reduce to about ¼ cup. Remove from heat, add cream and Hollandaise Sauce. Heat but do not allow to boil, and pour over fish. Serves 6-8.

KINGFISH UBSALA

4 medium-sized kingfish
¼ cup dry white wine
½ cup fish stock (p. 56) or bouillon
salt and pepper
2 cups White Wine Sauce (p. 31)

Put fish in buttered baking dish, add wine and fish stock or bouillon, season, and bake, covered, in moderately hot oven (350-375°) 30-45 minutes. Remove to serving platter to keep hot. Add White Wine Sauce to juices in pan and simmer until thick. Strain and pour over fish. Serves 4-6.

BAKED MACKEREL

1 (2½-3 pound) mackerel
1 pint cream
2 tablespoons butter
salt and pepper
1 tablespoon flour
1 tablespoon Sherry
parsley

Split mackerel and place, skin side down, in large pan. Add cream, which should about half cover fish. Season and dot with 1 tablespoon butter. Bake in moderate oven (350-375°) until tender, about 20 minutes. Remove fish to serving dish. Blend flour with rest of butter, add to liquid in pan, and cook until thickened. Stir in Sherry. Serve sauce separately. Serves 4.

MACKEREL BONNEFOY

½ cup chopped carrots
¼ cup chopped onions
¼ cup chopped leeks (white part only)
¼ cup chopped celery
½ cup chopped tomatoes
¼ cup butter
4 mackerel (approx. ¾ pound each)
¼ cup dry white wine
1 cup Brown Sauce (p. 28)
salt and pepper
chopped parsley

Sauté vegetables in butter until tender, remove, and brown fish quickly on both sides. Reduce heat, add vegetables, wine, and Brown Sauce, season, and simmer until fish is tender. Garnish with chopped parsley. Serves 4-6.

BAKED BLUEFISH, ITALIENNE

1 (4-4½ pound) bluefish
salt and pepper
1 cup dry white wine
1½ cups Sauce Italienne (p. 43)

Trim off fins and tail but do not remove head. Rub with seasonings and place in greased baking dish. Add wine and bake in moderate oven (350-375°) 20 minutes, basting frequently. Pour Sauce Italienne over and bake 15-25 minutes longer according to size. Serves 6 to 8.

COD CUTLETS FLEMISH STYLE

2 pounds cod cutlets
1 teaspoon salt
¼ teaspoon pepper
¼ teaspoon nutmeg
1 shallot or small onion, chopped
1 tablespoon lemon juice
1 small bouquet garni (p. 9)
2 cups dry white wine
3 tablespoons very dry bread crumbs

Place cutlets in well-buttered baking dish, add all other ingredients except crumbs, and bring to a simmer, then place in moderate oven (350-375°) for 10 minutes. Put cutlets on a serving dish, add bread crumbs to liquid, boil until it thickens, and pour over fish. Serves 4.

COD CUTLETS PORTUGUESE STYLE

2 pounds cod cutlets
2 tablespoons butter
salt and pepper
1 clove garlic, crushed and minced
1 medium-sized onion, chopped
1 tablespoon chopped parsley
1 sprig thyme, *or*
⅛ teaspoon powdered thyme
1 cup chopped tomato
1 cup dry white wine

Butter a casserole thoroughly, put in cutlets and all other ingredients. Place in moderate oven (350-375°) and cook 10 minutes after it begins to boil. Remove cutlets and keep hot. Reduce cooking liquor through boiling about ⅓. Pour it over fish. Serves 4.

COD STEAKS WITH OYSTER SAUCE

2 pounds cod steaks
salt and pepper
1 medium-sized onion, chopped
1 cup dry white wine
20 oysters
1 tablespoon flour
3 tablespoons butter
1 tablespoon lemon juice

Use a covered saucepan as small as possible, well buttered. Season steaks and add chopped onion, wine, and oyster liquor. Cover and simmer until cod is tender. Remove to hot serving dish. Make a roux of butter and flour, and add to liquid in which steaks were cooked. Add oysters and lemon juice, and cook very gently for a few minutes until oysters are plump and edges curled. Pour over fish. Serves 4.

FILET OF SOLE AU VIN BLANC

(From Hotel Lafayette, New York City)

Chop a few shallots, put in pan, and brown them in butter, add a glassful of white wine. Allow it to boil until the wine is almost completely evaporated. Then add *velouté de poisson* (p. 57) and a little cream. Stir the mixture, and add some salt and some red pepper. Then thicken with the yolk of an egg. Pour this sauce over the filets of sole, which have been previously poached, and serve very hot. Serves 6.

FILET OF SOLE WITH WHITE WINE

1 cup Sauterne
6 medium-sized mushrooms, thinly sliced
1 small onion, thinly sliced
salt and pepper
4 filets of sole (or flounder or halibut)
1 cup cream
1 tablespoon butter
1 tablespoon mayonnaise or Hollandaise Sauce

Bring wine, mushrooms, onion, and salt to a gentle boil and add filets. Simmer 2 minutes, turn with a pancake turner or spatula, and cook 2 minutes more. Remove fish carefully to an open casserole, or better still a sizzling platter. Then add cream, butter, and mayonnaise or Hollandaise to the wine sauce and simmer, but do not boil, for 6 minutes. Pour sauce over fish and put under broiler until fish is a delicate brown. Use any desired garnish—a few dashes of paprika, chopped parsley, or tender carrot tops. Do not add lemon—the flavor is just right without it. (If quick-frosted filets are used be sure they are thoroughly defrosted before cooking.) Serves 4.

FILET OF SOLE VERONIQUE

2 cups seedless white grapes
1 cup dry white wine
4-6 filets of sole or flounder
2 teaspoons chopped shallots
½ cup fish stock (p. 56)
1 tablespoon lemon juice
pinch of thyme
salt and pepper
2 tablespoons flour
2 tablespoons butter
½ cup cream
8-12 shrimps, or equal amount lobster meat

Bring wine to a simmer, add grapes, and cook 5 minutes. Remove and reserve. Place filets in saucepan, add wine in which grapes were poached, fish stock, lemon juice, and thyme and season to taste. Simmer gently 5 minutes. Remove and keep hot. Reduce sauce to half. Make a roux of flour and butter, add and cook 3 minutes, stirring constantly. Add cream, bring to a boil, and pour over filets. Arrange grapes around side, shrimp or lobster pieces on top, and brown lightly under broiler. Serves 4 to 6.

FILET OF SOLE OR FLOUNDER WITH CUCUMBERS AU GRATIN

4 filets of sole or flounder
1 teaspoon salt
1 large cucumber
¼ pound mild cheese, grated
¾ cup buttered bread crumbs
¾ cup Chablis or Riesling
½ teaspoon paprika

Cut filets in half and arrange them in baking dish on pieces of greased parchment paper cut about 1 inch longer and wider than the pieces of fish. Slice the cucumber about ¼ inch thick, place on top of the filets, and sprinkle with salt. Add the wine, cover with grated cheese, and top with buttered bread crumbs. Bake in a moderate oven (350-375°) 30 minutes. Remove each piece by slipping pancake turner or spatula under paper. In this way the fish can be slipped onto platter without breaking. Garnish with paprika. Serves 4.

FILETS IN RED WINE

3 tablespoons butter
3 medium-sized onions, chopped fine
4 fish filets (any kind)
salt and pepper
¾ cup dry red wine
1 tablespoon chopped parsley

Brown onions lightly in half the butter. Sprinkle them on the bottom of greased baking dish, lay in filets, season lightly, pour on wine, and dot with rest of butter. Bake in a moderate oven (350-375°) and baste frequently. When fish is no longer transparent, remove it to serving dish and pour over the sauce, which will be reduced to about ½ cup. Sprinkle with parsley. Serves 4.

FILET OF FLOUNDER À LA MARSHALL

4 tablespoons butter
1⅓ tablespoons vinegar
2 teaspoons thyme
1 teaspoon curry
½ cup Chablis
salt and paprika
1½ pounds filet of flounder

Brown butter, add vinegar, thyme, curry and wine, and season. Poach filet in sauce 4 minutes. Remove. Reduce sauce and pour over fish. Serves 4.

BAKED FILET VERMOUTH

4 fish filets
3 tablespoons melted butter
½ cup light cream
salt and pepper
dry bread crumbs
½ cup minced shallots
1 tablespoon minced chervil
1 teaspoon minced thyme
1 teaspoon minced marjoram
½ cup dry white wine
2 tablespoons dry Vermouth

Wipe filets, coat well with mixture of 2 tablespoons melted butter and cream, well seasoned, and cover with breadcrumbs. Place in very well-buttered baking dish, top with minced shallots and herbs, pour in wine and Vermouth, and bake in moderate oven (350-375°) until done, about 20 minutes. Pour off sauce and reduce by half, then add remaining melted butter. Put filets under hot broiler an instant and serve with sauce poured over. Serves 4.

FILETS OF LEMON SOLE DUGLERE

(From The Copley-Plaza, Boston, Mass.)

Cut 2 whole lemon or English sole so as to obtain 8 filets, saving the bones and trimmings for the later preparation of the fish stock.

Prepare a fish stock by boiling the trimmings and bones above together with a bouquet of kitchen vegetables, a pinch of thyme, ½ bay leaf, ¼ lemon, 2 ounces of fresh mushrooms, salt and pepper to taste, and enough water to cover. Boil for about 20 minutes, so as to reduce the quantity of liquor to about a pint, and strain through cheesecloth.

Cook 1 ounce of chopped shallots in a frying pan with 2 ounces of fresh butter until a golden blond color. Then add 6 ounces dry white wine (good quality) and boil 2 or 3 minutes longer. Finally add ½ pound of peeled and diced tomatoes, cooking all together for an additional 8 to 10 minutes.

Cook 3 tablespoons flour very slowly in a casserole in 2 ounces of butter, being careful not to allow the mixture to become brown. Set 2 ounces of the fish stock aside for later use, and stir in the remainder to form a cream sauce. Boil for 10 minutes, strain, and add the wine sauce. Add a little chopped parsley and season once more with salt and pepper if necessary. Set the sauce aside in a warm place to keep hot until ready to use.

Salt the filets of sole well and cook in a saucepan together with 1 tablespoon of lemon juice, 1 tablespoon of dry white wine, and the remaining 2 ounces of fish stock, being careful to cover the filets of sole with a piece of buttered or oiled paper to keep the filets nice and white during the cooking process. Bake in an oven (or very slowly on top of the stove) for 15 to 20 minutes. If any liquor is left in the casserole after cooking, stir into the sauce to strengthen it.

Arrange the filets on a serving platter and cover with the sauce. Serve very hot. Serves 6.

FILET OF SOLE MARGUERY

2 sole or flounder
1 pound coarse-meated fish, cut up
1 leek, white part only, sliced
½ cup sliced carrots
1 teaspoon chopped parsley
8 peppercorns
1 small bay leaf
2 quarts water
salt
cayenne
12 small oysters
12 cooked shrimp
¼ cup dry white wine
½ cup butter
4 egg yolks, well beaten

Have filets removed from sole or flounder. Place bones, skin, and heads in saucepan together with pieces of other fish, carrots, parsley, peppercorns, bay leaf, and water. Simmer until reduced to 2 cups. Strain. Place filets in buttered baking dish, pour one cup of stock over them, season, cover, and poach in moderate oven (350-375°) 15-20 minutes. Place on heat-proof serving dish. Cook oysters in fish stock, until plump and edges curled; garnish with oysters and shrimp and keep hot.

Pour remaining fish stock in pan in which filets were poached, simmer until reduced to 3 tablespoons, strain into double boiler, add wine and butter, and cook over low heat with very small quantity of water, just enough to steam top part. When butter is melted add egg yolks and stir constantly until sauce becomes consistency of a Medium White Sauce. Pour over filets, oysters, and shrimp and brown lightly under broiler. Serves 4.

FILETS OF FLOUNDER WITH WHITE WINE

1½ pounds filets
2 cups dry white wine
6 tablespoons heavy cream
2 egg yolks, lightly beaten
salt and pepper

Butter a small saucepan, put in fish, and cover with wine. Bring to a gentle simmer and poach for 10 minutes. Season to taste when about half done. Remove fish to serving platter, add cream to cooking liquid, and simmer 5 minutes more. Remove from heat, stir in egg yolks, and pour over fish. More wine may be added if a thinner sauce is desired. Serves 4.

FILETS OF TURBOT, BOGRATION

½ cup fish stock (p. 56)
4 filets of turbot
½ cup dry white wine
1 egg
1 cup White Wine Sauce (p. 31)
salt and pepper

Make fish stock from trimmings of turbot after fileting. Place filets in buttered casserole and add wine and fish stock, season and cook, covered, in moderately hot oven (375-400°) 30-45 minutes. Pick the meat from trimmings from which stock was made and put through food chopper two or three times, using finest blade. Mix in egg, season, and make into small balls about 1 inch in diameter. Poach them in fish stock 3 minutes. Serve separately in hot wine sauce. Serves 6-8.

FILETS OF TOTUAVA

(Mexican sea bass)

2 pounds filet of totuava
½ cup sliced mushrooms
1 tablespoon diced green peppers
2 cups fish stock (p. 56)
1 cup dry white wine
salt and pepper
1 tablespoon butter

Make fish stock from fish trimmings remaining after filets are removed. Place filets in saucepan, add mushrooms, diced green pepper, fish stock, and wine and season. Simmer until tender, 12-15 minutes. Remove fish, reduce sauce to one third, add butter and pour over fish. Serves 4.

BAKED FISH ESPAGNOLE

4 slices (about 3 pounds) firm white-meated fish
1 teaspoon salt
¼ teaspoon pepper
pinch of cayenne
pinch of nutmeg
2 tablespoons olive oil or vegetable oil
2 medium-sized onions, sliced thin
2 tablespoons pimiento, cut up
4 anchovy filets
4 slices tomato
2 tablespoons chopped chives
¾ cup sliced mushrooms
½ cup dry white wine
3 tablespoons butter
buttered bread crumbs

Season fish slices with mixed salt, pepper, cayenne, and nutmeg. Put oil in casserole, arrange onion slices and pimiento in a layer, then a layer of fish slices, with thick slices of tomato, topped with an anchovy filet on each. Sprinkle with chives and cover with sliced mushrooms. Add wine, dot with butter, and bake, covered, in moderately hot oven (375-400°) 20-30 minutes. Remove cover, sprinkle on buttered bread crumbs, and return to oven until browned. Serves 4.

FISH BAKED IN WHITE WINE

(Sole, flounder, halibut, swordfish, cod, or bass)

2 pounds fish (filets or slices)
1 large onion, sliced
1 cup Sauterne
3 tablespoons butter
2 sliced tomatoes,
½ green pepper, sliced
2 teaspoons Worcestershire sauce
1 teaspoon salt

Place fish and onion in a bowl or crock and cover with wine. Marinate for at least 1 hour. Use a shallow baking pan large enough not to crowd fish. Melt butter, add fish and onion with tomatoes and green pepper on top. Put in moderate oven (350-375°), and baste frequently with wine in which fish was marinated and to which the Worcestershire and salt have been added. Bake until fish is done, about 25 to 40 minutes, the time depending on the fish used. Serves 4.

CARP JEWISH STYLE

1 (2-3 pound) carp
¾ cup vegetable oil
1 large onion and 3 shallots, *or*
2 large onions, chopped
4 teaspoons flour
1¾ cups dry white wine
1¾ cups court bouillon (p. 55)
1 teaspoon salt
dash of cayenne
1 large bouquet garni (p. 9)
2 small cloves garlic, crushed and minced

Sauté onions and shallots in 4 tablespoons of oil until golden. Add flour and cook until thickened, then gradually add wine and court bouillon, stirring constantly. Add seasonings, bouquet garni, and garlic. Bring to a boil and put in fish, which should be sliced about 1 inch thick, and simmer for 20-25 minutes. Remove fish slices and arrange in serving dish. Take out bouquet garni and reduce sauce by boiling to one third. Remove from heat and pour in the rest of oil in a very fine stream, stirring vigorously, as in making mayonnaise. Pour over fish and chill. The sauce will jelly. Serves 4

FISH IN WINE ASPIC

4 cups any white fish, boned, cooked, and chopped
1 package aspic
dry white wine
2 cups peeled and seeded white grapes or seedless grapes
½ teaspoon salt
cucumber slices
watercress

Follow the directions on package for dissolving the aspic, substituting wine, heated to simmering, instead of water. Cover the bottom of a fish mold about ½ inch thick with this and when it has begun to set put in a few grapes evenly arranged. Add more aspic, then a layer of fish and repeat. End with aspic. Chill until set. To serve, dip mold an instant in hot water, put platter over top, and invert. Serve garnished with watercress and slices of cucumber cut thick, which have been soaking in brine in the refrigerator during the time the aspic was hardening. Serves 4.

BROILED FISH WITH WHITE WINE

2 pounds fish (filets, slices, or whole)
salt and pepper
1 teaspoon lemon juice
1 medium-sized onion, sliced
2 tablespoons butter
1 cup dry white wine
1 tablespoon flour
3 tablespoons hot water
6 stuffed olives, sliced

If a whole fish is used, split it lengthwise and place, skin side down, in a shallow pan, well buttered. Season with salt and pepper, and add lemon juice. Arrange sliced onions evenly and dot with butter. Place on rack under broiler and baste every few minutes with wine and liquid in pan. When fish separates easily with a fork, remove to a well-heated serving dish. Thicken basting liquid with flour mixed with hot water. Add sliced olives and pour over fish. Serves 4.

FINNAN HADDIE NEWBURG

3 tablespoons butter
1½ tablespoons flour
1½ cups milk
¼ teaspoon nutmeg
½ teaspoon paprika
2 cups finnan haddie, flaked
¾ cup cream
¼ cup Sherry
4 egg yolks, lightly beaten
salt
cayenne

Make a roux of butter and flour, add milk gradually, and cook, stirring constantly, until smooth and thickened. Add spices and fish, and bring to a boil. Simmer about 1 minute while stirring. Add egg yolks and Sherry mixed with cream, and reheat but do not allow to boil. Season to taste. Serves 4.

PICKLED EELS

Clean and skin as many eels as required. Cut in 2-inch pieces and cook in pickling liquid as for pickled oysters (p. 97) until tender. Place a layer in crock, cover with sliced onions, and repeat until all pieces are used. Cover with pickling liquid and keep cool.

EEL PIE

2 pounds eels
2 shallots, chopped, *or*
1 medium-sized onion, chopped
1 tablespoon chopped parsley
water
1/3 cup Sherry
3 tablespoons lemon juice
salt and pepper
1/4 teaspoon mace
2 tablespoons butter
2 tablespoons flour
biscuit dough or puff paste

Clean, skin, and bone eels and cut in 2-inch pieces. Choose a saucepan which the pieces of eel will nearly fill. Put in shallots or onion, parsley and water enough just to cover. Bring just to a boil. Remove eel and place in baking dish. Add wine, lemon juice, and seasonings to liquid in saucepan. Make a roux of butter and flour, add to liquid, and cook until thickened. Pour over eel. Cover the top with 3/4-inch layer of biscuit dough or puff paste. Bake 1 hour in moderate oven (350-375°). Serves 4.

BAKED EEL

1 (2 pound) eel
salt and pepper
6 tablespoons chopped shallots
1 bouquet garni (p. 9)
1/2 cup bread crumbs
2 tablespoons butter
1/2 cup boiling water
1/2 cup dry white wine
1 teaspoon flour

Cut the blanched and skinned eel in 3-inch pieces. Place upright in baking pan, sprinkle with chopped shallots, herbs, and bread crumbs, season, dot with 1 tablespoon butter, and pour in boiling water. Bake in a moderate oven (350-375°) until well browned and tender. Remove carefully to hot serving dish. Make a roux of remaining butter and flour, and add to gravy in baking pan. Add wine slowly, simmer 3 minutes, and pour around, not over, eel. Serves 4.

EELS FISHERMAN'S STYLE

(Matelote)

4 medium-sized onions, sliced
2 tablespoons butter
1 tablespoon flour
6 prunes, stoned and cut up
2 pounds eels, cut in 2½ inch pieces
2 cups dry red wine
4 cups water
salt and pepper

Brown onions lightly in butter, add flour, and stir. Add wine and water slowly, while stirring. Drop in prunes, season rather lightly, and simmer gently for 2 hours. Put in cleaned and skinned eels and cook 20 minutes. Serves 4.

BROILED SARDINES WITH WINE SAUCE

4 tablespoons butter
½ cup fresh bread crumbs
¼ cup very dry white wine
1 cup cream
2 hard-cooked eggs, chopped
few dashes Angostura bitters (optional)
salt, pepper, and paprika
1 can (7-oz.) boneless sardines *or* sardine filets
4 slices buttered toast, crusts trimmed

Melt butter over low heat. Add bread crumbs, wine, and cream. Stir until it just begins to simmer. Remove from heat and beat thoroughly. Add eggs and seasonings. Broil sardines until lightly browned, place on toast, pour sauce over, and serve at once. Serves 4.

ESCALLOPED FILETS OF SALMON

2 pounds salmon filets
2 tablespoons butter
1 cup sliced mushrooms
1 cup dry wine, either red or white
1 cup fish fumet (p. 56)
salt and pepper

Butter cooking dish well, put in fish and mushrooms, cover with wine and fumet, and poach for 15 minutes. Remove fish, reduce sauce by ⅓, season to taste, and pour over fish. Serves 4.

SALMON CUTLETS DORIGNY

4 slices salmon 1 inch thick
truffles
2 cups Chablis
1 cup heavy cream
2 tablespoons crawfish butter (p. 47)
1 dozen cooked crawfish
salt and pepper

Trim slices of salmon cutlet, shape, and lard with julienne of truffles cut very thin. Poach in Chablis, remove, and keep hot. Reduce wine until thick and sirupy. Stir in cream and crawfish butter. Serve sauce separately. Pile crawfish on platter and arrange cutlets, small end up, around them. Paper cutlet frills add an interesting touch. Serves 4.

SALMON CUTLETS BURGUNDY

2 pounds salmon cutlets
2 cups Burgundy

Poach the fish in the wine for 15 minutes. Remove and make a Red Wine Sauce (p. 29) out of wine in which fish was cooked. Pour over fish. Serves 6.

SALMON KEDGEREE

3 tablespoons butter
2 tablespoons chopped onion
1¾ cups fish fumet (p. 56)
1 sprig thyme, *or*
⅛ teaspoon powdered thyme
2 teaspoons chopped parsley
½ bay leaf
1½ cups rice
1½ cups White Wine Sauce (p. 31)
½ teaspoon curry powder
4 hard-cooked eggs, diced
3 cups cooked salmon, flaked

Brown onion in butter lightly. Add rice and stir until an even golden brown. Stir in fumet and herbs, and simmer, covered, until rice is tender. Do not stir more than is absolutely necessary to prevent sticking. Heat salmon and diced hard-cooked eggs in White Wine Sauce to which has been added the curry powder (this may be omitted if the flavor is not desired). Serve in a fairly shallow dish in alternate layers of fish and rice with rice as the top layer. Brown butter may be poured over the top. Serves 6.

SOUCHET OF PERCH

1 large carrot
8 stalks of celery
½ cup butter
1¼ cups water
1¼ cups dry white wine
½ teaspoon salt
6 medium-sized perch
2 tablespoons flour
1 tablespoon chopped parsley

Cut carrot lengthwise into very fine strips about 4 inches long. Cut an equal amount of celery in the same manner. Sauté for 10 minutes in 2 tablespoons butter, add wine, water, and salt, and simmer until vegetables are tender. Scale, clean, and trim fish and place side by side in a shallow dish. Strain boiling liquid over them, retaining the julienne vegetables. Cover and reduce heat to just below simmering point. Poach 12 minutes and place in a warm oven while making the sauce. Boil liquid until it is reduced one half. Make a roux of 3 tablespoons butter and flour. Add to liquid and boil, stirring constantly, 5 minutes. Remove from fire, add remaining butter, vegetables, and chopped parsley and pour over fish. Serves 6

POMPANO ROYAL POINCIANA

1 cup cooked shrimp
⅓ cup chopped mushrooms
½ cup cream
1 egg
2 tablespoons Sherry
salt
pepper
paprika
3 pounds pompano, boned
1 cucumber, sliced
French dressing

Put shrimp and mushrooms through food chopper twice, using finest blade. Beat egg and add ¼ cup cream and seasonings. Mix all together to a paste. Spread on pompano and skewer the two halves together. Place on parchment paper in greased baking dish and pour over remaining cream and Sherry. Bake in moderate oven (350-375°) 45 minutes. Serve garnished with thin slices of cucumber marinated in French dressing and dusted with paprika. Serves 3-4.

POMPANO EN PAPILLOTTE

(From Gabriel Lugot, Executive Chef, The Waldorf-Astoria, New York City)

8 filets of 4 pompano—1½ lb. each pompano
4 ounces sweet butter
2 tablespoons chopped shallots
1 tablespoon chopped chives
2 glasses excellent California dry white wine
6 double sheets of parchment paper—heart form—12 inches long
seasoning
little olive oil

Butter a flat saucepan, arrange the filets of pompano, already seasoned. Add shallots and white wine, cover with buttered paper and metal cover. Put to boil and cook in oven for 6 minutes. Remove filets. Reduce liquor to half-cup quantity. Add chives, also the mashed meat of 2 filets (no skin). Rectify seasoning. Reserve. Oil the papers (heart form) on both sides. Arrange 1 filet on one side of the paper. On top of each filet put a little of the preparation. Fold each paper hermetically in folding the edge. Put each papillotte in hot oven until golden color and soufflé is obtained. Serves 6.

SWEET SOUR FISH

1 cup water
1 cup vinegar
2 tablespoons brown sugar
6 whole cloves
½ teaspoon cinnamon
1 small onion, sliced
1 lemon, thinly sliced
1 cup dry red wine
2 tablespoons seedless raisins
1 tablespoon blanched and pounded almonds
salt and pepper
2 pounds any firm-meated fish, cut up
¼ cup gingersnap crumbs
4 egg yolks, well beaten

Simmer together water, vinegar, sugar, cloves, cinnamon, and onion until onion is tender. Strain and add lemon, wine, raisins, and almonds. Season. Bring to a boil and add fish. Simmer, covered, until fish is done. Remove fish to serving dish and keep hot. Add gingersnap crumbs, bring to a boil, remove from heat, and slowly add egg yolks, stirring constantly. Reheat but do not allow to boil after adding egg yolks. Serves 4-6.

Shad is one of the boniest fish in the world. For that reason, many people refuse to eat them when prepared in any of the ordinary ways. Here are two methods, both of which require extremely long cooking (twice the given time won't hurt), but at the end you will find that all the smaller bones have vanished completely and the larger bones have practically melted. These methods are also perfect for salmon and grilse.

SHAD AVIGNON STYLE

2 medium-sized onions, chopped
1 pound sorrel, chopped
4 tomatoes, chopped
1 clove garlic, crushed and minced
½ cup olive oil or vegetable oil
salt and pepper
4 tablespoons chopped parsley
¼ cup fresh bread crumbs
1 (3 pound) shad
1 cup very dry white wine

Heat oil in a large pan, add vegetables and seasonings, and sauté until onions are well browned. Drain off oil in another pan and fry shad until nicely browned. Meanwhile, mix together cooked vegetables, parsley, and bread crumbs and put half the mixture in the bottom of a covered dish. Lay in the fish. Cover with rest of the crumb mixture and add the wine. Cover and seal with paste of flour and water. Bake in moderate oven (350-475°) five hours. Serves 6.

BAKED SHAD WITH RAISINS

1 (3 pound) boned shad
3 tomatoes, sliced
3 tablespoons butter
¼ cup chopped parsley
2 cups seedless raisins
½ cup dry white wine
salt and pepper

Place fish in buttered baking pan. Arrange slices of tomato on top and dot with butter. Sprinkle raisins around fish and add wine. Sprinkle on chopped parsley, season, and bake in moderately hot oven (375-400°) 30-45 minutes. Serves 6.

SHAD MAINE STYLE

1 (3 pound) shad
1 cup vinegar
1 cup very dry white wine
salt
white pepper

Wrap the shad tightly in at least 5 or 6 yards of cheesecloth and tie it very securely. Place in a large vessel, cover with water, add vinegar, wine, and seasonings, and cook at least 5 hours. Add more water as required. Serves 6.

PLANKED SHAD

1 (3 pound) boned shad
salt, pepper, and paprika
1 tablespoon chopped parsley
½ cup dry white wine
3 tablespoons butter

Oil baking plank well and place shad on it, skin side down. Sprinkle with salt, pepper, paprika, and chopped parsley and bake in moderate oven (350-375°) 30 to 40 minutes, basting frequently with wine and butter. Serves 6.

SHAD ROE BAKED

2 pair shad roe
3 tablespoons butter
⅓ cup chopped onion
2 tablespoons chopped parsley
salt and pepper
1 cup sliced mushrooms
1 cup Riesling
1 teaspoon flour
lemon slices

Place roe in buttered baking dish, add onions, dot with 1 tablespoon butter, sprinkle with chopped parsley and season. Sauté mushrooms in rest of butter until just tender. and add mushrooms to roe but reserve butter. Bake in moderate oven (350-375°) 30 minutes, basting frequently. Blend flour with butter in which mushrooms were sautéed, add sauce from roe and wine, season, and stir until thickened. Place roe under broiler and brown lightly. Serve surrounded by sauce and garnished with lemon slices. Serves 4.

DEVILED SHAD ROE

2 pounds shad roe
1 tablespoon Worcestershire sauce
1 teaspoon anchovy paste
½ teaspoon mustard
dash of cayenne
2 tablespoons Sherry
¼ teaspoon Angostura bitters
1 tablespoon melted butter
4 slices buttered toast

Pour boiling water over roe and simmer very gently for 20 minutes. Drain and cut up in 1-inch pieces. Make a mixture of all other ingredients and roll roe pieces around in it until well coated. Arrange on buttered toast and put in hot oven 5 minutes. Serves 4.

SHAD ROE CREOLE STYLE

2 pounds shad roe
4 tablespoons butter
1 cup dry white wine
½ cup Creole Sauce (p. 41)
salt and pepper
3 cups cooked rice
croutons
2 tablespoons chopped parsley
4 tablespoons grated mild cheese

Do not parboil roe. Sauté gently in butter until light brown. Add wine and sauce, cover, and simmer 10 minutes. Season to taste. Serve surrounded with rice and croutons and topped with grated cheese and parsley. Serves 4.

TROUT WITH WHITE WINE JELLY

12 (½ pound) trout
2 cups court bouillon (p. 55)
White Wine Jelly (p. 56)
2 hard-cooked eggs, chopped
2 tablespoons parsley, chopped

Make the court bouillon with a medium dry Sauterne or Chablis and poach trout in it for about 10 minutes. Remove trout and place in mold. Make White Wine Jelly, using the court bouillon in which the trout was poached instead of the fish fumet. Cover the fish with the liquid jelly and as soon as it is cool add chopped hard-cooked eggs and parsley. Chill in refrigerator. Serves 6.

SALMON TROUT À LA CHAMBORD

1 (2-3 pound) salmon trout
1 sprig celery leaves
1 sprig thyme
1 sprig parsley
1 bay leaf
1 cup chopped mushroom stems
2½ cups dry red wine
1 cup water
salt and pepper
1⅓ tablespoons butter
1 teaspoon flour
24 mushroom caps, sautéed
croutons

Clean fish, remove head, and trim tail and fins. Wrap in cheesecloth and place in very well-greased baking dish. Add vegetables, herbs, wine, water, and seasonings. Bake in moderate oven (350-375°), allowing 10 minutes per pound. Baste frequently but do not turn. Remove carefully and skim. Strain cooking liquid and reduce one half. Stir in 2 teaspoons butter blended with flour and simmer, stirring constantly, until well thickened. Remove from heat and stir in rest of butter. Place trout on serving dish, pour sauce over, and garnish with mushroom caps. Serves 4 to 6.

PIKE—ANJOU STYLE

1 (2-3 pound) pike
3 tablespoons butter
1 cup Sauterne
salt and pepper
2 tablespoons chopped onion
¼ teaspoon dry mustard
dash nutmeg
3 tablespoons heavy cream
1 tablespoon lemon juice

Clean fish and cut in 2-inch pieces. Be sure to save liver. Sauté fish in foaming butter until lightly browned. Add wine, onion, and seasonings and simmer slowly about 20 minutes or until fish is done. Turn once. Mash liver to a paste and mix with cream. Remove fish slices, turn off heat, and when liquid in pan has stopped simmering, stir in the cream and liver mixture. Let stand a few minutes, add lemon juice, and pour over fish. Serves 4-6.

PIKE WITH MUSHROOMS

1 (2-3 pound) pike
½ pound mushrooms, sliced
1 cup Sherry
1 can condensed beef consommé
1 tablespoon butter
1 tablespoon brandy
2 tablespoons cream

Braise the pike and mushrooms, covered with the wine and consommé, until fish is done, about 25 minutes. When fish is tender, put on serving dish, surround with mushrooms, and keep hot. Reduce liquor in which it was cooked to about ½ cup, remove from heat and allow to cool slightly, add butter, cream, and brandy and pour over fish. Serves 4-6.

TROUT WITH FENNEL

12 (½ pound) trout
4 stalks fennel
½ teaspoon salt
dash of cayenne
1 cup dry white wine
1 tablespoon butter

Cut the fennel in 4-inch pieces and slice in matchlike strips; arrange these in the bottom of a buttered saucepan. Put in fish, wine, and seasonings and poach about 10 minutes. Remove trout and skin carefully. Place on serving dish and keep warm. Reduce poaching liquor ½, add butter, and pour over trout. Serves 6.

CHAPTER FIVE

Shellfish

There is a very definite affinity between shellfish and wine. There are recipes, such as Shellfish Newburg, which are classical, less known regional recipes, as, for example, shellfish pies, but best of all is the endless opportunity—and temptation—to experiment.

As with fish, beware—and again beware—of overcooking. When oysters plump up and their edges curl, they are done. Every additional second after that merely makes them tough. Clams and scallops the same. Crimes are committed against lobsters, shrimp, and crabs by well-intentioned cooks who just don't know when to quit.

Those of you who live near the seashore should get better acquainted with mussels. When their virtues are fully appreciated, they will undoubtedly, like calves' liver, become an expensive delicacy. As this is written they are one of the cheapest of seafoods.

Not the least attractive feature of shellfish is the ease of preparation. Bulk oysters require merely to be examined for stray pieces of shell. Shrimp are dropped in boiling water. Sea water is ideal for boiling shrimp, but, since that cannot usually be obtained, add 2 tablespoons of salt, a pinch of thyme, and 1 bayleaf to each quart of water. Bring water to a full, rolling boil and throw in shrimp. Cook 2 minutes after water resumes boiling. Allow to cool in the cooking liquor—do not place in cold water. When cool, shuck them and remove the black intestinal vein with the point of a sharp knife. The fact that few people bother to do this accounts for the grittiness so often found in otherwise delicious shrimp dishes.

Male lobsters are known as cocks or toms; females as hens, small chickens, or shorts; females with eggs as berry lobsters.

In the trade, lobsters are graded according to weight:

"Chicken" lobsters average 1 pound each
"Medium Quarters" average 1¼ pounds
"Large Mediums" average 1½-2 pounds
"Oversize" or "Jumbos" average 2¼ pounds and up

Chicken and jumbos are usually cheapest, not so much because of any difference in quality but because they are less popular with restaurants and hotels.

Buy lobsters alive if possible, and they should be active. To kill, insert a small, sharp knife between the head and body shells: this severs the spinal cord. Seize just behind the claws or grasp with vegetable tongs, straighten the tail, and plunge head first into rapidly boiling water to which 1 tablespoon of salt has been added to each quart. Boil 20 minutes. Cool, twist off large claws, crack them with a hammer or nutcracker, and pick out meat with a fork. Then turn lobster back down and with scissors cut lengthwise from head to tail. Discard the stomach or "lady," which is a small sac just behind the head. If you are careful, the intestinal vein which runs the full length of the body will come out with the "lady"; if not, it should be removed with the point of a knife. The green part is the liver and is edible. In female or hen lobsters the eggs or "coral" should be carefully preserved as they are decidedly a delicacy. The lungs are the spongy tissue between meat and shells and are not to be used.

Hard-shelled crabs are prepared in much the same manner as lobster. They should be washed thoroughly and plunged, head first, into boiling salted water (1 tablespoon salt to 1 quart water). Boil, covered, 20 minutes. Drain and cover with cold water. Break off claws and tail or "apron." Separate shells, beginning at tail end. The intestines, sand bags, and gills are spongy and fibrous and are found between the top shell and body and two halves of the body. These should be carefully removed; some scraping may be necessary. Remove meat in as large flakes as possible. Crack claws and remove meat with nutpick or small knife.

Be sure soft-shelled crabs are alive and vigorous when purchased. Rinse them, place them face down, lift the points at each end, and cut off spongy material beneath. Remove pointed apron on belly. However, if you buy them from a dealer, he will usually do this for you.

If you want to add the last touch of magnificence to either hard- or soft-shelled crabs, here is a method hitherto known to a very few.

Select specimens which are very lively and active, wash well, being careful to handle the little soft-shelled fellows very gently. Put them in a crock or bowl and cover with a rich eggnog made in the proportion of 2 lightly beaten eggs, ¼ cup Sherry, and a pinch of nutmeg to each cup of milk. Cover with a plate, weighted, if necessary, just enough to keep them from getting out. Let them remain in a cool but not cold place for 2 to 3 hours. The result will be far beyond your expectations. Don't worry if they show no signs of life when you take them out—they are simply dead drunk.

Recipes for crab meat and lobster meat are, in general, interchangeable.

Mussels, clams, and oysters in the shell should be alive before cooking. Discard any which are open and do not close at a touch. They should be rinsed in cold water. Both mussels and clams should be thoroughly and vigorously scrubbed with a stiff brush to remove sand. To open oysters insert a strong short knife between the shells near the thick end and run it around the edges. Mussels and clams may be opened by steaming. The hairy beard of mussels should be cut off and discarded.

The French method of opening mussels and clams is far superior to the plain steaming usually used here. A court bouillon of ½ cup dry white wine, an onion and a shallot, both chopped fine, half a dozen sprigs of thyme, half a bayleaf, salt, and pepper is used. Put mussels and court bouillon in tightly covered saucepan and bring to a brisk boil. Shake pan well every minute or two. In five or six minutes all the shells will be opened. This amount of court bouillon will open about two quarts of mussels.

Not everybody knows that the common snapping turtle or soft-shelled turtle makes gorgeous eating, comparable only to the lordly terrapin. They are decapitated with an axe and hung, head down, until the blood stops dripping, which may take an hour or more if you have a large one. Scrub thoroughly, and cook 10 minutes or more, or until the nails pull out easily. Drain, cover with cold water, and when cool enough to handle rub skin from legs and pull out nails. Cover with boiling water and cook, covered, until shell separates easily, about 30 minutes to 1 hour. Cool in same water. Starting at the tail end with the turtle on its back work the lower shell loose and remove it. Remove intestines, being especially careful not to break the gall bladder, which is a rather small sac near the head. If kept alive for twelve hours the gall bladder will be smaller and easier to handle. Reserve head, liver, and eggs, if any. Remove meat in as large pieces as possible and be sure to save all the green fat.

Terrapin, which usually weigh about 3 to 4 pounds each, are prepared in practically the same way except that they are not decapitated but are plunged, head first, into boiling salted water. They are done when the legs are tender after the second boiling, or in about 30 to 45 minutes, depending upon size. Pry shells apart with a heavy knife, remove sand bag, head, and gall bladder. Cut meat from shells, save liver and eggs, if any, and place in refrigerator until needed.

CLAM AND CHICKEN PIE

3 tablespoons butter
4 tablespoons chopped onion
1 cup chopped cooked chicken meat
2 cups cooked clams, from which hard parts have been removed and remainder chopped
5 hard-cooked eggs, diced
1 cup diced boiled potatoes
½ cup chopped celery
¼ cup Sherry
1 teaspoon salt
¼ teaspoon pepper
dash cayenne
½ cup milk
1 teaspoon flour
½ Pastry Recipe

Sauté onions in butter until they are soft but not brown. Add clams, chicken, potatoes, eggs, celery, seasonings, and Sherry. Bring just to a simmer and thicken with flour, add milk, and simmer 10 minutes. Put in casserole or baking dish, cover with pastry, and bake in hot oven (425-450°) 15 minutes, then reduce heat to moderate (350-375°) and bake 15 minutes more. Serves 6.

HASHED CLAMS ON TOAST

2 tablespoons butter
40 Little Neck clams, chopped fine
clam juice
2 tablespoons minced parsley
1 teaspoon minced chives
bread crumbs
2 tablespoons Sherry
salt
paprika
buttered toast

Melt butter, add clams and clam juice, parsley and chives; stir, bring to a simmer, and keep over very low heat for ½ minute. Thicken with bread crumbs, which should be fine and dry. Season to taste. Add Sherry and serve on buttered toast. Serves 4-6.

BAKED SOFT-SHELLED CLAMS

1 dozen soft shelled clams
1 clove garlic
1 slice bacon
1 pimiento
4 tablespoons butter
salt and pepper
4 tablespoons grated Parmesan cheese
4 tablespoons Sherry

Shell clams, wash very thoroughly in cold water, and cut off necks. Scrub 12 half-shells, wipe dry, and rub inside well with crushed clove of garlic. Arrange in shallow baking pan, and place a piece each of pimiento and bacon, cut in ½ inch squares, and ½ teaspoon butter in each shell. Add clams, season, and top with cheese and remaining butter. Bake in moderately hot oven (375-400°) 10 minutes. Baste with wine and bake 5 minutes more. Serves 4.

COURT BOUILLON FOR SHELLFISH

4 tablespoons butter
1 large carrot, minced
1 large onion, minced
3½ cups dry white wine
3½ cups water
1 bouquet garni (p. 9)
6 whole peppercorns
salt

Sauté carrot and onion in butter until tender. Add wine and water, and bouquet garni and peppercorns tied in a piece of muslin. Salt to taste. Simmer slowly for 45 minutes.

CRAB LEGS VOLTAIRE

(from Pierre Coste, Chef, Hotel St. Francis, San Francisco, Calif.)

Cook 2 crabs for 20 minutes. Pick the legs. Boil rest of crab meat in 1 pint double cream to obtain flavor, then strain. Next, brown very lightly in butter, ¼ pound sliced mushrooms, 2 ounces shallots, chopped fine and deglazed with 3 ounces Sherry. Add 1 pint cream and let reduce until thick. Then add legs, season to taste with juice of ½ lemon and ¼ pound sweet butter. Mix this well. Take it from stove and finish thickening the preparation with Hollandaise Sauce (p. 48) and a glass of Sherry (about 2 ounces). Serve hot with toast. Serves 4.

CRAB CUSTARD IN CASSEROLE

1 tablespoon grated onion
4 tablespoons butter
4 tablespoons flour
1 cup milk
½ cup light cream
1 teaspoon A1 sauce
dash cayenne
salt and pepper
4 eggs, beaten
2 tablespoons Sherry
3 cups flaked crab meat (fresh or canned)
½ cup buttered bread crumbs

Sauté onion in butter in double boiler until tender but not brown. Stir in flour, add milk and cream, and cook over hot water until thick. Add Sherry to beaten eggs and stir in. Place crab meat in casserole or individual baking dishes, pour on sauce, cover with buttered bread crumbs, and bake in moderate oven (350-375°) until knife comes out clean, about 1 hour. Serves 6.

STUFFED CRABS CUBAN STYLE

1 tablespoon butter
2 tablespoons chopped onion
1 small tomato, chopped
1 tablespoon chopped capers
1 tablespoon chopped parsley
½ small clove garlic, crushed and minced
1 teaspoon flour
1 tablespoon dry Sherry
1 tablespoon bread crumbs
1½ cups flaked crab meat (fresh or canned)
salt and pepper
¼ cup cracker crumbs
milk

Sauté vegetables in butter until tender but not brown. Stir in flour, add Sherry, bread crumbs, salt, and pepper and stir over very low heat for 2 minutes. Stir in crab meat. Pack in crab shells, or individual ramekins and top with cracker crumbs moistened with milk. Put in moderate oven (350-375°) until crumbs brown. Serves 4.

LORD BALTIMORE CRAB WITH CAPER SAUCE

3 cups flaked crab meat (fresh or canned)
1 egg, lightly beaten
1 teaspoon salt
1/8 teaspoon pepper
1 teaspoon dry mustard
1 teaspoon Angostura bitters
1 tablespoon Worcestershire sauce
1 tablespoon chopped parsley
1 tablespoon chopped chives
1/2 cup milk
1/2 cup rye cracker crumbs
Caper Sauce (p. 47)

Mix crab meat with seasonings and egg, and make into four cakes. Dip in milk and crumbs, and put on baking sheet in moderate oven (350-375°) until brown. Serve on toast with Caper Sauce. Serves 4.

Lobster or shrimp may be used instead of crab meat.

MARYLAND CRAB

4 cups flaked crab meat (fresh or canned)
1 cup cream
16 cooked shrimp (fresh or canned), diced
2 green peppers, minced
3 tablespoons butter
1 cup coarsely chopped mushrooms
1 teaspoon salt
1/2 teaspoon paprika
1/4 cup Sherry
12 slices thin toast

Sauté mushrooms and peppers lightly in butter. Cook crab flakes in cream, and add sautéed mushrooms and peppers and all other ingredients, the Sherry last. Serve on thin dry toast. Serves 6.

ECREVISSES (CRAYFISH) ST. FRANCIS

(from Pierre Coste, Chef, Hotel St. Francis, San Francisco, Calif.)

To 1 gallon of water add 2 quarts dry white wine and 1 quart vinegar, and boil. When boiling add 60 ecrevisses, 1 sliced onion, 3 sliced carrots, 1 stalk celery, 3 bay leaves, 1 pinch thyme, parsley, and 20 black peppercorns. Cook for 15 minutes and drain. Pick ecrevisses. In another pan add 1 pint dry Sherry to 1/2 pound chopped shallots and let reduce. Then add 1½ pints pastry cream, boil until thick, and season to taste. Sauté ecrevisses in butter, deglazed with white wine. Pass sauce through cheesecloth, pour over ecrevisses, and let boil 5 minutes. Remove from fire, add 4 ounces Hollandaise Sauce (p. 48) and a pinch of cayenne pepper. Serve hot with Wild Rice Polonaise. Serves 4.

DEVILED CRABS

2 cups flaked crab meat (fresh or canned)
¼ teaspoon mace
¼ teaspoon nutmeg
¼ teaspoon mustard
2 whole cloves
1 tablespoon melted butter
1 egg, separated
salt and pepper
½ cup Sherry
½ cup buttered bread crumbs

Stir together the crab meat, seasoning, melted butter, and well-beaten egg yolk. Add wine and season to taste. Fold in egg white beaten stiff but not dry.

If fresh crabs have been used, clean top halves of shells, inside and out, and bake mixture in these. Or use individual ramekins or a casserole. Top with buttered crumbs and bake in a moderate oven (350-375°) ½ hour. Serves 4.

CRAB STEW

4 tablespoons butter
3 tablespoons flour
2½ cups milk or light cream
1 teaspoon Angostura bitters
3 teaspoons Worcestershire sauce
2 tablespoons minced celery
4 cups flaked crab meat (fresh or canned)
¼ cup Sherry
salt and pepper
lemon slices

Make White Sauce of butter, flour, and milk or cream. Add Angostura, Worcestershire, and minced celery and cook until thick. Stir in crab meat, then bring to a simmer but do not boil. Season and stir in Sherry just before serving. Float halved lemon slices on top of each portion. Serves 4 to 6.

CRAB MEAT DEWEY

2 cups flaked crab meat (fresh or canned)
2 shallots, chopped
1 cup dry white wine
½ cup butter
3 tablespoons flour
¾ pound mushrooms, sliced very thin
⅓ cup heavy cream, scalded

Put crab meat in saucepan with shallots and wine, and simmer 7 minutes. Sauté mushrooms in butter over low heat, stirring frequently. Add flour and stir well. Add to crab-meat mixture, together with truffles and scalded cream, and simmer gently, stirring constantly, for 5 minutes. Place in casserole or individual ramekins and put under broiler until lightly browned. Serve with toast. Serves 6.

CREAMED CRAB MEAT

½ cup butter
4 tablespoons flour
2 cups milk
4 cups flaked crab meat (fresh or canned)
1 cup cream
1 teaspoon salt
dash cayenne
¼ cup Sherry

Make a white sauce with ¼ cup butter, flour, and milk. Sauté the flaked crab meat in remainder of butter for 3 minutes. Add white sauce, cream, and seasonings; simmer 3 minutes, remove from heat, and add Sherry. Serve with croutons or on toast. Serves 6

CRAB AND CHICKEN HASH ON TOAST

1 teaspoon butter
1 cup flaked crab meat (fresh or canned)
1 cup cooked chicken, chopped very fine
1 teaspoon finely chopped celery
½ cup light cream
½ teaspoon flour
salt and pepper
¼ cup Sherry
buttered toast

Melt butter and add crab meat and chopped chicken, celery, cream, flour, and seasonings. Simmer gently until quite dry, stirring constantly over very low heat. Stir in Sherry. Serve on crustless slices of buttered toast. Serves 4 to 6.

BAKED CRAB MEAT WITH AVOCADO

1 cup flaked crab meat (fresh or canned)
1 cup cooked, chopped spaghetti
3 tablespoons butter
3 tablespoons flour
1½ cups milk
½ teaspoon salt
⅛ teaspoon pepper
3 avocados
1 cup buttered bread crumbs
¼ cup Sherry

Mix crab meat with chopped spaghetti. Make white sauce with butter, flour, and milk. Add crab meat mixture and seasonings, and bring to a simmer. Split avocados evenly, remove pits, and fill hollows with mixture. Top with bread crumbs and sprinkle with Sherry. Brown under broiler. Serves 6.

LOBSTER À LA ALFREDO

4 tablespoons butter
1 shallot, chopped
salt
½ teaspoon paprika
1 (1½ pound) lobster, cooked
⅔ cup Chablis
1 cup canned tomatoes, without juice
2 tablespoons chopped chives
2 tablespoons brandy

Brown chopped shallot in butter with paprika. Add lobster meat cut in large pieces and cook 2 minutes. Add wine and simmer very gently for 10 minutes. Add tomatoes and simmer gently for 30 minutes longer. Remove from heat, and stir in chives and brandy. Serves 2.

LOBSTER CARDINAL

2 cups diced lobster meat
4 cups Cream Sauce (p. 28)
red coloring
24 ripe olives, sliced
¼ cup Sherry

Heat lobster meat, olives, and cream sauce together with very small amount of red food color, just enough to give the tint of a lobster shell. Add Sherry just before serving. Serve on toast or in patty shells. Serves 4 to 6.

LOBSTER EDWARD

2 cups lobster meat (fresh or canned) cut in ½ inch cubes
2 tablespoons butter
½ teaspoon dry mustard
salt
dash cayenne
¼ cup Sherry
juice 1 lemon

Melt butter; add mustard, salt, cayenne, and lobster. Stir 5 minutes over low heat. Add Sherry and lemon juice, simmer 1 minute, and serve. Serves 4.

LOBSTER NEWBURG
(From Hotel Lafayette, New York City)

Cut in large pieces the meat of 2 boiled lobsters, about 1½ pounds each. Put a nut of butter in a pan, add the lobster meat, season with salt and pepper, a pinch of paprika. Cook for a few minutes, then drop a cocktail glass of Sherry on top of the lobster. Let it simmer, then add a pint of heavy cream or Cream Sauce (p. 28). Let it boil slowly for 12 to 15 minutes. When ready to serve add a few spoonsful of Hollandaise Sauce (p. 48), or instead two yolks of eggs mixed with a nut of butter, but do not let it boil. Serves 2.

LOBSTER JAMBALAYA

2 medium-sized onions, chopped
2 tablespoons butter
1 cup uncooked rice
½ small bay leaf
2 cups flaked lobster meat (fresh or canned)
1 medium-sized tomato, chopped
2 cups boiling water
salt and pepper
½ cup Sherry

Sauté onions to a light golden brown in butter. Add rice and bay leaf, and sauté until rice begins to color. Add lobster, chopped tomato, and boiling water and boil rapidly, stirring frequently, until rice begins to get tender. Add more boiling water if necessary to prevent scorching. Reduce heat and simmer until rice is thoroughly done. Remove from heat, season, and add wine. Serve on toast. Serves 4.

CURRIED LOBSTER

2 cups diced lobster meat (fresh or canned)
3 tablespoons butter
½ to 1½ tablespoons curry powder
½ cup dry white wine
3 tablespoons finely chopped blanched almonds
2 tablespoons flour
2 cups condensed chicken consommé
juice of ½ lemon
salt and pepper

Sauté lobster 2 minutes in 1 tablespoon butter. Mix curry powder to paste with a little wine and stir into rest of wine. Add to lobster and simmer 5 minutes. (The amount of curry powder is governed by its strength and flavor desired.) Season, remove from fire, and keep hot. Brown almonds in remaining butter and stir in flour. Add consommé gradually, stirring constantly for 5 minutes. Add lemon juice, season, and pour over lobster. Serve in ring of fluffy boiled rice accompanied by shredded coconut and Indian chutney. Serves 4.

ROASTED LOBSTER

2 (1-1½ pound) lobsters
½ cup melted butter
1 cup dry white wine
2 tablespoons lemon juice
⅛ teaspoon thyme
⅛ teaspoon marjoram
⅛ teaspoon rosemary (optional)
salt
pepper

Prepare the lobster, taking out the lady and reserving the coral, if any.

Run a long skewer through each, lengthwise, to keep them from curling. Place them in a shallow dish in a very hot oven (450-500°), basting them frequently with the melted butter, wine, salt, and pepper. When the shell separates from the flesh and becomes brittle, remove the lobsters to the serving dish. Make sauce of basting liquid, spices, lemon juice, seasonings, and coral, if any, adding more wine if necessary. Simmer 3 minutes. Serve over lobster. May be served as broiled lobster, or meat may be removed from shell if desired. Serves 4.

LOBSTER À L'AMÉRICAINE

(This dish, by the way, originated in Europe)

2 (1-1½ pound) lobsters
½ cup olive oil
2 tablespoons butter
1 small carrot, diced
1 teaspoon chopped leeks
1 teaspoon chopped shallots
½ clove garlic, crushed and minced
2 small tomatoes, peeled and chopped
3 tablespoons brandy
¼ cup Sauterne
1 cup condensed chicken consommé
1 teaspoon chopped parsley
1 teaspoon chopped chervil
1 teaspoon chopped tarragon
salt
pepper
cayenne

Cut tail in pieces at joints and body in half lengthwise. Crush claws. Remove lady and intestinal vein and reserve coral, if any. Sauté in olive oil and butter, covered, six minutes. Add vegetables, brandy, wine, consommé, herbs, seasonings, and coral, if any. Simmer 20 minutes. Serve in soup plates on toast. Serves 4.

LOBSTER THERMIDOR

2 lobsters (1-1½ pounds each)
4 tablespoons butter
½ cup mushrooms, sliced
2 tablespoons dry mustard
2 cups Medium Cream Sauce (p. 28)
⅔ cup Sherry
½ cup buttered bread crumbs
2 tablespoons grated Parmesan cheese
salt and pepper
paprika

Split lengthwise, remove lady, and clean. Broil. Reserve coral, if any. Take out all the meat and slice. Sauté mushrooms in butter for 3 minutes. Add mustard and Cream Sauce, and blend well. Mix in lobster meat, coral, and wine, season, and fill shells with mixture. Cover with buttered crumbs and grated cheese, and bake in hot oven (400-450°) until browned. Sprinkle with paprika. Serves 4.

BELGIAN LOBSTER

½ cup finely chopped celery
¼ cup finely chopped carrot
1 large tomato, chopped
⅔ cup butter
2 cups dry white wine
1 baby lobster (boiled)
½ cup brandy
2 egg yolks
½ cup heavy cream
salt
pepper
toast

Sauté celery, carrots, and tomatoes in ⅓ cup butter until tender. Add wine and simmer over very low heat 30 minutes, stirring. In another saucepan sauté lobster meat, cut in as large pieces as possible, in rest of butter for 3 minutes. Add brandy, light it, and when flames have died out add to vegetable mixture, retaining a little liquid, 3 or 4 tablespoons, in the pan. Beat egg yolks in ¼ cup cream, add and simmer very slowly, stirring constantly, for ½ minute. Add rest of cream to liquid in which lobster was sautéed, season and reheat. Serve on thin toast with sauce poured over. Serves 4.

LOBSTER FARCI

1 cup light cream
2 cups milk
¼ cup butter
2 tablespoons flour
salt and pepper
2 teaspoons lemon juice
dash of mace
6 (1 pound) lobsters, cooked
⅓ cup Sherry
½ cup buttered bread crumbs
3 hard-cooked egg yolks, chopped fine
2 tablespoons chopped parsley

Make a white sauce with cream, milk, butter, and flour. Add seasonings and lemon juice. Add lobster meat, cut in large cubes, and Sherry, and bring to a simmer. Slip tail shells into body shells as containers. Fill with lobster mixture; top with bread crumbs, egg yolk, and parsley. Dot with butter and brown under broiler. Serves 6.

GOURMET LOBSTER

1 (1½-2 pound) lobster, cooked
2 tablespoons flour
2 tablespoons butter
1 cup stock in which lobster was cooked
½ cup heavy cream
¼ cup dry white wine
1 teaspoon chopped tarragon
1 egg yolk, well beaten
salt and pepper

Cut up meat from claws and tail of lobster in large size portions. Keep hot. Make roux of flour and butter, stir in stock, cream, wine, and tarragon and season to taste. Simmer, while stirring, about 5 minutes. Remove from heat and stir in egg yolk. Serve in tureen with sauce poured over. Serves 2 to 4.

LOBSTER MARTINIQUE

2 (1½ pound) lobsters, boiled
4 tablespoons butter
2 cups light cream or top milk
2 egg yolks, beaten
¼ cup Sherry
1 teaspoon salt
¾ cup bread crumbs

Remove meat in large pieces and clean shells. Make white sauce with 2 tablespoons butter, flour, and milk or cream. Add 4 tablespoons to egg yolks, mix thoroughly, and stir into white sauce. Add lobster meat, Sherry, and salt and heat for ½ minute, stirring. Fill shells with mixture, sprinkle with bread crumbs, and dot with rest of butter. Bake in moderate oven (350-375°) until browned, about 15 minutes. If canned lobster is used, place mixture in greased casserole instead of shells. Serves 4.

LOBSTER COCKTAIL

Meat of 2 (1½-2 pound) lobsters
½ cup French mustard
½ cup chili sauce
½ cup dry white wine
1 teaspoon onion juice
juice of 1 lemon
salt and paprika

Remove meat from shells and cut into 1-inch pieces. Mix all other ingredients, strain, and ice. Fill glasses ½ full of sauce and add lobster. Serves 8.

OYSTERS SCOTTO

30 medium-sized oysters
¼ teaspoon mace
½ teaspoon celery salt
½ teaspoon anchovy paste
2 tablespoons flour
2 tablespoons butter
1 cup cream
1 egg yolk
2 teaspoons lemon juice
2 tablespoons Sherry
6 slices buttered toast

Cook oysters in their own liquor until they are plump and the edges curled. Remove oysters. To the liquor add mace, celery salt, anchovy paste, and a roux of butter and flour. Cook slowly for 4 or 5 minutes. Add cream and beaten egg yolk and oysters. Cook for 3 minutes but do not allow to boil. Just before serving add lemon juice and Sherry. Serve on buttered toast. Serves 6.

OYSTER PATTIES À LA CARMEN

12 large oysters
2 tablespoons butter
3 tablespoons dry Sherry
1 teaspoon grated onion
1 teaspoon lemon juice
½ teaspoon salt
⅛ teaspoon white pepper
¼ teaspoon mace
½ cup sliced mushrooms
6 pimiento stuffed olives, sliced
¼ cup heavy cream
¾ cup oyster liquor
2 egg yolks
chopped parsley

Melt 1 tablespoon butter; add Sherry, lemon juice, and seasonings. Add oysters and cook until plump and edges are curled. Remove from heat. Melt remaining butter in small saucepan, and sauté mushrooms and onion slowly until tender. Add sliced olives, oyster liquor, and cream in which egg yolks have been beaten. Stir briskly until simmering point is barely reached. Add oysters and sauce in which they were cooked. Do not allow to boil after egg yolks and cream have been added. Serve in patty shells. Serves 4 to 6.

OYSTERS GRANDE DAME

1 clove garlic, crushed
2 dozen medium-sized oysters
2 tablespoons olive oil
3 tablespoons butter
2 tablespoons chopped shallots
2 tablespoons chopped parsley
⅛ teaspoon ground cloves
few drops tabasco sauce
1 tablespoon flour
juice of ½ lemon
salt and pepper
2 tablespoons dry white wine

Rub flat baking dish well with crushed clove of garlic. Add 1 tablespoon olive oil and 1 tablespoon butter. Put in oysters and pour over remaining oil. Sprinkle in chopped shallots, parsley, and seasonings and flour. Add lemon juice, wine, and ½ cup oyster liquor. Dot with remaining butter and bake in hot oven (400-450°) 15 minutes. Brown under broiler. Serves 3-4.

OYSTERS WITH CELERY

½ cup chopped celery
1 tablespoon butter
3 cups medium-sized oysters
2 tablespoons Sherry
salt and pepper
4 slices buttered toast

Sauté celery in butter until tender. Add oysters and their liquor, and simmer until plump and edges curled. Add wine, season to taste, place on toast, and pour over liquor. Serves 4.

OYSTERS AND MACARONI IN CASSEROLE

1 pint oysters
2 cups Medium White Sauce (p. 27)
3 tablespoons Sherry
2 cups cooked macaroni
¼ cup grated cheese
salt and pepper

Put one-half the macaroni in a well-buttered casserole and put in the oysters in an even layer. Add remaining macaroni. Stir together the white sauce, oyster liquor, and wine, season well, and pour over top. Top with grated cheese and bake in moderate oven (350-375°) for 15 to 20 minutes. Serves 4.

OYSTER RAREBIT

3 cups medium-sized oysters
3 tablespoons butter
½ pound grated cheese
salt
dash of cayenne
cream or evaporated milk
3 eggs, beaten
3 dashes Angostura bitters
1 tablespoon Sherry

Cook oysters in their own liquor until plump and edges curled. Drain oysters and keep hot. Reserve liquor. Melt butter, add cheese, and season. Stir until thick and add oyster liquor with enough cream or evaporated milk (undiluted) added to make 1 cup. Stir in eggs; stir until thickened but do not allow to boil. Remove from heat, add oysters and Sherry, and serve on toast. Serves 4 to 6.

PAN-BROILED OYSTERS

24 large oysters
2 tablespoons butter
salt
dash of cayenne
3 tablespoons Sherry
4 slices buttered toast

Melt butter, add oysters and seasonings, and stir until edges curl. Remove from heat, add Sherry, and serve on toast. Serves 4.

PICKLED OYSTERS

50 medium-sized oysters
1 cup white wine vinegar
1 cup water
2 teaspoons mixed pickling spices
1 tablespoon salt
dash of Tabasco or pinch of cayenne
2 cups very dry white wine

Simmer oysters in their own liquor until plump and edges curl. Remove oysters, add all other ingredients except wine, and simmer slowly 10 minutes. Strain, add wine, and pour over oysters. If not enough liquid to cover completely add half hot vinegar and water mixed with an equal amount of wine. These may be canned and will keep indefinitely.

Clams or mussels may be prepared in the same way. They may be served as a garnish or, well chilled, as appetizers.

OYSTERS POULETTE

2 dozen oysters
2 tablespoons butter
2 cups light cream
⅛ teaspoon celery salt
1 cup Hollandaise Sauce (p. 48)
3 tablespoons Sherry
8 slices toast

Gently sauté oysters in 2 teaspoons butter and all their own juice until edges begin to curl. In another pan bring cream, remaining butter, and celery salt to a simmer; add oyster mixture and Hollandaise Sauce, stirring constantly until it begins to thicken. Stir in Sherry and serve at once on hot toast. Serves 4.

MUSSELS À LA MARINIÈRE

Open mussels as described on page 82. Serve with both shells. Strain cooking liquor and add 2 tablespoons butter for each 2 quarts of mussels. Serve separately in individual dishes.

STUFFED MUSSELS

3 tablespoons olive oil
3 tablespoons chopped onion
2 leeks, white part only, sliced thin
2 medium-sized tomatoes, chopped
1 clove garlic, crushed and minced
½ teaspoon dried thyme
1 large bay leaf
½ teaspoon saffron
½ cup dry white wine
48 mussels, washed and scrubbed
salt and pepper
parsley

Sauté onions, leeks, tomatoes, and garlic in olive oil until onions and leeks are tender but not brown. Add thyme, bay leaf, saffron, and wine and bring to a boil. Add mussels and cover tightly, shake pan occasionally, and simmer gently for 5 minutes after all mussels are open. Remove mussels and allow sauce to reduce by one half. Strain. Meanwhile, remove mussels from shells, chop fine, and then stir into sauce. Reduce sauce further if necessary. Season to taste and stuff half the shells. Sprinkle with parsley before serving. Excellent either hot or cold. Serves 6.

MUSSELS BONNE FEMME

48 small or 42 large mussels
½ cup sliced mushrooms
2 stalks celery, cut julienne
2 tablespoons butter
¼ cup cream

Cook mussels in court bouillon as described on page 82 with the addition of mushrooms and celery. Reduce cooking liquor by half, strain, add butter and cream, and serve over mussels. Serves 6.

CURRIED SCALLOPS IN SHELL

1 pound scallops
3 tablespoons chopped onion
3 tablespoons butter
¾ cup dry white wine
1 bouquet garni (p. 9)
pinch of curry powder
2 tablespoons heavy cream
salt and pepper

Sauté scallops gently in butter with chopped onion until onion is tender but not brown. Add wine, bouquet garni, and curry powder and simmer 3 minutes. (The quantity of curry powder depends on its strength and your individual taste, but be very careful not to overdo it. Its flavor must not predominate, only suggest.) Remove scallops and place in heated shells. Strain sauce, reduce one half, add cream, and pour over scallops. Serve with rice. Serves 4.

SCALLOP STEW

1 quart scallops
1 quart milk
salt and pepper
1 tablespoon butter
1 tablespoon chopped parsley
½ cup bread crumbs
2 tablespoons Sherry
nutmeg

Boil scallops for 15 minutes in water enough to cover. Heat, but do not boil, the milk and add salt, pepper, butter, and parsley. Stir in bread crumbs. Add scallops and allow to just simmer. Just before serving, stir in Sherry and dust with nutmeg. Serves 4.

ANCHOVIED SCALLOPS

2½ tablespoons butter
2½ tablespoons flour
2 cups top milk or light cream
4 cups scallops
½ teaspoon salt
⅛ teaspoon pepper
½ teaspoon dry mustard
½ teaspoon Worcestershire sauce
⅛ teaspoon paprika
¼ cup Sherry
1 teaspoon anchovy paste
2 teaspoons lemon juice
½ cup buttered crumbs

Make a white sauce with butter, flour, and milk or cream. Add scallops, seasonings, and wine and simmer gently for 5 minutes, stirring constantly. Pour into greased casserole. Blend together anchovy paste, crumbs, and lemon juice and spread on top. Bake in hot oven (400-450°) until well browned, about 20 minutes. Serves 6.

SCALLOPS IN SHELLS BORDEAUX

3 tablespoons diced carrot
3 tablespoons diced onion
1 tablespoon diced shallots
1 teaspoon chopped parsley
1 bay leaf
1 pinch dried thyme
3 tablespoons butter
1 pound scallops
2 tablespoons brandy
3 medium-sized tomatoes, peeled and chopped
⅓ cup dry white wine
salt and pepper

Sauté carrots, onion, shallots, parsley, bay leaf, and thyme lightly in butter until vegetables are tender. (This is a Mirepoix Bordelaise.) If using the large sea scallops, cut them in 4 pieces, once across the grain and once with it. Stew gently in the Mirepoix, covered, for 10 minutes. Add brandy, light it, and when flames begin to die out add tomatoes and wine and cook slowly 10 minutes more. Remove scallops, reduce sauce, and season to taste. Serves 4.

SCALLOPS IN SHELLS AMERICAN STYLE

1 pound scallops
Mirepoix Bordelaise (p. 100)
3 medium-sized tomatoes, peeled and chopped
1 bouquet garni (p. 9)
3 tablespoons dry white wine
2 tablespoons cream
salt and pepper
2 tablespoons chopped chervil
1 tablespoon chopped tarragon

Sauté scallops in Mirepoix Bordelaise. Add tomatoes, bouquet garni, and wine and stew gently 10 minutes. Remove scallops and place in heated shells. Strain sauce, reduce one half, add cream, and pour over scallops. Sprinkle with chopped chervil and tarragon. Serves 4.

SCALLOPS IN SHELLS MORNAY

1 pound scallops
¾ cup dry white wine
¾ cup Mornay Sauce (p. 46)
4 teaspoons grated Parmesan cheese
salt and pepper

Poach scallops in wine for 15 minutes. Put 1 tablespoon of Mornay Sauce in each scallop shell, add scallops and rest of sauce, sprinkle with cheese, and brown under broiler. Serves 4.

SCALLOPS IN SHELLS BRETON

1 pound scallops, diced
1 shallot, minced
1 tablespoon chopped onion
3 tablespoons butter
3 tablespoons dry white wine
1 tablespoon chopped parsley
¼ to ½ cup bread crumbs
salt and pepper
½ cup buttered bread crumbs

Sauté scallops, shallot, and onion in butter until vegetables are tender. Add wine, parsley, and bread crumbs and simmer 7 to 8 minutes, until it has the consistency of a light sauce. Be careful to stir bread crumbs in gradually so as not to get sauce too thick. Fill scallop shells, sprinkle with buttered breadcrumbs, and brown under broiler. Serves 4.

SHRIMP AND NOODLES VERMOUTH

1 cup Medium White Sauce (p. 27)
2 tablespoons grated cheese
1 pound shrimp, boiled and peeled
¼ cup dry Vermouth
½ package (3 oz.) broad noodles
green vegetable coloring
salt

Blend cheese in White Sauce; add shrimp and Vermouth. Boil noodles in salted water to which a bit of green coloring has been added. Stir shrimp mixture and noodles together in greased casserole, and bake in hot oven (400-425°) for 20 minutes. Serves 4 to 6.

SHRIMP PIE

8 slices of bread, crusts removed
1 cup Sherry
1 pound shrimp, cooked, shelled, and ground
2 tablespoons butter
½ teaspoon pepper
¼ teaspoon mace
salt

Mash the bread and wine to a paste. Work in the shrimp, butter, and seasonings and bake in a buttered casserole in a moderate oven (350-375°) for 45 minutes. Serves 6.

SHRIMP ST. LAURENT

2 tablespoons butter
2 tablespoons flour
1 cup hot water
2 bouillon cubes
1 cup sour cream
1 teaspoon salt
⅛ teaspoon pepper
dash of cayenne
2 cups shrimp, coarsely chopped
¼ cup grated Parmesan cheese
¼ cup Sherry
buttered toast

Melt butter and blend in flour. Gradually add hot water in which bouillon cubes have been dissolved. Cook until thick and smooth. Add sour cream, seasonings, shrimp, and cheese. Simmer 10 minutes. Add Sherry. Serve on buttered toast. Serves 6.

SHRIMP SHORTCAKE

1 recipe biscuit dough
6 tablespoons butter
6 tablespoons flour
2 cups milk
2 cups cooked shrimp, fresh or canned
salt and paprika
½ cup chopped cucumber
½ cup dry white wine

Prepare biscuit dough. Pat dough ¼ inch thick and cut 12 rounds with 3-inch biscuit cutter. Place 6 rounds in shallow baking pan, brush with melted butter, and cover with remaining rounds. Bake in hot oven (425-450°) 15 minutes. Meanwhile make a roux of butter and flour, add milk gradually, and cook until thickened. Add shrimp, season, and simmer 2 minutes. Add cucumber and wine, and reheat just to simmering. Separate biscuit halves, cover bottom halves with shrimp mixture, lay on top halves, and cover with mixture. Serves 6.

Any shellfish or flaked firm-meated fish may be substituted for shrimp.

SHELLFISH NEWBURG

½ cup crab meat, flaked
½ cup lobster meat, coarsely chopped
½ cup shrimp, coarsely chopped
5 clams, coarsely chopped
6 tablespoons butter
2 tablespoons Sherry
2 cups cream
6 egg yolks, beaten
2 tablespoons lemon juice
salt
pepper
dash cayenne
toast
paprika

Sauté seafood in butter for about 2 minutes, add Sherry and 1½ cups cream, and bring to a boil. Stir beaten egg yolks in remaining cream, add to mixture, reduce heat, and stir constantly until mixture is thick. Do not allow to boil after egg yolks are added. Remove from fire, season, add lemon juice, spread on toast, and sprinkle liberally with paprika. Serves 4 to 6.

SHRIMP BRETONNE

1 cup Medium White Sauce (p. 27)
½ pound cheese
1 pound cooked shrimp, fresh or canned
1 cup Sauterne, not dry
1 cup avocado, cut in balls
½ cup buttered dry bread crumbs

Melt cheese in White Sauce. Add shrimp, wine, and avocado and mix well. Put in casserole and sprinkle with bread crumbs. Bake in moderate oven (350-375°) 20 minutes. Place under broiler to brown. Serves 4 to 6.

SEAFOOD STEW MAINE STYLE

1 quart milk
12 oysters, drained
¼ pound scallops
¼ pound cooked shrimp
¼ pound cooked crab meat
¼ pound cooked lobster meat
1 cup cream
3 tablespoons Sherry
2 tablespoons butter

Scald milk, add seafood, and simmer very slowly until oysters plump up and edges curl. Add cream and Sherry, reheat, and serve. Serves 6.

TERRAPIN BALTIMORE

Meat from 2 terrapins (p. 82)
2 cups (approximately) condensed chicken consommé
½ teaspoon beef extract
terrapin eggs, if any
½ cup butter
1 tablespoon brandy
¼ cup Madeira or Sherry
salt
pepper

Boil terrapin meat in enough consommé to just cover for 20 minutes. Remove terrapin meat and reduce consommé to ⅓. Remove from heat, add terrapin eggs and beef extract, and slowly stir in butter. Season, and add brandy and wine. Reheat but do not allow to simmer. Pour over terrapin. Serves 3 to 4.

TERRAPIN À LA MARYLAND

Meat from 2 terrapins (p. 82)
¼ cup butter
2 truffles, chopped (optional)
½ teaspoon salt
dash cayenne
dash mace
1 cup heavy cream
2 egg yolks, beaten
2 tablespoons Madeira or dry Sherry

Melt butter, and add terrapin meat, chopped truffles, and seasonings. Stir until thoroughly heated. Mix cream and beaten egg yolks, and add slowly, stirring constantly. Do not allow to boil. Stir in wine just before serving. Serves 3 to 4.

TERRAPIN CLUB STYLE

Meat from 2 terrapins (p. 82)
3 tablespoons butter
½ teaspoon salt
1 cup cream
3 egg yolks, beaten
2 tablespoons dry Sherry

Melt butter, add terrapin meat and salt, and heat thoroughly. Add cream and let boil gently while stirring for 2 minutes. Remove from heat and slowly stir in beaten egg yolks. Add wine just before serving. Serves 3 to 4.

TURTLE STEAK

1½ pound turtle steak
flour
2 eggs, beaten
2 cups bread crumbs
⅓ cup butter
½ cup Sherry
salt and pepper

Wipe turtle meat well with moist cloth. Flour thoroughly, and dip in beaten egg and then in bread crumbs. Brown in butter quickly on both sides. Reduce heat and sauté about 15 minutes, or until meat is tender, turning occasionally. Add Sherry and seasonings, cover, and simmer until wine is reduced one half. Pour wine over turtle meat and serve. (Veal cutlets are excellent treated in the same way.) Serves 6.

TERRAPIN CHESAPEAKE BAY

4 hard-cooked eggs
grated rind ½ lemon
juice of ½ lemon
¼ teaspoon nutmeg
2 tablespoons flour
1 cup bouillon
1 small onion, minced
¼ cup celery
meat from 2 terrapins (p. 82)
milk
2 teaspoons Worcestershire sauce
½ cup cream
2 cups Sherry
salt
cayenne

Mash egg yolks with lemon juice, grated rind, nutmeg, and flour. Blend in bouillon, add onion, celery, terrapin meat, sliced terrapin liver, and eggs, if any; add enough milk to cover. Cook in double boiler until meat separates from bones. Remove bones and add chopped egg whites, Worcestershire, cream, and Sherry. Season to taste, reheat, and serve on toast. Serves 6.

FROG LEGS COOKED IN WHITE WINE

(From Alphonse Raes, Chef-Steward, Park Plaza Hotel, St. Louis, Mo.)

2 large frog legs
1 large white onion
1 ripe tomato
3 ounces dry white wine
3 ounces fresh cream
salt and pepper
1 tablespoon butter
1 teaspoon flour
a little chopped chives and parsley
juice of ½ lemon

Chop onion finely and sauté in a little butter until cooked (not brown) and add frog legs. Add 2½ ounces of wine, 3 ounces of cream, salt and pepper, and tomato chopped in large pieces. Cook slowly for 15 minutes, with cover. Mix teaspoon of flour with equal amount of soft butter and put in the preparation while stirring and boiling. Finish with a pinch of sugar, ½ ounce of wine, finely chopped chives, and parsley and lemon juice. Mix well and then serve. Mushrooms added to this preparation will improve the taste. Serves 1.

FROG LEGS A LA NEWBURG

4 pair large or 8 pair small frog legs
½ cup soup stock or consommé
½ cup Madeira or Sherry
salt
cayenne
1 cup cream
3 egg yolks, slightly beaten

Skin legs. Drop in boiling salted water and simmer 20-25 minutes or until tender. Heat stock or consommé, add wine, season to taste, and boil 3 minutes. Mix cream and egg yolks, add and simmer 2 minutes, stirring constantly. Pour over frog legs. Serves 4.

FROG LEGS POULETTE

(from Hotel Lafayette, New York City)

Take two pounds of medium-sized frog legs and about 8 heads of fresh mushrooms. Slice mushrooms, and put them in a copper pan with the frog legs, 3 chopped shallots, a glass of dry white wine, and a nut of butter; cover and let cook on top of stove for about 14 minutes. Then add a pint of heavy cream, season with salt and cayenne pepper, let cook again 10 minutes. When ready to serve, add some chopped chives and thicken the sauce with a ladleful of Sauce Hollandaise (p. 48) or instead, with two yolks. Serves 2.

CHAPTER SIX

Meats

The use of wine in meat cookery goes back almost to the dawn of history. It is frequently mentioned in the Bible, the Koran, the writings of Confucius, and even the stone writings of the Babylonians and Phoenicians and the Aztecs and the Mayas. Yet, in the average American kitchen, it is practically unknown.

A pity! Because the use of wine in combination with meat serves a double purpose. In addition to adding a wide range of new and delightful flavors, it tenderizes. Marinating is a common thing in Europe; less so in America except among professional chefs. It is nothing except the prolonged immersion of meat in a solution of a fruit acid which may be either vinegar, lemon juice, or dry wine, or a combination of them with or without water. The process transforms the tough connective tissues to which meat owes its toughness to collegan, a gelatin-like substance, and makes the toughest cuts as tender as the most expensive and, by the way, often superior in flavor.

To convince yourself of this, once and for all, try the recipe for Hamburger de Luxe on page 123. Cook half in the regular way and half as directed. Let your palate and your family be the judges.

And marinating is not expensive, in spite of the relatively large quantities of wine sometimes required, since the solution has salt added and can be frequently re-used if kept covered in a cool place and with a thin film of oil on top.

If the marinated meat is to be roasted, you will want to baste it with the marinating liquid. Use what is left in the pan for a sauce, thickened or not as you prefer.

A plain marinade is made in the proportion of two parts of water to one part of wine and salt in the proportion of one tablespoon to a quart of liquid. In many cases you will want to add herbs and spices according to the dish you are preparing.

Tradition calls for the service of red wine with red meat and white wine with white meat. For this reason and none other, many chefs carry this rule into the kitchen. These ultra-purists will be shocked by many of the following recipes in which this rule is ignored, but just try one or two and then go on and do some experimenting on your own initiative.

You may be inclined to question the low roasting temperatures in the following recipes. Try them first. They are the result of thousands of experiments by the Bureau of Home Economics of the U. S. Department of Agriculture and the home economics departments of colleges and food manufacturers everywhere. Slow cooking with wine is especially advisable as the very high temperatures (400-500° F.) give a "burnt" flavor to the wine which may be very disagreeable.

When you use wine for basting, stop basting about fifteen minutes before the roast is done. This will not only give a better "finish" to the roast but will thicken the gravy which you can make into any sauce you desire.

The liquid in which meat is boiled usually develops a scum which you are invariably directed to remove. But don't. This scum is made up of some of the most nutritious elements in the meat, and to throw it away is as wasteful as discarding the water in which vegetables are cooked.

Have you a meat thermometer? If not, you'll find it very well worth its comparatively small cost. It takes all the guesswork out of roasting. At best, the time and temperature method is not always reliable. A small roast, for example, takes longer per pound than a large one. Because bone is a heat conductor, a boned and rolled roast may take as much as fifteen to twenty minutes more per pound than one with the bone left in. The meat thermometer guarantees that your roast will be exactly as you want it, every time.

Quick-frozen meats may seem a bit expensive; but, when you consider that they are of top quality and practically without waste, the difference, if any, is slight. Remember, almost every butcher trims your meat after he weighs it.

And, if it is possible, always let meat reach room temperature before cooking. It will be noticeably more tender and better flavored, and, of course, the cooking time will be shortened. This is especially important in the case of roasts, and it may require four or five hours to lose the refrigerator chill.

On page 131 you will find instructions for baking ham in a dough envelope. The same method may be used with meat of any kind—fresh pork, ham, or shoulder with Sauterne are particularly distinctive.

ORGANS

Dietitians advise us to eat more organs. Twice a week at least, they say, brains, tongue, sweetbreads, heart, tripe, liver, or kidneys should be given the place of honor on our menus. Without going into technicalities, each of these contains substances valuable to our well-being which are not found in sufficient quantities in other portions of the animal.

One reason, perhaps, that they are not more generally used is the belief that they are expensive. This is far from the truth. With the exception of sweetbreads and calf liver, which usually cost about as much per pound as tenderloin steak, the rest will not strain the most sensitive budget, and don't forget that the waste is almost microscopic.

Here is as good a place as any to discuss their selection and preliminary preparation.

Brains and sweetbreads may be considered together as they require the same initial treatment. If you decide on brains you may take your choice of calf, lamb, pork, sheep, or beef, and there is slight difference between them. The price of all is about the same, but, if market conditions result in a margin in favor of one kind, take advantage of it. Use one pair of beef brains, two pairs of calf or pork brains, or four pairs of lamb brains per portion.

It is imperative that both brains and sweetbreads be absolutely fresh when purchased and prepared immediately upon reaching your kitchen. Just rinse them well, cover with cold salted water, and let stand about half an hour. Drain and cover with boiling water to which one teaspoon each of salt and vinegar or lemon juice have been added. Cool and remove outside membranes and tubes. Keep under refrigeration until ready to use.

When it comes to tongue you again have your choice of veal, lamb, pork, or beef, but there is a considerable difference in price, texture, and cooking time. Beef tongues will run from four to six pounds each, calf one to two pounds, pork one-half to three-quarters pound and lamb one-quarter to one-third pound. The smaller ones are not only more delicate in flavor and texture but cook more quickly.

The method of preparation is the same for each. First, scrub thoroughly with a stiff brush, cover with boiling water, and simmer, covered. Add about one-half teaspoon salt per pound when they are nearly done. Allow to cool in cooking liquid and, when cool enough to handle, skin and remove gristly root end. The cooking time will be three to four hours for beef tongue, two to three hours for calf tongue, one and a half to two hours for pork tongue, and one to one and a half hours for lamb tongue. Pickled, smoked, or corned tongue should be covered with cold water instead of boiling. If very salty, corned tongue may have to be soaked in cold water for three or four hours before boiling. Allow about one fourth to one third pound per portion.

Exactly the same advice for the selection of tongues applies to hearts, except that there is not much difference in the price per pound of the various sizes, and the cooking time pound for pound and the amount per portion is about the same.

To prepare them, first, wash out all the clotted blood and remove the gristle, large arteries, and veins. Cover them with boiling water and simmer until tender.

In the finest restaurants of both Europe and America, tripe holds a high place of honor. Unfortunately, as it is prepared in the average restaurant or home, it just makes enemies. It can be one of the most economical of luxuries, or it can take second place to the sole of a tennis shoe.

Part of the secret lies in its selection and preliminary preparation. Insist on honeycomb tripe. It is easy to distinguish because the name describes it perfectly. Choose either fresh or pickled, whichever is cheaper. There won't be any difference when it gets to the table.

Wash, cover with cold water, and bring slowly to a boil. Drain, cover with boiling water, and simmer, covered, until tender—until you can cut it easily with a fork. If you are using fresh tripe add one-half teaspoon salt when nearly done. Allow one quarter to one-third pound per person.

Did you ever read a description of an English breakfast that didn't mention grilled kidneys and bacon? Curiously, while they are a staple in every home there, they are far from being as well known here as their delicacy, economy, and high nutritive qualities entitle them to be.

Again, you have your choice of lamb, veal, pork, mutton, or beef kidneys, in order of their desirabilities.

Wash, cut in halves lengthwise, and with a very sharp pointed knife remove white centers and tubes thoroughly. Soak in two or three changes of cold salted water for one-half to two hours according to size. If very old or large, cover with cold, salted water, bring to a boil, and simmer 15 to 20 minutes. Drain on absorbent paper or a towel. Allow about half a beef kidney, one veal or pork kidney, or one and a half to two lamb kidneys per portion.

Your grandmother never thought of paying for liver. Your mother paid a few cents a pound. Dog and cat owners found it an economical addition to the diet of their pets. A few years ago the medical profession discovered that it was almost a specific for pernicious anemia, hitherto considered incurable; furthermore, that it would work wonders in convalescent and undernourished conditions of all kinds. In one short year calf liver jumped in price to the luxury class.

Habit is strong. We are so accustomed to thinking of "liver" as "calf liver" that we forget the other kinds that richly deserve our consideration. Maybe you think you can tell the difference between it and lamb or pork liver. Maybe you can, if so you are one out of a hundred. Remember pork is from animals not over one year old. Beef liver is not so tender or delicate in flavor, but it is very inexpensive and five minutes' parboiling improves it immensely. In "made" dishes it may even be preferable on account of its firmness. And remember, too, from the standpoint of health and nutrition, liver is liver.

If possible, buy liver in one piece and slice it yourself to avoid loss of juice. Drop it into rapidly boiling water. Drain and remove skin and veins. Few people go to this trouble, but it makes a surprising difference. And here is a secret few people know: for a really de luxe dish, soak the liver in milk for three or four hours. Evaporated milk, undiluted, is even better than natural milk and not much is needed, just enough to coat the liver well. Turn the pieces several times while soaking.

The reason liver, especially when fried, is so frequently tough and flavorless is because it has been cooked too slowly and too long. When perfectly done, the juices are pinkish. Why is broiled liver so seldom met? Try it next time for a change. The flavor is quite different, nuttier. Have slices cut at least a half inch thick, wipe but do not dredge with flour, spread well with butter, and have broiler well greased. Five minutes to a side is about right.

BEEF CORNED IN WINE

Corned beef is, traditionally, a rather low-brow sort of dish. But, prepared as described here, it reaches epicurean heights.

The first point of difference is the cut used. Even the best commercial corned beef uses brisket. In this recipe use chuck or rump, bottom or top round, or, for a particularly festive occasion, rib roast boned and rolled.

Not too large a piece, because the beef should be thoroughly corned all through—5 or 6 pounds at most. Put meat in a large crock or vessel (not aluminum); pour in a mixture of ½ dry red wine and ½ water to half cover the meat. Remove the meat and add 1 cup salt, 4 bay leaves, 1 teaspoon pepper, and 1 tablespoon poultry seasoning for each quart of liquid. Stir until salt is dissolved. Return meat to liquid. Keep at room temperature for at least 72 hours. Turn frequently.

Simmer in corning liquor until tender. Time will depend on cut of meat used, about 20-30 minutes per pound. Do not "freshen" as this takes away the wine flavor.

Red cabbage, quartered, may be added to cooking liquor 20 minutes before beef is done.

If a pressure cooker is used (and this method of cooking prevents loss of wine flavor), cooking time is about 5 minutes per pound.

When done, remove meat and reduce 2 cups of cooking liquor by boiling until it begins to thicken. Pour over beef and cabbage, and serve. Remainder of cooking liquor may be placed in covered container and saved for future use.

FILET OF BEEF CREOLE

1 whole filet of beef, 4-6 pounds
salt pork for larding
salt and pepper
1 medium-sized onion, sliced
1 bay leaf
4 whole cloves, crushed
3 tablespoons butter
2 tablespoons beef extract
3 tablespoons water
¾ cup Sherry
¼ cup water

Remove outer skin and fat of filet. Cut pork for larding in ⅛-inch strips; lard evenly in 4 or 5 rows about 1 inch apart. Rub well with salt and pepper. Spread sliced onion, bay leaf, and cloves in bottom of baking dish just large enough to hold filet. Lay filet on top, larded side up, and dot with 1 tablespoon butter. Roast in hot oven (400-450°) for 30 minutes or to 140° if you are using a meat thermometer. (It should be quite rare.) Do not add water.

To make sauce, melt remaining 2 tablespoons butter, add beef extract dissolved in 3 tablespoons water, and wine and water, stirring constantly. Pour around filet before serving. Serves 12 to 18.

LARDED FILET OF BEEF RENAISSANCE

1 (2 pound) filet of beef (center cut of tenderloin), larded
1 medium-sized onion, sliced
1 medium-sized carrot, sliced
1 stalk celery, diced
2 whole cloves
2 bay leaves
10 peppercorns
3 tablespoons butter, melted
½ cup Madeira or Sherry
1 tablespoon flour, browned
2 cups beef stock
salt
pepper

Skin filet and remove all fat. Place vegetables, cloves, bay leaves, and peppercorns in small roasting pan, lay filet on top, and brush all over with melted butter. Season and place in very hot oven (450-500°) 45 minutes. Baste quickly every 10 minutes *but do not add water*. When well browned, remove to serving dish and keep hot. Brown vegetables in pan until all liquid disappears. Stir in browned flour, add stock, and simmer very slowly 15 to 20 minutes. Add wine, strain, reheat, and pour over filet. Serves 4 to 6.

CREPINETTES OF BEEF (POLISH)

1 pound tenderloin of beef
4 tablespoons butter
1 cup sliced mushrooms
⅓ cup chopped onion
1 tablespoon flour
½ cup tomato soup
¼ cup Sherry or Madeira
salt and pepper

Have tenderloin cut in 4 equal pieces and flattened to about ½ inch thick. Sauté in 2 tablespoons butter until medium well done, about 3 minutes, on each side. Meanwhile, sauté onions and mushrooms in another pan in rest of butter until tender. Blend in flour thoroughly, then slowly add tomato soup and wine, and simmer slowly while stirring until quite thick. Season to taste, pour over meat, cover, reduce heat very low, and let simmer for 3 minutes more. Serves 4.

FILETS STROGONOFF

1 onion, grated
2½ tablespoons butter
2 pounds filets of beef or pork, sliced ⅛ inch thick
1 tablespoon flour
¼ cup beef bouillon
¼ cup dry white wine
1 cup sour cream
1 tablespoon Worcestershire sauce
1 tablespoon chopped parsley
salt and pepper

Sauté onion in butter until tender but not brown. Add meat and brown it lightly. Sprinkle in flour while meat is cooking. Add all other ingredients except parsley and cook until sauce is a golden yellow. Serve sprinkled with parsley. Serves 6.

FILET OF BEEF WITH OLIVES

6 slices beef tenderloin, 1 inch thick
1½ tablespoons olive oil
2 tablespoons butter
¾ cup stock or bouillon
1 teaspoon vinegar
1 tablespoon mushroom catsup
1½ tablespoons flour
salt and pepper
⅔ cup dry red wine
¼ cup sliced olives

Have filets flattened to ½ inch thick. Brown in very hot butter and olive oil 3-4 minutes. Make paste of catsup, flour, and stock, add wine and olives, season, and simmer 3 minutes, stirring constantly. Pour around meat on hot platter. Serves 6.

ROAST BEEF AND SHERRIED MUSHROOMS

4 (1½-inch thick) slices cold roast beef
½ cup butter
½ pound mushrooms
2 cups (approximately) thick gravy
½ cup orange juice
1 cup Sherry

Brown beef slices lightly in butter. Remove to serving dish and keep hot. Sauté mushrooms in butter, add gravy, orange juice, and Sherry, stir until very smooth, and simmer gently about 5 minutes. Pour over beef and serve. Serves 4. Excellent with rice.

SALMI OF BEEF

2 tablespoons butter
1 tablespoon flour
1 cup broth, *or*
1 bouillon cube dissolved in 1 cup hot water
4 thick slices cold roast beef
1 teaspoon lemon juice
1 tablespoon Worcestershire sauce
½ cup dry red wine

Brown butter and flour together, add broth, and stir until it begins to thicken. Add meat and heat thoroughly. Add lemon juice, wine, and Worcestershire. Serve at once. Serves 4.

BEEF STEW I

½ cup vegetable oil
2 medium-sized onions, minced
2 pounds stewing beef, cubed
3 tablespoons chopped olives
2 tablespoons flour
1 teaspoon salt
¼ teaspoon pepper
1 cup boiling water
1 cup dry white wine

Heat oil and brown onions lightly. Add beef and brown. Add olives and flour, and mix well. Season. Add water and wine, cover, and simmer until meat is tender. Serves 6.

BEEF STEW II

1 pound diced beef
½ cup vegetable oil
½ clove garlic
1 cup diced onions
1 cup tomato sauce
salt and pepper
1 cup dry red wine
2 tablespoons flour
1 bay leaf
¼ teaspoon ground cloves
¼ teaspoon thyme

Brown beef in oil. Add onions and garlic. Add flour and brown lightly, then add tomato sauce, seasonings, and ½ cup wine. Cook until beef is tender. Remove meat and boil sauce until thick. Add rest of wine and heat gently. Pour over meat. Serves 4.

TOMATO BEEF STEW WITH WINE

2 pounds lean beef, cut in 1-inch cubes
suet or vegetable oil
salt
pepper
1 clove garlic, minced
1 cup diced celery
1 cup diced carrots
3 cloves
1 bay leaf
1 cup dry red wine
8 small potatoes, cut in halves
1 pound tomatoes, peeled and quartered, *or*
3 cups solid-pack canned tomatoes
2 tablespoons browned flour

Brown beef cubes in hot fat. Sprinkle with salt and pepper, and add garlic, celery, cloves, and bay leaf. Add wine and enough water to cover the meat (about 1 cup). Cover kettle and simmer for one hour. Add potatoes and tomatoes. Continue simmering for an hour longer, or until very tender. Mix flour with water to make quite a thin paste; stir into stew and cook five minutes longer. Serves 6 to 8.

OLD FASHIONED BEEF STEW

2 pounds lean beef, cut in 1-inch cubes
½ cup chopped suet
1 teaspoon salt
¼ teaspoon pepper
2 medium-sized onions, chopped
3 stalks celery, chopped
1 cup dry red wine
½ cup condensed tomato soup
1 small bay leaf
⅛ teaspoon powdered thyme
1 small clove garlic, crushed
2 tablespoons flour

Heat suet until it begins to smoke. Add beef, salt, and pepper and brown well. Add vegetables, sprinkle in flour, and stir well. Add herbs, wine, tomato soup and stir until it begins to boil. Cover and place in hot oven (375-400°) for 2½ hours. Remove meat, strain sauce, and boil until reduced one-half. Skim off fat and pour sauce over meat. Serve very hot. Serves 6 to 8.

NOISETTE OF BEEF ROSSINI

1½ pounds tenderloin of beef
2 tablespoons butter
2 tablespoons olive oil or vegetable oil
½ pound chicken livers
¼ pound mushrooms, sliced
1 cup Madeira or Sherry
½ cup thick Brown Sauce (p. 28)
toast

Have tenderloin sliced thin and flattened to ¼ inch thick. Heat butter and oil until it just begins to smoke, reduce heat, and sauté beef 7 minutes. Remove and keep hot. Slice chicken livers thickly and sauté with mushrooms until latter are tender. Meanwhile reduce wine by one half and add Brown Sauce. Place one slice of meat on each slice of very thin toast, top with chicken liver and mushrooms, and add sauce. Serves 4 to 6.

ESTOUFFADE OF BEEF BURGUNDY STYLE

(From Gabriel Lugot, Executive Chef, The Waldorf-Astoria, New York City)

2 pounds hip of beef, large dices and tender
1 pound salt pork, cut in small dices
2 large onions
2 carrots
2 tablespoons flour
1 small clove garlic, chopped
1 bouquet garni (made with parsley, bay leaf, and thyme)
½ pound small onions
½ pound mushrooms
1 quart good California red wine
1 pint good stock

Parboil cut salt pork. Put to fry 4 minutes in a flat saucepan and then remove. In this grease put to fry very nicely the cut hip beef, already seasoned, with carrots and large onions cut in small parts. When fried, add garlic and flour, cook 1 minute, then pour in red wine and stock. Add bouquet garni, cover, and let cook slowly in oven for 1 hour. Clean small onions and cook them with little butter in a medium pan. When cooked, add mushrooms (washed and cut in four parts). Reserve. Take out each piece of meat from the saucepan and put them with the small onions, mushrooms, and salt pork. Reduce the sauce to a quart of volume. Strain it over top of meat. Rectify seasoning. Put to boil 10 minutes and serve very hot. Serves 6.

STEAMED SPICED BEEF (SAUERBRATEN)

4 pounds lean beef
1 teaspoon salt
¼ teaspoon pepper
1 teaspoon dry mustard
½ teaspoon thyme
⅛ teaspoon sage
⅛ teaspoon allspice
12 whole cloves
⅔ cup vinegar (preferably tarragon)
1½ cups dry red wine
2 bouillon cubes
4 tablespoons butter
6 ginger snaps, crushed
¾ cup (1 6-oz. can) tomato paste
1½ tablespoons Sherry or Madeira

Put beef in about six-quart enamel, earthenware, or stainless steel kettle with tight-fitting lid. Mix wine, vinegar, seasonings, and bouillon cubes, pour over meat, and leave at room temperature for 4 days, turning frequently.

Remove meat and sauté in butter in frying pan until lightly browned. Remove meat to heavy kettle or Dutch oven. Blend flour into drippings, gradually add the marinating liquid and the crushed gingersnaps, and cook until thickened. Add to meat and cook over low heat until meat is very tender, 3 hours or more according to cut used. Add water if necessary. Remove meat. Stir tomato paste and wine into gravy. Slice meat thickly across grain and pour sauce over. Serve with potato dumplings, potato pancakes, or boiled potatoes. Serves 8 to 12.

BOILED BEEF BORDELAISE

6 shallots, minced
½ cup dry white wine
3-4 tablespoons beef marrow
¼ cup hot water
2 tablespoons Sauce Espagnole (p. 35)
salt and pepper
8-12 slices cold boiled beef

Add minced shallots to wine and simmer gently until wine is reduced one half. Mash beef marrow, melt in hot water, and add, together with Sauce Espagnole. Simmer gently for 15 minutes, stirring frequently. Add beef (sliced across grain), season, and heat for 10 minutes. Serve with croutons. Serves 4 to 6.

POT ROAST WITH RED WINE NO. 1

4 pounds beef
¼ cup flour
2 teaspoons salt
⅛ teaspoon pepper
⅛ teaspoon ground cloves
¼ cup chopped suet
4 cups dry red wine
4 cups meat stock or consommé
4 medium-sized onions, sliced
6 medium-sized carrots, sliced
6 stalks celery, cut up
1 cup seedless raisins
flour
milk

Select a solid, lean piece of meat, either top sirloin, top or bottom round, rump, or chuck. Wipe with damp cloth and dredge thoroughly with mixture of flour and spices. Try out suet in heavy kettle or Dutch oven until golden; do not allow it to smoke. Brown meat well on all sides, add wine and consommé, and cook over low heat, until meat is tender, 3-5 hours, according to cut used. Add vegetables and raisins during last ½ hour. Remove meat. Drain off liquid, measure, and skim off fat. For each cup of brown gravy use 2 tablespoons each of browned flour and fat; blend and cook until light brown; stir in liquid slowly, using skimmed gravy from kettle with enough milk or stock to make necessary quantity. Simmer 5 minutes. Slice meat thick and serve gravy separately. Serves 10 to 12.

ENGLISH "HOT POT"

1 pound lean beef, cubed
flour
salt and pepper
4 tablespoons chopped suet
4 medium-sized potatoes, thinly sliced
3 medium-sized onions, sliced
½ cup Sherry
boiling water

Roll beef pieces in seasoned flour and place in casserole; add suet and onions and a layer of potatoes on top. Pour in Sherry, season again, and add boiling water until potatoes are just covered. Cover and cook 2 hours in slow oven (250-325°). Remove cover and bake until potatoes are browned, about 1 hour longer. Serves 6.

POT ROAST WITH RED WINE NO. II

3 to 4 pounds lean beef
1½ cups dry red wine
2 large onions, sliced
1 lemon, sliced
2 tablespoons sugar
1 tablespoon salt
1 teaspoon ginger (may be omitted)
12 whole black peppers
4 tablespoons fat
2 tablespoons flour

Place meat in deep bowl, and add all of the ingredients except the fat and flour. The meat should be more than half covered with wine. Marinate 18 to 24 hours, turning occasionally. Remove meat from liquid, drain thoroughly, then brown all over in 2 tablespoons hot fat in heavy kettle. Add liquid in which it was marinated, cover kettle, and let simmer 3 to 4 hours, adding a little water if necessary. When tender, lift meat out and strain remaining liquid. In the kettle melt 2 tablespoons fat, stir in the flour, and brown lightly. Add the liquid and cook, stirring, until slightly thickened. (If too thick, thin with hot water to desired consistency.) Add more salt if needed, put meat back into gravy, and heat 5 minutes longer. Serve sliced across grain on hot platter, pouring gravy over meat. Serves 8 to 12.

CORDON BLEU GOULASH

¼ pound prunes
1 pound lean beef, cut in 1-inch cubes
1 pound lean veal, cut in 1-inch cubes
3 tablespoons vegetable oil
½ cup chopped onion
1 teaspoon salt
1 teaspoon paprika
1 cup strained tomatoes
6 medium-sized potatoes
1 teaspoon saffron (optional)
½ cup dry red wine

Cook prunes until soft, remove pits, and chop coarsely. Sauté meat and onion slowly in oil, stirring occasionally, until onions are golden brown. Add seasonings and tomato, and simmer 1 hour. Add potatoes and prunes, and cook ½ hour more or until potatoes are nearly done. Add saffron and wine, and cook 10 minutes more. Serves 6.

BEEF JULIENNE

1 tablespoon butter
3 tablespoons chopped onion
1 tablespoon flour
1 cup bouillon (canned or made with cubes)
salt and pepper
Worcestershire sauce
½ cup dry red wine
Thick slices of cold roast beef

Melt butter in frying pan and fry onion until golden brown. Blend in flour, mix well, then add bouillon and cook, stirring, until blended. Season to taste. Add wine and continue stirring. Put in sliced roast beef and let heat slowly. If you have gravy left over from the night before, that simplifies everything. Merely mix the wine with the gravy you already have and add to the meat. Serves 6.

BEEF AND NOODLES WITH BURGUNDY SAUCE

1 pound noodles or spaghetti
1 egg, lightly beaten
¼ cup milk
½ teaspoon salt
⅛ teaspoon pepper
3 tablespoons vegetable oil
1 tablespoon flour
1½ cups stock or bouillon
1 tablespoon lemon juice
½ cup Burgundy (or Claret)
1½ pounds (approximately) cooked beef, sliced thin
parsley or watercress

Cook noodles or spaghetti in rapidly boiling salted water about 9 minutes or according to directions on package. Drain and rinse in cold water. Stir egg, milk, and seasoning together and stir into noodles or spaghetti. Pour in a greased mold, place in a pan of hot water, and bake in a moderate oven (350-375°) about 20-30 minutes or until firm. Blend flour with hot oil; add stock or bouillon slowly, stirring until smooth. Add wine and lemon juice, and when it begins to simmer add meat, cover, and cook 5 minutes. Unmold noodles or spaghetti on serving dish, arrange meat around them, cover with sauce, and garnish with parsley or watercress. Serves 6.

BEEF ROULADE LORRAINE

(From Camil Virla, Chef, Hotel Mark Hopkins, San Francisco, Calif.)

2 pounds hamburger meat
12 ounces bacon cut in strips 3 x ½ inch
1 pound small silver onions, peeled
¾ pound carrots, cut in large dices
3 stalks celery, cut in large dices
1 stalk parsley
1 bay leaf
4 cloves garlic
1 teaspoon black pepper
1 teaspoon salt
1 pint Claret
1 tablespoon flour
½ pound fresh mushrooms
¼ pound butter
1 cup beef stock

Divide hamburger in 8 equal parts, roll in balls, then flatten in circles of 3 to 4 inches in diameter. Place 1 strip of bacon in center of each roll, then bind each extremity with white thread so they will not open. Place in ½-gallon jar with carrots, onion, celery. Tie the parsley, bay leaf, garlic, and black pepper in a little bag of cheesecloth tied with white thread. Add wine, bag of spices, and salt and let pickle in a cool place or icebox for 3 days. Drain meat and vegetables separately. Fry meat and onions in butter. When brown, sprinkle on flour, allow flour to brown about 1 minute, then add the rest of the ingredients except mushrooms, bring to a boil, skim, let simmer for 2 hours, remove bag of spices. Fry mushrooms in butter; add to sauce 15 minutes before meat is done. Rectify seasoning. Serve with noodles au gratin. Serves 8.

HAMBURGERS DE LUXE

1 pound chopped beef
1 teaspoon poultry seasoning
salt and pepper
2 tablespoons Smithfield ham spread
⅓ cup dry red wine
2 tablespoons butter

Mix the seasonings, ham spread (if available), salt, pepper, and ¼ cup of the wine thoroughly into chopped meat. Cover and place in refrigerator 4 to 8 hours. Make into patties and brown well in butter. Add remaining wine and simmer slowly until sauce is sirupy, turning patties several times. Serve on hot platter with sauce poured over. Serves 4.

BRAISED SIRLOIN

1 (2-pound) sirloin steak
2 tablespoons vegetable oil
2 medium-sized carrots, cut julienne
1 small turnip, peeled and sliced very thin
2 medium-sized onions, sliced thin
2 tablespoons flour
½ teaspoon peppercorns
1 teaspoon salt
½ teaspoon paprika
1 cup beef consommé, *or*
1 cup water and 2 beef cubes
2 tablespoons capers
½ lemon, sliced very thin
1 cup sour cream
½ cup dry white wine

Heat fat almost to smoking and brown steak well on both sides. Reduce heat, add vegetables and seasonings, and sauté until vegetables begin to get tender but do not allow them to brown. Sprinkle in the flour, stir well, add consommé, and bring just to a boil. Place steak in casserole and strain sauce over, reserving vegetables. Place in moderate oven (350-375°) for 1½ hours. Add reserved vegetables, capers, lemon, and wine. Stir and return to oven for 15 minutes. Serve with noodles or rice. Serves 4.

LANGUEDOC BEEF

1½ pounds lean beef (round, rump, chuck, or flank), cut in cubes
2 tablespoons vegetable oil
½ cup chopped onions
1 small clove garlic, crushed and minced
1 bay leaf
1 teaspoon thyme
8 olives, sliced
2 cups dry red wine
flour

Brown beef well in oil, then add onions and stir until they are a light golden brown. Add all other ingredients except flour, cover, and simmer slowly for at least 3 hours. If necessary, add a very little hot water. When beef is very tender remove it, strain sauce, and thicken it slightly with a little flour and water to a creamy consistency. Serves 4.

STUFFED STEAK

1½ pounds top round of beef
dry red wine
2 bay leaves
1 teaspoon dried thyme
2½ teaspoons salt
½ pound lean veal
1 medium-sized onion
1 egg
¼ cup Chablis
2 teaspoons poultry seasoning

Pound beef until about ¼ inch thick; trim off ragged edges. Cover with dry red wine, add bay leaf, thyme, and 2 teaspoons salt, cover, and allow to marinate 24 hours. Put veal, trimmings from beef, and onion through food chopper twice. Mix in egg, wine, poultry seasoning, and ½ teaspoon salt, cover, and allow to marinate same length of time as beef. Spread chopped veal on steak, roll up, fasten with toothpicks, and tie. Roast in moderately slow oven (325-350°) about 2½ hours, basting frequently with marinating liquid. Remove to serving dish. Skim fat from liquid in pan and use it to make a roux with 2 tablespoons flour. Add to liquid to make gravy, adding a little milk if too thick. Serve gravy separately. Serves 4 to 6.

TENDERLOIN OF BEEF AND VEAL KIDNEYS À LA DEUTCH

(From J. B. Heguy, Head Chef, Hotel Pennsylvania, New York City)

2 pounds minced beef tenderloin
½ pound veal kidneys
1 ounce butter
1 glass Burgundy
2 mushrooms
1 medium-sized onion
1 green pepper
2 cups Sauce Madère (p. 36)
1 pinch chopped parsley

Fry in butter together minced beef tenderloin and veal kidneys until all has browned, for about 5 minutes. Add wine, then mushrooms, onion and green pepper nicely minced, and let this mixture cook for 10 or more minutes. Add Sauce Madère, let boil for 5 minutes, and then finish with a piece of butter and chopped parsley. Serve in a very hot casserole with a few German-fried potatoes on top. Serves 4.

TENDERLOIN OF BEEF, RED WINE SAUCE

2 slices fat salt pork, diced
1½ pounds tenderloin of beef, ¾ inch thick
½ cup flour
½ teaspoon salt
dash of pepper
1 medium-sized onion, chopped
¾ cup sliced mushrooms
2 cups thick Brown Sauce (p. 28)
1 cup dry red wine

Fry salt pork until light brown and crisp. Roll tenderloin pieces in flour, to which seasonings have been added. Brown quickly on both sides in pork fat, which should be very hot. Remove and keep hot. Sauté onion and mushrooms until tender. Add to Brown Sauce, stir in wine, season to taste, bring to simmering point, and pour around tenderloin on hot platter. Serves 4 to 6.

MIRONTON OF BEEF

2 pounds beef, cut in 1-inch cubes
3 tablespoons butter
3 tablespoons flour
1½ cups dry red wine
1½ cups chopped onion
1 cup chopped mushrooms
1 bouquet garni (p. 9)

Cover beef with cold water, bring to simmering point, and stew gently for about 1 hour or until almost tender. Melt butter, add flour, and stir until well browned. Slowly add 1½ cups broth from meat. Bring to a boil, and add wine and all other ingredients. Add sauce to meat and allow to simmer ½ hour or until meat is very tender. Strain sauce. Serve on a deep platter with sauce poured over meat and a border of dry, flaky rice. Serves 6.

SIRLOIN STEAK BORDELAISE

2 pounds sirloin steak or 2 T-bone steaks
2 tablespoons butter
2 tablespoons chopped shallots or onion
1 cup dry red wine
salt and pepper

Pan broil steak slightly under customary time for rare, medium, or well done. Add butter and shallots or onions, and cook about 5 minutes or until they are soft. Add wine and simmer 5 minutes more. Serve on hot platter with sauce poured over. Serves 4.

BROILED STEAK WITH BURGUNDY

6 shallots or 1 small onion, chopped fine
1 cup dry red wine (Burgundy preferred)
¼ pound butter
2 teaspoons lemon juice
3 beef cubes
2 tablespoons hot water
1 tablespoon minced parsley
1 2-pound sirloin steak or 2 T-bone steaks
salt and pepper

Put chopped shallots or onion in small saucepan with wine and boil until wine is reduced one half. Cream butter and mix in lemon juice, beef cubes dissolved in hot water, and minced parsley.

Broil steaks as desired. Melt butter mixture and stir in wine slowly. Bring just to simmering point. Serve meat on hot platter with sauce poured around, not over, the steak. Serves 4.

BROILED STEAK PIQUANTE

Broil sirloin steak until it is medium rare. Cover one side with a paste made as follows:
2 tablespoons crumbled Roquefort cheese
1 tablespoon Sherry
1 tablespoon butter
½ teaspoon Worcestershire sauce
salt and pepper
paprika

Return to broiler until paste is melted. Serve immediately.

BEEF AU VIN

1 (1½ pound) round steak
3 tablespoons butter or vegetable oil
4 medium-sized onions, sliced
1 clove garlic, crushed and minced
4 carrots, sliced or julienne
1 teaspoon mixed sweet herbs
salt and pepper
dry red wine

Cut meat in 1-inch pieces. Put in heavy skillet with onions, garlic, and carrots and brown slowly in fat. Remove to casserole and add drippings from pan, herbs, and salt and pepper to taste. Add enough wine to cover. Cover and simmer slowly until meat is very tender, 2 to 3 hours. Thicken gravy slightly before serving. Serves 4.

STEAK EN CASSEROLE

6 medium-sized potatoes, sliced
3 medium-sized onions, sliced
1 pound top round steak, cut in 1-inch cubes
1 tablespoon flour
1 teaspoon salt
1/8 teaspoon pepper
2 tablespoons butter
1 1/2 cups dry red wine
1 teaspoon Angostura bitters

Arrange potatoes and onions in casserole in two alternate layers, then a layer of steak cubes, then a layer of onions and another of potatoes. Mix flour, salt, and pepper, sprinkle over each layer, and dot with butter. Add Angostura to wine and pour over all. Bake covered in moderate oven (350-375°) 2 hours. Serves 6.

STEAK ROLLS

2 pounds round steak, sliced 1/4 inch thick
1 large or 2 small dill pickles, sliced crosswise
3 medium-sized onions, sliced thin
8-10 slices bacon
salt
pepper
cooking fat
1 cup water
1 teaspoon prepared mustard
1 teaspoon paprika
2 tablespoons lemon juice
1 cup dry red wine
1 teaspoon Angostura bitters
2 tablespoons flour

Cut steak in pieces about 4 by 6 inches. Place one slice each of pickle, onion, and bacon on each slice of steak. Salt and pepper, roll up, and fasten with toothpicks. Brown well all over in hot fat in skillet. Add all other ingredients except flour and simmer gently, covered, for about 1 hour or until meat is fairly tender. Blend flour with 4 tablespoons gravy, stir in well, and cook 15 minutes longer. Serves 6.

Veal steak may be used instead of beef. In this case, use white wine instead of red.

TUESDAY NIGHT BEEF

1 medium-sized onion, chopped
1 tablespoon butter
½ tablespoon flour
½ cup broth or 1 bouillon cube dissolved in ½ cup hot water
1 pound (approximately) left-over roast beef, cut in ½ inch slices
salt
pepper
½ cup dry red wine
½ teaspoon sugar

Brown onion in butter, stir in flour, and gradually add bouillon. Drop in roast beef slices; salt and pepper quite generously. Simmer slowly. As gravy begins to thicken, add wine gradually. Finally add sugar. Serves 4.

BRAISED OXTAIL

1 oxtail (approximately 2 lbs.) cut in 2-inch pieces
1 cup flour
4 tablespoons bacon drippings or vegetable oil
1 cup canned tomatoes
1 cup water
1 teaspoon salt
⅛ teaspoon pepper
¼ cup chopped celery
¼ teaspoon ground cloves
1 large bayleaf
4 medium-sized carrots, diced
1 clove garlic, crushed and minced
1 cup sliced mushrooms
¼ cup Sherry

Wash and wipe oxtail, roll in flour, and brown well in half the fat. Add tomatoes, water, and seasonings and simmer gently, covered, about 3 hours or until meat can be separated from bone. Brown carrots, onion, and garlic lightly in rest of fat with mushrooms and add to meat during last ½ hour. Add Sherry during last 5 minutes and serve. Serves 4.

MOLDED BEEF À LA MODE

4 pounds bottom round steak
1 cup dry red wine
¼ cup tarragon vinegar
1 bay leaf
1 sprig thyme
2 sprigs parsley
2 whole cloves
1 clove garlic, crushed
2 onions, sliced
2 pimientos, sliced
2 carrots
salt and cayenne
gelatin

Marinate beef in wine and vinegar, to which spices, garlic, and onion have been added, for at least 12 hours. Put into cooking dish with marinating liquid and carrots, and add enough cold water to cover. Bring to a boil and simmer 5 hours, adding more water if necessary. Cool and when fat hardens remove it all carefully. Take out meat, and strain and measure stock. For each 2 cups of stock soften 1 tablespoon gelatin in ½ cup cold stock, and add to remainder and reheat until gelatin is thoroughly dissolved. Wet the inside of a mold with gelatin mixture and put in refrigerator to chill slightly. Arrange pimiento strips crosswise on bottom about an inch apart and continue up sides. Slice carrots and arrange evenly between pimiento strips. Put in meat carefully and pour in broth very slowly to fill. Chill. Chill broth that is left over and when ready to serve, chop and surround the dish and sprinkle with finely chopped parsley. Serves 8 to 10.

BAKED HAM

1 slice ham, 2 inches thick
½ cup brown sugar
1½ cups water
½ cup raisins
1 tablespoon butter
1 tablespoon cornstarch
½ cup dry white wine

Combine sugar and cornstarch; add butter and water. Cook 3 minutes, stirring constantly. Take from fire, and add raisins and wine. Place ham in greased baking dish and cover with sauce. Bake uncovered in a moderate oven (350-375°) about 1 hour. Serves 6.

BAKED HAM À LA WALDORF

1 (10-12 pound) ham
1½ cups grated fresh pineapple, *or*
1½ cups crushed canned pineapple
½ cup brown sugar
5 cups sifted flour
1½ cups shortening
⅔ cup cold water
⅓ cup Sherry

Bake ham according to time specified on wrapper. Remove from oven and take off skin but no fat. Cut fat in 1-inch squares down to lean. Mix pineapple with brown sugar and spread on ham, rubbing in well. Make dough with flour, shortening, and water; roll into sheet ¼ inch thick to completely cover ham. Press down well. Make 1-inch hole in center. Bake in hot oven (400-425°) for about 35 minutes or until pastry is lightly browned. Pour Sherry through regular or paper funnel slowly into hole in top. Put back in oven and bake until pastry is well browned. Remove pastry and slice.

HAM AND VEAL PIE

1½ pounds ham, sliced thin
1½ pounds veal, sliced thin
½ cup flour
1 teaspoon poultry seasoning
1 teaspoon grated lemon rind
1 tablespoon chopped parsley
salt and pepper
cayenne
¼ cup water
½ recipe plain pastry
¼ cup beef stock or consommé
3 tablespoons Sherry

Roll veal slices in flour, which has been mixed with seasonings. Place in quart casserole in alternate layers of veal and ham and add water. Wet edges of casserole and cover with pastry rolled to fit. Slash pastry and make hole in center. Bake in moderate oven (350°) about 1½ hours. Add stock and Sherry, using small funnel or paper cone, through hole in center of pastry, and return to oven with heat turned off and door opén for 10 minutes. Serve hot or cold. Serves 6 to 8.

FRESH MUSHROOMS WITH KENTUCKY HAM AMBASSADOR

(From Hotel Ambassador, Chicago)

For each portion, two small pieces of Kentucky ham and six fresh mushrooms. Sauté in butter until done. Remove from pan, then remove excess fat from pan and add five ounces of rich cream, and one ounce of brandy. Allow this to simmer for a few minutes until thickened. Strain, add one ounce Madeira wine and two pieces of butter. Place mushrooms and ham back in the sauce and allow to heat on side of range. Do not allow the sauce to boil after adding the butter and wine.

HAM AND NOODLES WITH WINE

3 cups cooked ham, cut up
3 ounces (½ 6 oz. package) noodles
1 can condensed mushroom soup
2 medium-sized onions, sliced
½ cup Sherry
½ cup Sauterne
salt
cayenne

Cook noodles in boiling water 12 to 15 minutes or according to directions on package. Drain. Blend soup, onions, and wine and stir into noodles. Add ham, mixing well. Put in greased casserole, cover, and bake in moderate oven (350-375°) 45 minutes. Serves 6.

EPICUREAN HAM

1 small ham (8-10 pounds)
cloves
brown sugar
1 small can (4 slices) pineapple
1 cup Sherry
1 tablespoon gelatin

Skin ham, stick with cloves, moisten, and cover as thickly as possible with brown sugar. Lay pineapple slices over top. Bake in slow oven (275-300°) until meat thermometer registers 150°, or according to directions on wrapper. Baste with pineapple juice and Sherry. As baking proceeds, sugar will run down in pan and caramelize. Watch carefully and as soon as well caramelized add water. There should be 2 cupfuls when ham is done. Remove ham. Add gelatin, dissolved in cold water, to liquid in pan, pour into dish, and chill. Cut in small cubes and serve as a garnish with the cold ham.

GLAZED HAM WITH CRANBERRIES

2 slices ham, 1 inch thick
whole cloves
2 cups cranberry sauce
½ cup light corn sirup
2 cups dry red wine

Stick fat of ham generously with cloves and place one slice in greased casserole. Mix cranberry sauce and sirup and pour half of mixture over 1 ham slice. Put second slice on top and cover with rest of mixture. Bake in moderate oven (350°) until tender, about 1½ hours, basting frequently with wine until last ½ hour of baking. Serves 6.

HAM WITH PORT

1 (2 pound) slice ham
2 tablespoons Port
1 orange, sliced
parsley or watercress

Place ham in baking dish and add Port. Cover and bake in moderate oven (350-375°) 1 hour. Place on hot platter and garnish with sliced orange and parsley or watercress. Serves 6.

SUGAR HAM

1 (10-12 pound) ham
1½ cups brown sugar
½ cup prepared mustard
½ cup water
3 cups granulated sugar
1½ cups red cinnamon drops
1 cup seeded or seedless raisins
2 cups water
½ cup Sherry

Boil ham according to directions on wrapper. (Note: some tenderized hams require no preliminary boiling.) Skin ham and score fat in diamonds. Make a paste of brown sugar, mustard, and water and rub well over all the ham. Bake in hot oven (425-450°) 15-20 minutes per pound (or according to directions on wrapper).

Meanwhile add granulated sugar, cinnamon candy, and raisins to 2 cups water and simmer gently until ham is ready to remove from oven.

Allow ham and sauce to cool 24 hours or more. When ready to serve, slice ham and heat in sauce, to which Sherry has been added.

FRESH HAM WITH SAUERKRAUT

¼ pound bacon, diced
1 1-inch slice (about 1½ pounds) fresh (uncured) ham steak
2 quarts sauerkraut
2 teaspoons caraway seeds
2 medium-sized onions, grated
3 cups very dry white wine
salt and pepper

Fry bacon until crisp, remove, and drain. Fry ham steak slowly in bacon fat about 45 minutes. Drain sauerkraut and, if very salty, rinse with cold water. Mix in fried bacon and caraway seeds, and season. Place ham steak in bottom of casserole, pile sauerkraut on top, add wine, cover tightly, and bake in moderate oven (350-375°) until sauerkraut is tender, about 30-45 minutes. Serves 4 to 6.

BAKED SMITHFIELD HAM

1 Smithfield ham
4 medium-sized onions
6 stalks celery, including leaves
12 stalks parsley
6 green apples, if obtainable
1 teaspoon mace
white pepper
cloves
light brown sugar
4 tablespoons mustard
1 quart Sherry (approximately)

Soak ham in lukewarm water 1 hour to overnight, according to size and age. Scrub thoroughly with stiff brush. Put in pan with water to cover, bring to a boil, and after 30 minutes skim and add vegetables, apples, parsley, mace, and 6 cloves. Reduce heat and allow to simmer until the swelling of the fat changes the center of gravity and causes it to turn over. About ½ hour per pound will be required. Turn off heat and allow ham to cool in its own stock. As soon as cool enough to handle, pull off skin with hands covered with a cloth. Sprinkle fat liberally with pepper. (Virginians advise ¼ pound for a large ham.) Next, coat with light brown sugar and mustard. (If sugar has been exposed to air and become dry and hardened, steam until quite moist.) Put on as thick a layer as possible. With care and perhaps an occasional dampening, a depth of one inch may be achieved. Pour Sherry around, not over, the ham and place in a very slow oven (250°). Be sure not to have oven too hot. If it is kept at the proper temperature very little of the sugar will run off, most of it being absorbed by the ham. Definite baking time cannot be given as it varies widely with the age and size of the ham, but when sugar has all been absorbed or run off into pan, increase heat to moderately hot (375-400°) and baste with Sherry and drippings until well browned. Pour drippings over top of ham and allow to cool. Approximately 1/4 pound per portion.

HAM BARBECUE STYLE

1 1/2 pounds ham, 1 1/2 inches thick
1 tablespoon prepared mustard
1/4 teaspoon black pepper
1 tablespoon fat or vegetable oil
3 tablespoons vinegar
1 1/2 tablespoons flour
1 cup water
1/2 cup dry red wine

Mix mustard and pepper, and spread on both sides of each slice of ham. Brown lightly in skillet on both sides. Add vinegar and simmer, covered, about 30-35 minutes, turning when half done. Remove ham and keep hot. Blend flour into hot fat, add water gradually, and stir until smooth. Add wine, bring to a simmer, and pour over ham. Serves 4 to 6.

JAMBONNEAU

1 (4 pound) picnic ham
2 medium-sized onions, quartered
2 medium-sized carrots, sliced
4 cups dry white wine
1/8 teaspoon thyme
12 peppercorns
rind of 1/4 orange
1 bay leaf

Soak ham at least 8 hours in cold water unless it is a tenderized ham. Drain, and add rest of ingredients and enough water to cover. Bring to a boil and simmer until tender. Allow to cool in stock.

An excellent variation is to slice ham wafer-thin, strain stock, add 1 tablespoon gelatin to each pint of stock, pour over ham in mold, and allow to cool.

CANADIAN BACON WITH SHERRY

1 pound Canadian bacon, thinly sliced
1½ cups (approximately) Sherry

Place bacon in frying pan, cover with Sherry, and let it stand at least ½ hour. Then simmer, covered, over very slow fire until Sherry practically disappears, 20-25 minutes. Excellent with waffles. Serves 4-6.

COTTAGE HAM WITH WINE SAUCE

1 (3-4 pound) cottage ham
⅓ cup condensed beef consommé
1½ cups dry red wine
1 teaspoon sugar
2 cloves
1 small onion, sliced
1 teaspoon lemon juice
rind of ½ lemon, grated
¼ cup Tokay

Parboil ham 25-30 minutes per pound. Boil together for a few minutes consommé, red wine, sugar, cloves, and onion. Pour over ham and bake 45 minutes in moderate oven (350-375°), basting frequently. Remove ham, skim sauce, add lemon juice, grated rind, and Tokay, and simmer gently until it begins to get sirupy. Pour over ham. Serves 8 to 10.

VIRGINIA HAM MOUSSE IN ASPIC

2 pounds Virginia ham, finely ground
1 cup Cream Sauce or Velouté (p. 28)
1 teaspoon paprika
1 cup tomato sauce
½ cup Sherry
salt
pepper
Tabasco
3 tablespoons gelatin, softened in cold water
1 pint heavy cream, whipped

Add ham to Cream Sauce or Velouté, tomato sauce, and wine. Season and cook for ½ hour. Then stir in gelatin and mix well. Strain through a fine strainer and stir while cooling. Fold in whipped cream, pour into a mold, and chill. Serves 6 to 8.

PORK CHOPS ST. ODILE

(From Paul Debes, Chef, Hotel Sir Francis Drake, San Francisco, Calif.)

Medium-sized pork chops are seasoned with salt and pepper and fried in foaming butter to a golden color. Remove pork chops from skillet and fry some shredded onions until brown. In an earthen casserole place one layer of brown onions, sliced raw potatoes, and pork chops. Repeat with onions and potatoes. Season again and cover with a good Riesling wine. Cover the casserole, bake in oven for 40 minutes, and serve.

PORK CHOPS PORTUGUESE

8 pork chops
1 large bouquet garni (p. 9)
1 clove garlic, crushed and minced
2 cups dry white wine
2 tablespoons bacon fat
2 teaspoons flour
salt and pepper

Marinate chops in wine with bouquet garni and garlic for from 1 to 3 days. Use enamel, earthenware, or stainless steel vessel and turn chops frequently. Sear in 2 tablespoons bacon fat, pour off fat, and reserve. Season, cover, and sauté 20-25 minutes. Make roux of flour and reserved fat, gradually add strained marinating liquid, and stir well until thickened. Serve separately. Serves 4.

CHESHIRE PORK PIE

1 recipe plain pastry
8 loin pork chops
salt and cayenne
nutmeg
3 medium-sized tart apples, sliced
½ cup sugar
½ cup Sherry

Trim most of fat from chops; season well with salt, cayenne, and pinch of nutmeg mixed together. Line baking dish with pastry rolled ¼ inch thick. Arrange a layer of chops, a layer of apples, sprinkle with sugar, and repeat until dish is full. Add Sherry and put on ¼-inch-thick top crust, gash and put in moderate oven (350-375°) for 2 hours. If top crust begins to get too brown, cover with pie plate. Good served hot or cold. Serves 4 to 8.

PIG IN A POKE

1 (5-6 pound) pork loin (center cut), boned
2 cups dried bread crumbs
1 egg, lightly beaten
2 teaspoons poultry seasoning
1 medium-sized onion, chopped
milk, if necessary
5 cups sifted flour
⅔ cup shortening
¾ cup water
salt
pepper
1 cup dry white wine

Simmer bones in enough water to cover for 45 minutes. Increase heat and boil until reduced to 1 cup. Make stuffing of bread crumbs, egg, poultry seasoning, onion, and pork stock. It should be quite dry, but, if more moisture is needed, add a little milk. Season to taste. Spread on cut side of meat, roll, and tie.

Make pastry of flour, shortening, water, and 1 teaspoon salt. Use a little more water than for pie pastry. Roll ½ inch thick, place meat on it, and cover meat completely with pastry. Wet hands and smooth it over so that no opening remains. Place in greased baking pan with the side you were working on down. Examine ends again to see that there are no holes or cracks. Roast in moderately slow oven (325-350°) 3½ hours. Cover pan if pastry gets brown too soon. Thirty minutes before roast is done, insert small funnel through pastry and pour in 1 tablespoon of wine at a time until all the wine is used. Serve part of pastry with each portion. Serves 6 to 8.

LAMB CHOPS IN WINE

8 lamb chops
2 tablespoons butter
1 cup button onions
4 medium-sized carrots, cut julienne
½ cup dry white wine
2 cups sliced mushrooms
salt
pepper

Brown chops, onions, and carrots in butter. Add wine, mushrooms, and seasonings, cover, and simmer slowly for 30 minutes. Serves 4.

LAMB CHOPS D'ARCY BERCY

8 lamb chops
6 tablespoons butter
2 shallots, chopped *or*
1 medium-sized onion, chopped
1 cup dry white wine
4 bouillon cubes
½ cup hot water
1 tablespoon chopped parsley
salt
pepper

Sauté chops in ½ the butter. Remove to serving dish and keep hot. Sauté shallots or onion until soft; add wine and bouillon cubes dissolved in hot water. Add rest of butter and bring just to a simmer. Season to taste, add parsley, and pour over chops. Serves 4.

LAMB CHOPS WITH WINE SAUCE

8 lamb chops
½ cup dry red wine
salt and pepper

Pan-fry chops and place on hot platter. Pour off all but about 2 tablespoons of fat. Add wine, salt, and pepper and reduce by boiling to about ¼ cup or less. Pour around chops and serve. Serves 4.

BAKED CHOPS SUPREME

6 shoulder chops, lamb or pork
1 clove garlic, crushed
salt
pepper
2 tablespoons cooking fat
2 medium-sized onions, chopped
2 cups diced cooked carrots
4 tablespoons flour
4 tablespoons chili sauce
½ cup dry white wine

Rub chops with crushed clove of garlic, sprinkle with salt and pepper, and brown on both sides in hot fat in frying pan. Remove to baking dish. Sauté onions and carrots in pan until onions are soft. Add flour, chili sauce, and wine and cook until thickened. Place a mound of carrot mixture on each chop and bake in a moderate oven (350°) 45 minutes or until done. Serves 6.

LAMB EN CASSEROLE

2 lamb shanks
boiling water
1 clove garlic
1 bay leaf
2 teaspoons salt
1 can condensed tomato soup
½ pound mushrooms, sliced
1 large onion, sliced
1 teaspoon chopped parsley
1 teaspoon poultry seasoning
1 cup Sherry
1½ cups mashed potatoes
2 tablespoons butter

Cover shanks with boiling water, add garlic and bay leaf, and boil 5 minutes. Skim and simmer until meat can easily be separated from bones, about 3 hours. Add 2 teaspoons of salt when half done. Remove meat and cool. Reduce stock to 1 cup, add all other ingredients except mashed potatoes and butter, and simmer 25 minutes. Place meat in casserole, cover with sauce, top with mashed potatoes, dot with butter, and bake in a moderate oven (350-375°) until potatoes are brown. Serves 4 to 6.

LAMB PIE

2 cups diced cooked lamb
1 onion, chopped fine
⅔ cup diced celery
1½ teaspoons salt
1 cup diced potatoes
⅓ cup diced green peppers
⅔ cup canned tomatoes
2 cups meat stock or beef bouillon
⅓ cup dry red wine
½ recipe biscuit dough

Simmer all ingredients, except the wine, together for 10 minutes, then add wine and simmer 5 minutes longer. Put into baking dish and cover with a biscuit dough about ¼ inch thick. Bake in hot oven (450-475°) 20 minutes or until crust is nicely browned. Serves 4.

Veal may be used in place of lamb. In this case, use white wine in place of red.

ROAST LEG OF LAMB PROVENÇAL

1 cup stale bread crumbs
¼ cup milk
½ pound fat salt pork, ground
¼ cup minced parsley
1 egg, lightly beaten
1 (6 pound) leg of lamb, boned
4 medium-sized onions, sliced
4 small carrots, sliced
2 teaspoons salt
¼ teaspoon pepper
2 cups dry white wine
2 cups boiling water

Mix together bread crumbs, milk, half the salt pork, egg, and parsley. Stuff lamb with mixture and sew up. Put rest of salt pork in large cooking vessel and cook until pork is lightly browned. Add meat and turn until well browned on all sides. Add vegetables and cook until golden. Add wine, boiling water, salt, and pepper. Cover and simmer slowly until meat is tender, about 1½ to 2 hours. Serve sliced with sauce poured over. Serves 8.

ROAST LEG OF LAMB WITH WHITE WINE

1 (5-6 pound) leg of lamb
1 cup sliced onion
½ cup sliced carrot
1 tablespoon poultry seasoning
1 clove garlic, crushed
1 quart Riesling
2 teaspoons flour
salt and pepper

Skin leg of lamb and remove all fat. Place in enameled, earthenware, or stainless steel vessel, cover with wine, and add vegetables and seasonings. Cover and marinate from 1 to 3 days, turning frequently. Remove and roast in moderate oven (350-375°) 30 to 35 minutes per pound or to 180° by meat thermometer. Baste occasionally with marinating liquid. Remove lamb. Reduce marinating liquid to 2 cups and strain. Blend flour with drippings in pan and stir in reduced marinating liquid. Cook until thickened. Serve separately. Serves 6 to 8.

White currant or gooseberry preserves make an excellent accompaniment for this roast.

LEG OF LAMB EN DAUBE

1 (5-6 pound) leg of lamb, boned and larded
2 large cloves garlic, sliced in strips
2 teaspoons ground cloves
2 teaspoons ground cinnamon
2 teaspoons pepper
4 tablespoons salt
4 slices salt pork
2 medium-sized onions, sliced
2 medium-sized carrots, sliced
2 cups dry red wine
2 cups dry white wine

Have lamb larded with about ¼ pound salt pork. Insert thin garlic slices in gashes on outside. Mix all seasonings and rub well into meat. Line bottom of baking dish with salt pork slices, add the vegetables in a layer, place meat on top, and cover with wines. Cover tightly and keep in cool place for 24 hours. Bake, covered, 6 hours in slow oven (250-325°). Strain juices in pan and pour over meat. Serves 6 to 8.

MEAT AND POTATOES GRECIAN

½ cup olive oil or vegetable oil
1 clove garlic, crushed and minced
6 medium-sized potatoes, sliced very thin
1 pound beef, veal, or lamb, chopped
2 medium-sized onions, chopped
salt and pepper
1 cup dry red wine
½ cup water
½ cup tomato paste or condensed tomato soup
1 2-inch stick cinnamon
2 medium-sized bay leaves

Sauté garlic lightly in oil. Add potatoes and cook until tender but not brown, then remove. Knead chopped meat, onions, salt, and pepper together and fry about 3 minutes, stirring so that it does not cake. Arrange potatoes and meat in alternate layers in greased casserole or baking dish. Mix together tomato paste or soup, water, wine, and oil from frying pan and pour over. Put cinnamon and bay leaves on top and bake, covered, in moderate oven (350-375°), for 1 hour. Remove cinnamon and bay leaves before serving. Serves 4 to 6.

KAVKASKII SHASHLIK

2 pounds lean lamb, skin removed
¼ cup olive oil
1½ teaspoons salt
¼ teaspoon pepper
dash of cayenne
2 medium-sized onions, grated
dry red wine
large onions sliced ¼ inch thick

Cut lamb in 1½-inch cubes. Mix seasonings and grated onion with oil, and rub very thoroughly into meat. Put in enamel or earthenware dish, cover with wine, and marinate 24 hours. Stick pieces of meat and onion slices alternately on 8- to 10-inch skewers, beginning and ending with meat. Broil slowly with pan underneath to catch juices. Serve with fluffy rice with juice poured over. Serves 4.

COUNTRY SAUSAGE GASTRONOME

1 pound bulk sausage
4 cups mashed potatoes
1 cup Red Wine Sauce (p. 29)
¼ cup medium cheese, grated

Make sausage into patties and fry. Add grated cheese to Red Wine Sauce and simmer, stirring, until completely blended. Make a bed of mashed potatoes on serving dish, place sausage patties on top, pour sauce over, and put briefly under broiler. Serve very hot. Serves 4 to 6.

SAUSAGES IN WINE SAUCE

1 cup Sherry
½ cup chili sauce
½ cup tomato catsup
1 tablespoon Worcestershire sauce
½ teaspoon Angostura bitters
12 small pork sausages
1 tablespoon flour

Put all ingredients except flour in double boiler and cook 25 minutes. Take out sausages. Skim off all grease, reserving about 2 tablespoons. Blend this with flour and add gradually to sauce while stirring. Continue cooking until sauce is slightly thickened, about 5 minutes. Serve sausages in heated dish with sauce poured over. Serves 4.

BAKED SAUSAGES IN WINE

1 pound link sausages
4 tablespoons melted butter
½ cup flour
½ teaspoon salt
⅛ teaspoon pepper
1 cup dry white wine

Dip sausages one by one in melted butter and roll in flour, to which seasonings have been added. Arrange in baking dish, add wine and remainder of butter, and bake uncovered in a moderate oven (350-375°) for 45 minutes. Serves 4.

VEAL KNOTS

1½ pounds veal steak
1 cup flour
½ teaspoon salt
⅛ teaspoon pepper
½ cup butter
1 small bay leaf
½ cup Sauterne

Have steak cut in strips about ½ inch thick and 1 inch wide, and tie each in a tight knot. Roll in seasoned flour. Brown well in butter, add bay leaf, cover, and cook over very low heat until tender, about 20 minutes, turning twice. Add wine, season to taste, bring just to a simmer, and serve quickly. Serves 4.

SCALOPPINI OF VEAL AU MARSALA

1 (1½ pound) veal cutlet
½ cup grated Parmesan cheese
6 tablespoons butter or vegetable oil
1 cup sliced mushrooms
salt and cayenne
1 teaspoon beef extract
2 tablespoons hot water
¼ cup Marsala or Sherry

Have veal cut about 1 inch thick. Place on board, sprinkle with cheese, and pound with back of heavy knife. Do this on both sides until all cheese is used and cutlet is about ½ inch thick. Cut in 3-inch pieces and season. Sauté gently in ¼ cup butter or oil until lightly browned. Meanwhile sauté mushrooms in remaining butter. Add drippings from veal and beef extract, dissolved in hot water. Season and stir until well blended. Add wine, pour over veal, and serve. Serves 4.

VEAL SCALOPPINI ADVISORY

1 (1½ pound) veal cutlet
¼ pound cooked Virginia ham, sliced very thin
½ teaspoon sage
2 tablespoons olive oil or butter
½ cup dry white wine
½ cup Brown Sauce (p. 28)
3 cups cooked spinach, drained and chopped
6 hard-cooked eggs

Have veal prepared as for Scaloppini of Veal au Marsala. Lay a slice of ham on each cutlet and dust with very small pinch of sage. Roll and tie with string or fasten with toothpicks. Sauté gently in oil or butter 10 or 15 minutes, turning so they are evenly browned. Add wine, Brown Sauce, and salt and bring to a simmer. Serve on bed of spinach and garnish with eggs cut in half. Serves 4.

VEAL CUTLETS LOUISANNE

1 veal cutlet (approximately 1½ inches thick)
2 tablespoons butter
2 scallions, including tops, cut up
18 medium-sized mushrooms
1 small bay leaf
1 cup Sauterne
¼ cup Sherry
½ teaspoon Angostura bitters
salt and pepper

Brown cutlet well in butter, add all other ingredients, cover, and simmer gently until veal is very tender, 30-40 minutes. Remove meat to hot platter and reduce sauce until sirupy, stirring constantly. Pour over veal and serve. Serves 4 to 6.

BLANQUETTE OF VEAL

2 cups cooked veal, cut in small strips
1½ cups Medium White Sauce (p. 27) *or* brown gravy
¼ cup Sherry
mashed potatoes
parsley, finely chopped

Heat veal in sauce or gravy. Add Sherry just before removing from flame. Serve in a border of mashed potatoes and garnish with chopped parsley. Serves 4.

SCALOPPINI OF VEAL NEAPOLITAN

1 pound veal cutlets, sliced thin
1/4 cup butter
1/3 cup chopped mushrooms
1 tablespoon chopped shallots or chives
1/2 tablespoon flour
1/2 cup meat stock or bouillon
1 tablespoon Italian tomato paste
salt and pepper
1 tablespoon Sherry
2-3 cups hot cooked rice

Have cutlets flattened to 1/8 inch thick. Cut in 4-inch squares. Sauté veal in butter until golden. Remove and keep warm. Put in mushrooms, shallots or chives and sauté until tender. Stir in flour and cook, stirring constantly, until brown. Add meat stock gradually, then tomato paste, and stir steadily until slightly thickened. Add veal and Sherry, and simmer about 5 minutes. Serve with border of rice. Serves 4.

ROULADE OF VEAL ASTOR

(from Lucien Toucās, chef, Hotel Astor, New York City)

6 ounces butter
2 onions, finely chopped
1/4 pound spinach, chopped
10 green olives, chopped
6 filets of anchovies, chopped
1 soupspoonful fines herbes, chopped
salt and pepper
10 slices veal (very thin, about 5 ounces each)
5 slices bacon, half cooked and cut in two
1 pint dry white wine
1 small can tomato paste or 6 large fresh tomatoes, peeled

METHOD OF PREPARATION

Put into a sauté-pan 2 ounces of butter and 1 onion and allow to attain a golden brown; now add the chopped spinach, olives, anchovies, a little fines herbes, salt and pepper, and let simmer for a few minutes.

Arrange your slices of veal flat on the table together with the half slice of bacon on each; besprinkle with a little salt and pepper, and garnish with the sautéed spinach, olives, anchovies, etc. Now roll your slices of veal with spinach and insert toothpick to hold into shape.

COOKING OF ROULADE OF VEAL

Put 4 ounces of butter in a sauté-pan; when the butter is hot arrange your roulade of veal in pan and let brown on both sides; then add remaining onion and allow to simmer for a few minutes; add wine, the can of tomato purée or fresh tomatoes, and let cook slowly for about 10 minutes. Arrange your roulade on a serving dish; reduce the sauce to half the quantity and strain; now pour sauce over roulade and sprinkle with the remaining fines herbes. Serve with a boiled potato and string beans. Serves 5.

VEAL CHOPS ZINGARA

4 veal chops (1 inch thick)
5 tablespoons butter
¼ cup chopped onion
1 cup sliced carrots
2 medium-sized tomatoes, peeled and sliced
½ cup dry white wine
salt and pepper
1 cup mushrooms

Have chops cut with kidney in. Brown in 3 tablespoons butter. Add onions, tomatoes, carrots, and wine and season to taste. Cover and simmer 45 minutes. Just before serving add mushrooms, which have been sautéed in rest of butter. Serves 4.

A DELICATE DISH OF VEAL

2 pounds breast of veal
3 tablespoons butter
2 tablespoons flour
3 cups water
1 onion
4 cloves
1 bayleaf
1 tablespoon chopped parsley
2 slices of lemon
nutmeg, salt, and pepper
½ cup dry white wine

Cut veal into small pieces. Put into saucepan with a roux of butter and flour. Add water and onion stuck with cloves, parsley, bay leaf, lemon slices, nutmeg, salt and pepper, and wine. Cook slowly for 1½ to 2 hours. Remove veal, strain sauce, and add sufficient water and flour (in proportion of 1 tablespoon flour to 1 cup water) to make 2 cups sauce. Serves 4.

VEAL CUTLETS MARENGO

1 (1½-2 pound) veal cutlet
5 tablespoons butter
3 tablespoons tomato paste
½ cup dry white wine
½ cup chopped onion
1 clove garlic, minced
2 tablespoons vegetable oil
1 cup condensed tomato soup
salt and pepper
1 cup sliced mushrooms

Brown cutlet in 3 tablespoons butter. Add tomato paste and wine. Sauté onions and garlic in 2 tablespoons oil in another pan until tender. Add tomato soup and pour over cutlet. Season to taste, cover, and simmer slowly for 2 hours. Just before serving, sauté mushrooms in remaining butter and add. Serves 4.

GOLDEN GATE CUTLETS

1½ pounds veal cutlets (1 inch thick)
3 tablespoons butter or vegetable oil
¼ pound liver sausage
½ cup Sauterne
1 teaspoon onion juice
salt and pepper
¼ cup orange juice
grated peel ½ orange
1 egg yolk
1 cup seeded white grapes

Make a paste of sausage, wine, onion juice, salt, pepper, and egg yolk. Brown veal in butter or oil, spread with sausage mixture, place in baking dish, and pour over fat from skillet. Add orange juice, grated orange peel, and grapes. Bake in moderate oven (350-375°) about 45 minutes to 1 hour, basting often. Serves 4 to 6.

VEAL CHOPS MERIDA

6 veal chops (¾ inch thick)
2 tablespoons olive oil or butter
1 medium-sized onion, chopped fine
6 tomatoes, peeled
6 tablespoons uncooked rice
salt and pepper
dash cayenne
1 cup dry white wine

Brown chops in oil or butter and place in baking dish large enough to hold them all in one layer. Arrange chopped onion around and between chops. Put 1 tablespoon uncooked rice on top of each chop. Cut 1 thick slice (¾ inch) from center of each tomato and place on top of rice. Chop rest of tomatoes and arrange over chopped onion. Season, add wine, and bake, tightly covered, in moderate oven (350-375°) until chops are very tender, about 1½ hours. More wine may be added if necessary. Serves 6. Pork chops may be used if preferred.

FRENCH VEAL IN CASSEROLE

1 tablespoon sugar
½ cup sliced onion
2 pounds veal steaks, cut in pieces for serving
boiling water
3 tablespoons butter
3 tablespoons flour
salt and pepper
½ cup Sauterne
¾ cup cream or rich milk

Melt sugar in a heavy kettle; when brown add the onion and stir until coated. Add meat, sear and add boiling water to cover, and bring to a rapid boil. Cover closely and simmer until almost tender. Make a roux of butter and flour. Add to meat, cooking and stirring until gravy is thick and smooth. Season to taste. Add wine and cream. Cover and continue to simmer until meat is tender. Serves 4.

BRAINS IN BLACK BUTTER

4 pairs calf brains, or equivalent (p. 110)
½ cup butter
½ cup white wine vinegar
pinch of chervil
pinch of thyme
salt and pepper
½ cup dry white wine

Prepare brains (p. 110) and slice. Melt butter over brisk heat until chocolate brown, dash in vinegar, add herbs, season, and bring to a brisk boil. Add wine and sliced brains. Cover, bring to a simmer, and serve at once. Serves 4.

LIVER AND RICE IN CASSEROLE

2 tablespoons vegetable oil
3 large onions
1 teaspoon paprika
dash of cayenne
salt and pepper
1 cup (uncooked) brown rice
2 cans condensed bouillon
6 slices bacon
1½ pound lamb liver
2 tablespoons flour
½ cup water
1 cup Sauterne
1 tablespoon lemon juice

Put oil in frying pan over low flame. Slice onions into it, and add seasonings and uncooked rice, which has been washed and drained well. Cook slowly for 10 minutes, or until rice begins to pop. Add 1 cup bouillon, cook until dry, then add remaining bouillon a little at a time, and let cook dry after each addition; stir constantly to prevent burning. Fry bacon in another pan until half done and drain on paper. Fry floured liver in bacon fat until browned on both sides, but not thoroughly cooked. Place most of cooked rice in casserole, put liver on top of it, and cover with remaining rice. Make gravy by stirring 2 tablespoons flour into fat remaining in pan after frying liver; when browned, add water and wine, and cook, stirring, until smoothly thickened. Add lemon juice and more seasonings if needed. Pour gravy over rice and liver, cover casserole, and bake in moderate oven (350-375°) for 30 minutes. Remove cover, arrange partially cooked bacon over top, then put back into oven until bacon is crisp. Serves 6.

LIVER ITALIAN COUNTRY STYLE

2 medium-sized onions, sliced
3 tablespoons butter or olive oil
2 pounds calf liver (or lamb or pork) sliced
salt and pepper
¼ cup dry red wine

Sauté the onions in butter or olive oil until golden brown. Remove. Flour liver, salt and pepper to taste, and brown in same fat. Have fat as hot as possible without smoking. Do not overcook. Add onions and wine, bring to a simmer, and serve. Serves 6.

RISOTTO (ITALIAN)

2 tablespoons olive oil or vegetable oil
1 cup uncooked rice
4 medium-sized onions, chopped
½-1 clove garlic, crushed and minced
1 tablespoon chopped parsley
¼ teaspoon dried thyme
½ teaspoon saffron (optional)
salt and pepper
dash cayenne
2 cups meat stock *or*
4 bouillon cubes and 2 cups hot water
6 slices bacon
1 pound pork or liver, or chicken or
  chicken livers, chopped fine
½ cup flour
1 tablespoon lemon juice
2 slices lemon, chopped
1 cup dry white wine

Sauté rice, onions, and seasonings in oil gently for 10 minutes, stirring constantly. Add 1 cup stock and allow to simmer over low heat until liquid is nearly all absorbed. Add rest of stock and cook until it also has practically all been taken up with rice mixture.

Fry bacon until just crisp but not brown and remove. Sauté chopped meat or liver in bacon fat for 10 minutes, stirring occasionally. Blend in flour, add rest of ingredients, and stir until smooth. Place rice mixture in greased casserole, pour in contents of saucepan, and place bacon slices on top. Bake in hot oven (425-450°) 10 minutes. Serves 6.

CALF LIVER IN WINE

1 whole calf liver
¼ pound salt pork (about)
¾ cup melted butter
2 bay leaves
2 teaspoons salt
½ teaspoon pepper
3 cups dry white wine

Have liver well larded by butcher. Melt butter in casserole; add liver, wine, and seasonings. Cover and simmer very slowly about 5 hours. Serves 8 to 10.

LIVERGEMS

1 pound liver
⅓ cup cream
3 tablespoons Sherry
2 teaspoons chopped parsley
1 teaspoon chopped thyme
1 teaspoon chopped marjoram
salt and pepper
1 cup (approximately) bread crumbs

Parboil liver for not more than ½ minute. Remove skin and large tubes, and put through food chopper, using medium-sized blade. Add cream, Sherry, herbs, and seasonings and just enough bread crumbs so it can be molded into cakes. It should be quite moist. Divide into 8 patties and fry in hot fat until quite crisp. Serves 4.

Variations: Use dry red wine instead of Sherry. Two tablespoons mild cheese, crumbed and added before bread crumbs. Or a raw oyster hidden in the center of each patty. Watch for surprised looks if you try this. After all, that would be the last place one would expect to meet an oyster.

SWEETBREADS IN CASES

2 tablespoons chopped onion
½ cup chopped mushrooms
½ small clove garlic, crushed and minced
1 tablespoon minced parsley
2 tablespoons butter
3 pairs prepared sweetbreads (p. 110), well larded
½ cup Sherry or Madeira
½ cup Sauce Espagnole (p. 35)
salt and pepper
6 puff pastry cases

Sauté onion, mushrooms, garlic, and parsley in butter slowly until onion is tender but not brown. Divide sweetbreads in half, add with wine, and place in hot oven (400-450°) until sweetbreads are delicately browned, turning occasionally. Remove sweetbreads and keep hot. Add Sauce Espagnole and bring to a simmer. Season to taste.

Have ready 6 puff pastry cases, about 4″ x 3″ x 1½″. Put on baking sheet, place ½ sweetbread in each, and pour gravy over. Put in oven for 5 minutes. Serves 6.

BRAISED SWEETBREADS

2 pairs sweetbreads
¼ pound (approximately) salt pork, cut for larding
1 cup sliced carrots
1 cup sliced onions
⅛ teaspoon powdered thyme
1 bay leaf
2 tablespoons butter
1 cup meat stock (preferably veal)
¼ cup dry white wine (preferably Chablis)
salt and pepper

Lard prepared sweetbreads (p. 110) with salt pork. Make a bed in a casserole of carrots, onions, thyme, and bay leaf and lay sweetbreads on top. Dot with butter. Bake in hot oven (400-450°) until vegetables are browned. Add wine and meat stock; season, reduce heat to 350°, and braise for 1 hour, basting frequently. Serves 4.

BRAISED SWEETBREADS, FINANCIÈRE

2 pair sweetbreads
1 tablespoon pickling spices
2 teaspoons salt
2 teaspoons vinegar
¾ cup butter
⅔ cup dry white wine
1 cup chopped mushrooms
½ cup pitted and chopped olives
½ cup chopped shallots
1 tablespoon parsley
1 teaspoon chervil
½ teaspoon marjoram
½ teaspoon thyme
salt and pepper

Place sweetbreads in boiling water enough to cover, to which spices, salt, and vinegar have been added, and simmer, covered, 20 minutes. Drain, cover with cold water, and remove membranes and tubes. Sauté in ½ the butter about 10 minutes, until light brown. Put in casserole or baking dish with ⅓ cup wine and bake in moderate oven (350-375°) for 30 minutes. Sauté mushrooms, olives, shallots, and herbs in remaining butter until mushrooms are tender. Add remaining wine and reduce one half. Stir in sauce from baking pan and serve over sweetbreads. Serves 4.

SWEETBREADS IN CASSEROLE

3 pairs prepared sweetbreads (p. 110)
1 cup sliced mushrooms
2½ cups Sauce Poulette (p. 49)
24 oysters, coarsely chopped

Cut sweetbreads in ¾-inch dice. Put in casserole with mushrooms and sauce. Bake, covered, in moderate oven (350-375°) 30 minutes. Remove from oven, add chopped oysters, and season to taste. May be served from casserole or in patty cases. Serves 6.

SWEETBREADS LUCULLUS

2 pairs prepared sweetbreads (p. 110)
1 cup Chablis
2 tablespoons bacon fat
½ teaspoon beef extract *or*
1 beef cube dissolved in 1 tablespoon water
salt
paprika
3 cups cooked wild rice
2 cups Brown Sauce (p. 28)

Simmer sweetbreads gently in wine for 5 minutes, covered. Turn only once. Add bacon fat, beef extract, salt, and paprika and glaze over moderate heat, turning twice. Place in ring of wild rice; pour cooking sauce over sweetbreads and Brown Sauce over wild rice. Serves 4.

SWEETBREADS À LA NEWBURG

3 tablespoons butter
3 tablespoons flour
1 cup milk
¼ teaspoon salt
⅛ teaspoon pepper
2 eggs, separated
1 cup heavy cream
3 pairs prepared sweetbreads (p. 110), diced
2 tablespoons Sherry

Make a White Sauce with butter, flour, and milk. Add sweetbreads and season. Add beaten egg yolks, cream, and Sherry and reheat in double boiler. Fold in stiffly beaten egg whites. Cover and let cook about three minutes or until whites are set. Serves 6.

TRIPE À LA MODE DE CAËN

2 pounds honeycomb tripe
6 slices bacon
6 thin slices pork tenderloin
2 small onions, quartered
2 cloves garlic, crushed and minced
¼ cup chopped celery
1 cup sliced carrots
2 cups chopped tomatoes
1 calf's foot, cut in quarters
3 whole cloves
1 bay leaf
2 teaspoons chopped parsley
1 cup brandy
1 cup very dry white wine
salt and pepper
chicken broth

Prepare tripe (p. 111). Layer the bottom of a heavy casserole with bacon and pork. Put in tripe and add all other ingredients and broth sufficient to cover. Cover, moisten top of cover and edges of casserole, and seal tightly with a thick paste of flour and water. Bake in slow oven (250-275°) 6 to 8 hours. Serves 4 to 6.

DEVILED KIDNEYS NO. I

6 lamb kidneys or equivalent (p. 111)
2 tablespoons butter
2 tablespoons chopped onion
½ clove garlic, crushed and minced
½ cup chopped mushrooms
1 teaspoon salt
2 tablespoons Sherry
2 tablespoons water
4 bouillon cubes
3 egg yolks, lightly beaten
1 teaspoon minced parsley
dash of cayenne
½ cup buttered bread crumbs

Chop prepared kidneys (p. 111) quite fine and sauté gently in butter about 3 minutes. Add onions, garlic, mushrooms, salt, Sherry, and bouillon cubes dissolved in the water. Cook 15 minutes longer. Remove from heat and stir in beaten egg yolks, parsley, and pepper. Put in casserole, cover with buttered crumbs, and brown under broiler. Serves 4 to 6.

DEVILED KIDNEYS NO. II

2 beef kidneys or equivalent (p. 111)
3 tablespoons butter
1 tablespoon English mustard
1 teaspoon curry powder
2 tablespoons Worcestershire sauce
½ teaspoon Angostura bitters
1 cup dry red wine
salt, pepper, and cayenne

Slice prepared kidneys (p. 111) very thin. Sauté gently in butter about 2 minutes. Add all other ingredients, season quite highly, and boil 5 minutes. Serves 4 to 6.

KIDNEYS SAUTÉ

3 veal or 6 lamb kidneys
¼ pound mushrooms, sliced
3 tablespoons butter
1 tablespoon flour
1 cup condensed consommé
⅔ cup cream
salt and pepper
2 tablespoons Sherry

Prepare kidneys (p. 111) and cut in ¼-inch slices. Sauté gently in butter with mushrooms until slightly brown. Sprinkle in flour and stir. Gradually add cream and consommé, stirring constantly. Season, cover, and simmer until tender, about 10-15 minutes. Stir in Sherry and serve on toast. Serves 4 to 6.

LAMB KIDNEYS SAUTÉ CHASSEUR

6 lamb kidneys
1 tablespoon flour
½ pound mushrooms
½ cup Sherry or Madeira
½ cup dry white wine
½ teaspoon finely chopped shallots
¼ teaspoon finely chopped parsley
salt and pepper

Cut prepared kidneys (p. 111) into slices and season. Fry rapidly in very hot butter, sprinkle shallots over them, and stir for a few moments over the fire. Add flour and brown lightly, then add both wines and bring to a boil; add mushrooms, previously sautéed. Season to taste, simmer 5 minutes, place on dish and sprinkle with parsley. Serves 4 to 6.

KIDNEY STEW

3 veal or 6 lamb kidneys
¼ cup butter
1 tablespoon finely chopped onion
¼ pound mushrooms, finely chopped
2 tablespoons flour
1 cup bouillon
1 cup dry white wine
salt and pepper
2 tablespoons Sherry

Cut prepared kidneys (p. 111) in ¼-inch slices and sauté, together with onions and mushrooms, in butter for 3 minutes. Stir in flour, add bouillon and white wine, and season. Cover and simmer 25 minutes. Add Sherry just before serving. Serves 4 to 6.

BRAISED TONGUE

1 fresh beef tongue
2 tablespoons butter
2 medium-sized onions, sliced
4 medium-sized carrots, sliced
1 calf's foot
½ cup dry white wine
salt and pepper

Brown tongue in butter. Add vegetables, calf's foot, wine, and water to cover. Simmer, covered, until tender, about 3-4 hours. Season when about half done, using about ½ teaspoon salt per pound. Skin tongue, remove root, and serve with onions and carrots. Strain gravy and pour over.

TONGUE IN ASPIC

1 beef tongue
2 medium-sized onions, minced
1 bay leaf
2 tablespoons butter
4 cups condensed consommé
4 tablespoons gelatin
½ cup Sauterne
salt and pepper

Prepare tongue (p. 110). Brown onions lightly in butter. Add consommé and bay leaf, and boil until consommé is reduced to 3 cups. Add wine and cook 3 minutes longer. Strain and season. Soften gelatin in 1 cup of consommé and wine, and add to remainder. Pour over tongue in suitable mold. Serves 6 to 8.

TONGUE WITH CHEESE, EN CASSEROLE

1 pound tongue, sliced
3 cups tongue stock
¼ cup wine vinegar
1 teaspoon pickling spices
1 teaspoon salt
⅛ teaspoon pepper
1 cup browned bread crumbs
½ cup grated sharp cheese
½ cup dry white wine

Simmer cooked tongue (p. 110) in stock, vinegar, spices, and seasoning 10 to 15 minutes. Place a layer of tongue slices in greased casserole, sprinkle with crumbs and grated cheese mixed together, and repeat until all is used, finishing with crumb and cheese mixture. Add wine and bake in moderate oven (350-375°) until top is browned. Serves 4.

CHAPTER SEVEN

Poultry and Game

Of all the foods that come to our table, chicken is perhaps the most versatile. A famous French chef once wagered that he could prepare 365 menus, one for every day of the year, and each containing chicken in a style completely different from any of the others. And won.

And yet the average American housewife, good cook though she is, is apt to confine herself to a rather limited repertoire—fried, broiled, boiled, or roasted, with the usual croquettes, hashes, and creamed dishes to take care of leftovers.

In the following pages you will find many recipes which are about the same as those you use except for the addition of wine. If you are just getting acquainted with wine cookery, you will be interested in trying one of them first. There is no surer way to make a convert.

In Chapter Six on page 109 we told you of the low temperatures advised by the Bureau of Home Economics of the U. S. Department of Agriculture in the cooking of meats. The same practice is strongly advocated for all kinds of poultry, except a few game birds, and, in addition, if the bird is to be roasted, it should be placed breast down in a shallow, not a deep, pan. Do not cover and do not add water. Small or medium-sized birds should be turned every half hour, very large ones every hour, and basted with pan drippings, melted butter, or vegetable oil and whatever wine you are using. Use only as much wine as necessary for each basting. Do not put it all in at once.

Do not use a fork in turning. Protect the hands with thick folded cloths and lift by head and feet. To tell when the bird is done, use a sharp fork or skewer. Run it in the thigh near the breast and into the thickest part of the breast. If the flesh is tender and the juice is clear—not pinkish—it is just right.

If possible, stuff the bird the day before, particularly if wine is used in the stuffing, as considerably more of its flavor is absorbed.

A time table is at best only an approximate guide, as birds differ so much in age and tenderness. The one below is fairly accurate for young birds.

	Weight of Bird	Oven Temperature	Time
	Pounds	° F.	Hours
Chicken	4-5	350	1½-2
Duck (except wild)	5-6	350	2-2½
Goose	10-12	325	3-4
Guinea	2-2½	350	About 1½
Turkey	6-9	325	2½-3
	10-13	300	3-4
	14-17	275	4½-5½
	18-25	250-275	6-8

One important point to remember is to have every kind of poultry or game at room temperature no matter what method of cooking you use. The difference in flavor and tenderness is marked.

In general, the same methods apply to game as to domestic fowl and animals with one notable exception. Freshly killed game lacks both flavor and tenderness and must be "hung"—just how long depends on the age of the bird or animal, the temperature at which it is kept, and your own taste. In a cool room about three to four days will bring about the right results for the average taste. Foreign recipes frequently give directions to wait until the tail feathers can be plucked easily. Such birds are definitely "high," and few Americans will tolerate them.

Game birds should not be plucked or drawn until after being hung. Epicures demand that woodcock be not drawn.

Wild ducks have a strong, gamey flavor. This can be subdued, if it is objected to, by roasting the bird with an orange or two or three, according to the size of the bird, in the body cavity. Throw the oranges away when the bird is done. Of course, if you want stuffing, you'll have to bake it separately.

Deer, elk, and moose require from one to three weeks' hanging, and if, in addition, you marinate it from one to three days in red wine an old buck will be as tender as lamb.

Wild geese, as a rule, are much better in the bag than on the table. Only young specimens are worth cooking, and even these are apt to be greatly inferior to the domestic product. The best methods of cooking are braising, boiling, or some form of salmi. If the hunter insists on roasting, use a slow oven and frequent basting.

FRENCH ROAST CHICKEN

1 (3½-4 pound) roasting chicken
1 clove garlic, crushed
1 cup Sherry
1½ cups canned tomatoes
½ cup chopped celery
2 medium-sized onions, sliced
1 tablespoon chopped parsley
2 cups mashed potatoes
2 tablespoons melted butter
½ cup seedless raisins
½ cup chopped pecans
pinch of thyme
salt and pepper

Rub chicken well inside and out with crushed clove of garlic. Place in covered dish with ½ cup Sherry, add water to half cover, and simmer, covered, for 2 to 3 hours or until chicken is tender, adding ½ teaspoon salt per pound after first hour. Remove chicken. Mix mashed potatoes, melted butter, raisins, nuts, and thyme, season to taste, and stuff chicken with mixture. Sew up, place in casserole, and brown in moderately hot oven (375-400°). Add tomatoes, celery, onion, and parsley to liquid in which chicken was cooked and boil until onion and celery are tender. Serve in separate dish. Pour ½ cup Sherry over chicken just before serving. Serves 6.

CHICKEN SAUTÉ BONNE FEMME

1 (2½-3 pound) chicken, disjointed
flour
salt and pepper
¼ cup butter
2 cups diced mushrooms
½ cup chopped ripe olives
1 cup cream, scalded
2 egg yolks, beaten
¼ cup Sherry

Roll chicken in well-seasoned flour and brown well in very hot butter. Add mushrooms and bake, covered, in moderate oven (350-375°) 35-45 minutes or until tender. Remove and keep hot. Pour off all but ¼ cup fat. Add cream, egg yolks, and chopped olives, and stir until thickened. Add Sherry and season to taste. Pour over chicken and serve. Serves 4.

CHICKEN SAUTÉ HUNGARIAN STYLE

½ cup butter
½ cup sliced onions
2 (2-2½ pound) frying chickens, disjointed
flour
½ cup dry white wine
2 teaspoons paprika
1 cup cream
salt and pepper
2 cucumbers, thinly sliced

Sauté chopped onion in hot butter until tender but not brown and remove. Dredge chicken in flour and sauté until chicken is tender. Add onions, wine, paprika, and cream. Simmer slowly 5 minutes and serve garnished with cucumber. Serves 4 to 6.

YOUNG CHICKEN SAUTÉ SAN SOUCI

(From The Copley-Plaza, Boston, Mass.)

Quarter 3 young fresh chickens weighing about 2 to 2½ pounds each so as to obtain 2 legs and 2 breasts from each one. Season the quarters with salt and pepper.

8 ounces salt pork, diced and blanched
8 ounces diced fresh mushrooms
18 pieces small onions
1 pint good Claret
5 ounces sweet butter
¾ pint Brown Sauce (p. 28)
2 tablespoons wheat flour
1 small clove garlic, chopped

Fry the mushrooms, onions, and salt pork in the butter. When done, remove the onions and mushrooms from frying pan, and set aside in a warm place. Use the same pork and butter to fry the chickens. When done, add the onions and mushrooms once more, cover the frying pan, and place in the oven for about 25 minutes. Remove and place the chickens on a serving dish, arranging the garniture neatly around. Skim the fat from the frying pan, and add chopped garlic and Claret. Reduce the quantity to a half by boiling. Add the Brown Sauce. Mix 4 ounces sweet butter with a tablespoon of wheat flour, and add to the Claret and Brown Sauce. Boil for a few minutes, strain through a Chinese strainer, and pour over the chickens. Serves 6.

CHICKEN SAUTÉ À LA GRENOBLOISE

(From P. Moreau, Chef, Hotel St. Regis, New York City)

1 (2½ pound) chicken, cut in four
1 small onion, chopped
1 glass dry white wine
1 cup cream
1 cup tomato purée
1 small bay leaf
1 small clove garlic, crushed
thyme
parsley
salt and pepper

In a flat saucepan sauté the chicken slowly with the chopped onion, bay leaf, garlic, and thyme until golden brown. Place the pieces of chicken in a large earthenware casserole and keep aside. In the saucepan add the white wine, cream, and tomato purée. Reduce by half on fire. Add a few pieces of sweet butter. Season to taste, strain, and pour over chicken. Garnish with small quarters of *courgettes,* tomatoes and artichokes sautéed in oil, and a few round potatoes *persillées*. Serves 4.

BREAST OF CHICKEN DOUBLE WINE SAUCE

Breasts of 3 (2½-3 pound) chickens
larding pork
6 tablespoons butter
6 slices bread, crusts trimmed, and toasted on one side only
2 tablespoons chopped shallots
1 cup mushrooms in julienne slices
2 tablespoons Sherry
2 tablespoons Sauterne
½ cup heavy cream
salt
dash cayenne

Remove skin from chicken breasts and lard well. Place in pan with 4 tablespoons butter in hot oven (400-450°) until golden brown. Remove and keep hot. Fry both sides of bread in same pan. Place with chicken breasts to keep hot.

Sauté shallots and mushrooms in remaining butter until tender. Add wines, season, and cook to consistency of heavy cream; add cream and bring just to a simmer. Arrange chicken breasts on toast and pour sauce on top. Serves 6.

CHICKEN SAUTÉ WITH FINES HERBES

1 (3-3½ pound) chicken, disjointed
flour
¼ cup butter
¼ cup vegetable oil
2 tablespoons fines herbes (p. 9)
½ cup dry white wine
1 tablespoon chopped chives
¾ cup sour cream

Dredge chicken with flour and brown well on all sides over fairly low heat. Sprinkle in herbs, add ½ the wine, season, and simmer, covered, about 1 hour or until chicken is very tender. Remove chicken to serving dish and keep hot. Add rest of wine and simmer until it begins to get thick, add cream and chives, and pour over chicken. Serves 4.

CHICKEN SAUTÉ CREOLE

2 (1½-2 pound) broilers, disjointed
flour
salt and pepper
bacon fat
1 green pepper, chopped fine
1 onion, chopped fine
1 clove garlic, crushed and minced
2 sprigs parsley, minced
2 tablespoons olive oil
2 tablespoons chili sauce
¼ cup dry white wine

Dredge chicken pieces in seasoned flour and sauté in bacon fat. Meanwhile, sauté chopped pepper, onion, garlic, and parsley in olive oil until tender. Add chili sauce and wine, and season to taste. Reheat and pour over chicken. Serves 4.

ROASTED BROILER WITH SHERRY

1 broiler, split in half
2 tablespoons butter
salt and pepper
½ cup Sherry

Sauté the broiler halves in butter to a light brown. Place in casserole or baking dish, season, pour on wine, and bake in a slow oven (300-325°) for 45 minutes, basting every 10 or 15 minutes. Add more wine if necessary and use thickened sauce for gravy. Serves 2.

CHICKEN HUNTER STYLE

1 (2½-3 pound) chicken, disjointed
¼ cup flour
½ teaspoon salt
⅛ teaspoon pepper
4 tablespoons butter or vegetable oil
1 cup Sauterne (not too dry)

Wipe pieces of chicken with damp cloth, dredge with mixed flour and seasonings, and fry slowly in butter or oil until golden brown. Add wine and reduce heat. Simmer gently, turning occasionally, until chicken is tender. Serves 4.

CHICKEN MARENGO

1 (3-4 pound) chicken, disjointed
¼ cup olive oil or vegetable oil
½ cup sliced mushrooms
¼ cup chopped white onions
1 bay leaf
1 small clove garlic, crushed and minced
¼ cup condensed tomato soup or tomato paste
salt and pepper
2 tablespoons flour
1 cup dry white wine

Brown pieces of chicken in oil on all sides and put in casserole. Sauté mushrooms, onions, and garlic until tender but not brown. Put in casserole together with tomato soup or paste and seasonings. Cover and place in moderate oven (350-375°) for about 1 hour or until chicken is very tender. Add water, a little at a time, if necessary. Remove chicken to serving dish and keep hot. Blend flour into a little of liquid in pan, add to remaining liquid, and slowly stir in wine. Simmer gently until it thickens. Pour over chicken and serve with border of rice. Serves 5 to 6.

CHICKEN BURGUNDY

(From Paul Debes, Chef, Hotel Sir Francis Drake, San Francisco, Calif.)

Disjoint a chicken in four, season with salt and pepper, and fry in foaming butter until golden brown. Add some finely chopped shallots and blanched bacon cubes. Cover with a good Burgundy wine and simmer for 20 to 25 minutes. Thicken with a Beurre Manié (p. 34), add fresh chopped parsley, and serve. Serves 2.

CHICKEN TETRAZZINI

1 (3-4 pound) chicken, disjointed
2 teaspoons salt
¼ pound mushrooms, sliced thin
½ cup butter
½ pound spaghetti
2 tablespoons flour
1 cup heavy cream
¼ cup dry Sherry
½ pound grated Parmesan cheese

Cover chicken with cold water, add salt, and bring to a boil. Simmer, covered, until meat can be separated from bones, and cool in broth for 3 hours. Remove meat and skin from bones, cut meat in small chunks, and put bones and skin back into broth; bring to a boil and simmer, covered, for 45 minutes. Uncover and boil rapidly until reduced to 2 cups. Strain.

Cook spaghetti according to directions on package. Sauté mushrooms in 1 tablespoon butter until light brown and remove. Melt rest of butter, blend in flour, stir in broth slowly, and simmer 2 minutes. Remove from heat and stir in cream and Sherry. Add cut-up chicken to half the sauce, and mix spaghetti and mushrooms with other half. Line sides and bottom of greased casserole or individual ramekins with spaghetti-mushroom combination and pour in chicken mixture in center. Sprinkle with the cheese and bake in moderate oven (350-375°) until very lightly browned. Serves 6.

CHICKEN BERCY

(From J. B. Heguy, Head Chef, Hotel Pennsylvania, New York)

3 (2 pound) chickens, disjointed
4 ounces sweet butter
1 soupspoon chopped shallots
1 glass dry white wine
¼ cup glacéd meat
juice of ½ lemon
6 heads fresh mushrooms, minced
pinch of chopped parsley
salt and pepper

Pan-fry chickens in sweet butter. When cooked, place them aside on a plate. In the same butter, cook chopped shallots for 2 minutes; then add one Delmonico glass of wine and reduce to half. Add glacéd meat, lemon juice, and mushrooms. Season to taste. When done, pour on chickens all of the pan's contents. To finish, sprinkle with chopped parsley. Serve very hot. Serves 6.

CHICKEN BREASTS IN SAUTERNE

breasts of 2 (3-3½ pound) chickens
½ cup flour
salt and pepper
1 clove garlic, crushed
2 cups Sauterne (approximately)
1 cup cream
2 tablespoons chopped parsley

Split breasts through center to make 4 pieces. Wipe with moist cloth and dip in seasoned flour. Rub the inside of a shallow baking dish or casserole with crushed clove of garlic. Lay in breasts and add wine, which should barely cover them. Cover and bake in moderate oven (350-375°) for 1 hour. Stir in cream and bake uncovered 15 minutes more. Garnish with parsley. Serves 4.

CHICKEN SAUTÉ ITALIAN STYLE

2 (1½-2 pound) broilers, disjointed
⅓ cup olive oil or vegetable oil
½ cup minced Italian ham
1 clove garlic, crushed and minced
1 tablespoon chopped parsley
½ cup Chablis or Reisling
salt and pepper

Sauté chicken until it is light brown, stir in other ingredients, and simmer, turning chicken occasionally, until chicken is tender, about 20 minutes. Remove chicken, increase heat slightly, and reduce wine to about one half. Serves 4.

CHICKEN PROVENÇAL

2 (2-2½ pound) frying chickens, disjointed
¼ cup olive oil or vegetable oil
4 small cloves garlic, crushed and minced
¾ cup Riesling or Chablis
1 cup chopped tomatoes
¼ teaspoon thyme
2 tablespoons chopped parsley
1 cup chopped ripe olives
salt
cayenne

Brown chicken well in oil, add all other ingredients, and simmer, covered, until chicken is tender. Remove to hot serving dish, increase heat, and stir sauce until well thickened. Serve over chicken. Serves 4 to 6.

CHICKEN WITH OLIVES ITALIAN STYLE

1 cup dried Italian mushrooms
1 cup dry white wine
1 (3-4 pound) chicken, disjointed
flour
4 tablespoons olive oil or butter
¼ pound black Italian olives, pitted and chopped
1 cup cream
1 teaspoon salt
⅛ teaspoon pepper
1 teaspoon ginger

Wash mushrooms and soak in wine until plump, about ½ to ¾ hours, adding more wine if necessary. Roll chicken pieces in flour and brown well in olive oil or butter. Add all other ingredients, cover, and simmer gently, turning occasionally, for about 1½ hours or until chicken is tender. Serve with rice. Serves 4 to 6.

POULET SAUTÉ LOUISETTE

1 (3½ pound) chicken, disjointed
4 tablespoons butter
2 tablespoons vegetable oil
1 medium-sized onion, chopped
1 clove garlic, crushed and minced
1 tablespoon flour
½ cup dry white wine
½ cup stock
1 bouquet garni (p. 9)
salt and pepper
½ cucumber, sliced
¼ cup chopped cooked ham
2 egg yolks
3 tablespoons light cream

Brown chicken in oil and ½ of the butter. Add garlic and onion, and stir until onion is lightly browned. Sprinkle in flour, stir, and add stock, wine, and bouquet garni. Season and bring to a gentle simmer. Cook, covered, until the chicken is very tender. Remove chicken and keep hot. Sauté cucumber in remaining butter until transparent, add chopped ham and the strained chicken liquor, and simmer 5 minutes. Mix the egg yolks and cream, and stir in slowly. Do not allow to boil after egg yolks and cream are added. When thickened pour over chicken on serving dish. Serves 4 to 6.

FRENCH CHICKEN

1 (4 pound) roasting chicken, split in half
¼ cup vegetable oil or fat
2 cups dry white wine
1 small clove garlic, crushed and minced
½ teaspoon marjoram
½ teaspoon thyme
2 teaspoons salt
⅛ teaspoon pepper
flour
⅓ cup Swiss cheese, grated

Brown chicken well in fat. Add wine and seasonings, cover, and simmer slowly about 1 hour or until very tender. Place chicken on platter. Measure liquid in pan and add enough flour to make a Medium Brown Sauce (p. 28). Pour over chicken, sprinkle with grated cheese, and place under broiler until lightly browned. Serves 6.

BRUNSWICK STEW MANSION STYLE

Practically every restaurant in the country lists a Brunswick Stew on its menu, and it is a safe gamble that the name is the only point of similarity. Here is a recipe of the type served to the Southern lords of the manor in Colonial days, considerably modernized.

1 (4-5 pound) chicken, disjointed
½ pound bacon, chopped
1 cup dry white wine
½ cup chopped onion
2 cups canned tomatoes
1 cup canned corn
1 cup lima beans
½ cup Sherry
salt and pepper

Fry bacon until crisp and remove. Brown chicken and onions in bacon fat, and put in pot. Cover with boiling water, add white wine, cover, and simmer until meat can easily be separated from bones, about 3 hours. Add ½ teaspoon of salt per pound after first hour of cooking. When done, remove chicken, pick off meat, and cut up in fairly large pieces. Return to stock, add vegetables, bring to a boil, and simmer until vegetables are cooked and stock is thickened. Season and add Sherry. Serves 6 to 8.

CHICKEN VERMOUTH NO. 1

2 (2-2½ pound) frying chickens, disjointed
flour
¾ cup butter
3 tablespoons chopped parsley
3 tablespoons chopped chives
salt
paprika
2 tablespoons shaved Brazil nuts
1 cup dry Vermouth

Shake pieces of chicken in paper bag with flour and brown well on all sides in butter almost hot enough to smoke. Reduce heat, stir in parsley, chives, seasonings, nuts, and ¾ cup Vermouth. Simmer gently, stirring occasionally, about 45 minutes or until chicken is tender. Add rest of Vermouth as sauce thickens. Serves 4.

CHICKEN FLORENTINE

2 (2-3 pound) frying chickens, quartered
½ cup olive oil or vegetable oil
¼ cup butter
½ teaspoon sage
2 cloves garlic, crushed and minced
salt and pepper
½ cup dry white wine

Brown pieces of chicken well on both sides in oil and butter over low heat. Add seasonings and wine, and simmer about 15 minutes or until chicken is tender. Serves 4.

CHICKEN MOUSSE

6 cups cooked chicken meat
1 cup whipped cream
¼ cup Sherry
3 eggs, separated
salt
white pepper

Put chicken meat through food chopper (using finest blade) three times at least. Beat egg yolks until creamy. Mix chicken to a paste with the Sherry, add whipped cream and egg yolks, and season. Beat egg whites until stiff but not dry. Fold into chicken mixture. Put in well-buttered mold. Place in pan of hot water and bake in a moderate oven (350-375°) until it begins to draw away from the edges very slightly, about ½ hour. When tested with a toothpick the center will be slightly sticky. Brains or sweetbreads may be substituted for part or all of the chicken. Serves 6 to 8.

CHICKEN VERMOUTH NO. 11

2 (1-1½ pound) broilers, disjointed
3 tablespoons butter
2 leeks (white part only), chopped, *or*
3 tablespoons chopped white onions
salt and pepper
1½ cups sweet Vermouth
1 tablespoon tomato paste or condensed
tomato soup
1 pinch cinnamon
1 pinch mace
dash tabasco or cayenne

Sauté chicken in butter until golden brown and fairly tender. Add leeks or onions and seasonings, and cook until soft. Remove chicken and contents of pan, and keep hot. Put Vermouth in skillet, heat, and ignite. Before flames die down put in chicken and gravy, and stir in tomato sauce and rest of seasonings. Serves 4.

CHICKEN STEW BAVARIAN STYLE

1 (3-3½ pound) chicken, disjointed
6 tablespoons butter
6 leeks or medium-sized onions, chopped
1 clove garlic, crushed and minced
2 tablespoons flour
2 cups condensed beef consommé
2 tablespoons tomato paste
¼ teaspoon Worcestershire sauce
¼ teaspoon Angostura bitters
salt and pepper
1 cup dry red wine
1 bouquet garni (p. 9)
½ pound mushrooms, sliced and sautéed
parsley

Brown chicken, including cut-up giblets, in 4 tablespoons butter and place in casserole. Sauté leeks or onions in same pan until golden. Add remaining butter, blend in flour, and gradually stir in consommé, tomato sauce, Worcestershire, Angostura, wine, and seasonings, also bouquet garni tied loosely in a cloth. When thickened, pour over chicken in casserole and simmer, covered, until tender, about 1 hour. Remove bouquet garni, stir in sautéed mushrooms, and serve garnished with parsley. Serves 4.

Guinea fowl, rabbit, or duck may be used if preferred.

CHICKEN CARIOCA

1 (3½-4 pound) chicken, disjointed
¼ cup butter
1 medium-sized onion, chopped
12 green onions, cut up
2 tablespoons chopped parsley
1 sprig thyme *or*
⅛ teaspoon dried thyme
2 cups sliced mushrooms
1 can chicken consommé
1 cup Sauterne
salt and pepper
1 tablespoon Sherry
1 tablespoon rum
1 tablespoon lemon juice
flour

Brown the chicken and cut up giblets in butter. Put in casserole with onions, parsley, thyme, and mushrooms. Add consommé, Sauterne, and all seasonings. Cook, covered, in moderate oven (350-375°) for 2½ hours. Remove chicken and keep hot. Strain gravy, measure, and thicken with flour in the proportion of 2 tablespoons to the cup. Add Sherry, rum, and lemon juice and pour over the chicken in the casserole. Serves 4-6.

CAPON CHANTECLAIR

1 (6-7 pound) capon, disjointed
4 cups dry red wine
½ cup chopped onion
1 cup chopped carrot
½ cup chopped celery
3 cloves garlic, crushed and minced
salt and pepper
flour
½ cup butter
2 cups sliced mushrooms
¼ pound bacon, diced
1 teaspoon chopped fresh tarragon

Marinate capon with onion, carrots, celery, and garlic in wine for 24 to 36 hours. Drain, season, dust with flour, and sauté in butter until well browned. Put in marinating liquid with mushrooms and bacon, and simmer until very tender. Remove capon, add tarragon to sauce, and reduce one half. Serve with sauce poured over. Serves 6 to 8.

ARROZ VALENCIANO

1 cup cooked chicken meat
1 cup cooked fish
½ cup chopped clams
½ cup cooked beans
4 small sausages, cut in 1-inch pieces
2 tablespoons chopped green pepper
2 tablespoons chopped onion
½ cup chopped tomato
1 clove garlic, crushed and minced
3 tablespoons olive oil or vegetable oil
2 cups boiling water
1 cup rice
1 cup dry white wine
salt and pepper
dash of cayenne

Sauté chicken, fish, clams, beans, sausage, peppers, onion, tomato, and garlic in oil until peppers and onion are tender. Add rice and boiling water, and cook until rice is tender, 20 to 25 minutes. Add wine and reheat. Serves 6.

Since this is a Spanish recipe designed to use up leftovers, it is susceptible of infinite variation. The above recipe will give you the general idea.

CHICKEN IN PARCHMENT

1 (3-3½) pound chicken, disjointed
2 cups Sauterne
2 tablespoons chopped onion
1 tablespoon chopped parsley
1 cup chopped mushrooms
½ teaspoon chervil
¼ teaspoon thyme
salt
white pepper

Marinate chickens for 3 hours in wine, to which all other ingredients have been added. Turn occasionally. Moisten a full-sized sheet of cooking parchment (about 24 inches square) and lay it in baking dish. Put in chicken and marinating liquid. Gather together corners and sides of paper to form a sack, and tie very tightly together with white cord, finishing with a slip knot. Bake in moderate oven (350-375°) 1 hour. Serves 4.

Note: If pressure cooker is used, the same results may be obtained in 12 minutes without using parchment.

CHICKEN POMPADOUR

8 breasts of frying chickens
16 small pork sausages
4 tablespoons chopped onion
3 truffles (optional)
½ cup chopped mushrooms
1 cup dry white wine (Chablis preferred)
½ cup chicken broth
1 teaspoon salt
½ teaspoon paprika
3 egg yolks, lightly beaten
⅓ cup cream
1 tablespoon butter
½ teaspoon lemon juice

Prick sausages and fry them lightly. Add chicken breasts, onion, truffles, mushrooms, wine, and chicken broth and seasonings. Cover and simmer, turning chicken occasionally, about 20 minutes or until chicken is tender. Remove chicken and sausages to hot serving dish. Add egg yolks stirred into cream, butter, and lemon juice. Simmer until thick. Pour over chicken. Serves 4.

CHICKEN À LA FARNSWORTH

1 (4-5 pound) chicken
4 prepared sweetbreads (p. 110)
4 tablespoons flour
6 tablespoons butter
4 artichoke bottoms, cut in quarters
¾ cup Sherry
1 pint light cream
4 link sausages
salt and pepper
12 1-inch diamond-shaped croutons
12 stuffed ripe olives

Boil chicken until very tender. Remove meat and cut up coarsely. Break up sweetbreads into approximately ¾-inch pieces. Roll chicken and sweetbreads in flour, and brown lightly in butter. Add artichoke bottoms and wine, and simmer gently while stirring until mixture is quite thick and liquid is reduced about two thirds. Add cream and simmer very gently 15 minutes longer. Fry sausages, cut in 1-inch pieces, and add. Season, place in serving dish, and garnish with olives and croutons. Serves 6.

CHICKEN PERIGORD

½ pound ham, cut in small cubes
¼ cup butter
1 (3-4 pound) chicken, disjointed
flour
4-5 small white onions, quartered
1 small clove garlic, crushed and minced
1 tablespoon chopped parsley
¼ teaspoon dried thyme
1 cup chopped truffles *or*
1 cup chopped mushrooms
salt and pepper
2 tablespoons brandy
1 cup dry red wine

Sauté ham cubes in butter for 3-4 minutes. Dredge chicken in flour and brown well. Add onions, garlic, parsley, thyme, and truffles or mushrooms and season. Bring to a simmer, pour on brandy, and light it; blow out flame before it goes out. Add wine, cover, and simmer about 1 hour or until chicken is tender. Serves 6.

CHICKEN SAUTERNE

1 (4 pound) roasting chicken, disjointed
⅓ cup butter or vegetable oil
4 medium-sized mild onions, sliced
6 carrots, sliced
4 medium-sized potatoes, sliced or cut in balls
½ teaspoon thyme or marjoram
1½ teaspoons salt
⅛ teaspoon pepper
4 cups dry Sauterne
flour
1 tablespoon chopped parsley

Brown chicken well in butter or vegetable oil. Place in casserole. Brown vegetables slightly in same pan. Cover chicken with wine and add seasonings. Cover and simmer until chicken is tender, about 2 hours. About 1 hour before it is done add the vegetables. Thicken the gravy to the consistency of medium cream sauce, add parsley, and serve over chicken. By adding more potatoes this makes a one-dish meal. Serves 6.

SUPREME DE POULET MARJOLAINE

Breast of 3½-pound roasting chicken
nutmeg
powdered mixed herbs (rosemary, bay leaf, thyme, and marjoram)
salt and pepper
¾ cup butter
½ cup Sherry

Season the breast of chicken with nutmeg, mixed herbs, salt, and pepper. Melt 4 tablespoons of butter and cook each side of seasoned breast for 7 minutes. Remove chicken and add to the pan ½ cup Sherry. Simmer until sauce is reduced about one third. Remove from fire, and add remaining butter gradually and enough more seasonings to taste. Pour sauce over chicken. Serves 2.

CHICKEN EN CASSEROLE

1 cup chopped carrots
¾ cup chopped celery
¼ cup minced onion
¼ cup butter
1 (3-3½ pound) fowl, disjointed
1 teaspoon salt
1 cup cream
⅓ cup Sherry

Lightly brown vegetables in butter and remove. Put in chicken and sauté until golden brown all over. Put in casserole with vegetables on top and add salt, cream, and wine. Cover and bake in moderate oven (350-375°) until chicken is tender, about 1 hour. Serves 4 to 6.

CHICKEN PATTIES

4 tablespoons butter
4 tablespoons flour
2 teaspoons onion juice
½ cup chicken stock
½ cup cream
½ cup dry white wine
2 cups diced cooked chicken

Melt butter, blend in flour, and add onion juice, chicken stock, and cream. Simmer while stirring for 1 minute. Add wine and chicken. Bring to a simmer and serve on toast or in pastry shells. Serves 4.

CHICKEN MONTAGNE

1 (2½-3 pound) chicken, disjointed
salt and pepper
4 tablespoons butter
1 cup chopped mushrooms
2 tablespoons chopped truffles
¼ cup Sherry
1 cup cream

Season chicken and brown well on both sides in very hot butter. Bake, covered, in moderate oven (350-375°) 20-25 minutes or until chicken is fairly tender. Add mushrooms and bake about 15 minutes more or until chicken is done. Remove and keep hot. Add truffles and Sherry to drippings in pan, bring to a boil, add cream, and reheat but do not allow to boil. Pour over chicken and serve. Serves 4.

CHICKEN TARRAGON

¼ cup fresh tarragon leaves
½ cup Chablis or Riesling
2 (2-2½ pound) frying chickens, disjointed
¼ cup butter or vegetable oil
salt and pepper

Soak tarragon in ¼ cup wine for 3 or 4 hours. Brown chicken well in hot fat, add ¼ cup wine, season, and simmer about 20-30 minutes or until chicken is tender. Add tarragon and rest of wine, and bring to a boil. Serves 4.

CHICKEN CREAMED WITH SHERRY

3 cups cooked chicken flaked, *or*
1½ cups chicken and 1½ cups diced prepared sweetbreads (p. 110)
½ cup chicken stock
1 cup Thick White Sauce (p. 28)
¾ cup Sherry
1 hard-cooked egg
6 slices buttered toast, crusts removed

Simmer chicken (and sweetbreads) slowly in stock 10 minutes and gradually add White Sauce, Sherry, and grated egg yolk. Simmer 5 minutes longer. Serve on toast garnished with chopped egg white. Serves 6.

JERRY'S CHICKEN HASH

4 cups cooked chicken meat, coarsely chopped
1 cup Sauterne
2 teaspoons flour
½ cup chicken fat
¼ cup finely chopped onion
1 teaspoon finely chopped parsley
2 cups diced boiled potatoes
¼ cup heavy cream
salt and pepper

Pour the wine over the chopped chicken and allow to soak for 3 to 4 hours. Brown onions and parsley lightly in melted chicken fat. Stir in flour, add chopped chicken meat and wine, and simmer 3 minutes. Add potatoes, which should not be overcooked, and cream, and bring to a simmer. Season to taste. Serve on buttered toast. Serves 6.

CHICKEN À LA KING DE LUXE

5 tablespoons butter
4 tablespoons flour
1 cup milk
1 cup chicken broth or canned chicken soup
1 cup heavy cream
¼ minced green pepper
1 cup sliced mushrooms
1 pimiento, sliced thin
¼ cup chopped ripe olives
2 cups coarsely chopped cooked chicken
¼ cup dry Sherry
2 egg yolks, lightly beaten

Make White Sauce using 2 tablespoons butter, flour, milk, and chicken broth. Add cream and bring just to a simmer. Sauté green pepper and mushrooms in rest of butter about 10 minutes or until tender. Add to sauce together with all other ingredients except egg yolks and wine. Stir while simmering for 5 minutes. Add egg yolks and stir over low heat 1 minute but do not allow to boil. Remove from heat and add wine. Serves 6.

Suggestions: Besides the conventional Melba toast, it may be served on very crisp, well-buttered waffles or in individual casseroles lined with hot mashed potatoes or on French toast with small rashers of bacon accompanied with pickled peaches.

CHICKEN HASH

1 (4 pound) fowl
2 cups sliced mushrooms
¼ cup butter
2 cups Medium Cream Sauce (p. 28)
2 egg yolks, beaten
½ cup Hollandaise Sauce (p. 48)
¼ cup Sherry
1 package (8 ounces) spaghetti, cooked
1 cup whipped cream

Boil fowl, remove meat, and cut in small pieces or chop very coarsely. Sauté mushrooms in butter, add Cream Sauce, beaten egg yolks, Hollandaise Sauce, and Sherry and stir in chicken meat. Bring to a simmer and stir until thickened. Put cooked spaghetti in buttered, heated casserole, add chicken mixture, top with whipped cream, and put under broiler until brown. Serves 8 to 10.

MINCED CHICKEN REGAL

1 (3½ pound) fowl
1½ quarts boiling water
1 teaspoon salt
½ cup butter
2 shallots, chopped fine
3 teaspoons flour
½ cup dry Sherry
2 cups milk
1 pound noodles
½ cup whipped cream
3 egg yolks, beaten
3 tablespoons grated Parmesan or other sharp cheese

Boil fowl until very tender, adding salt when nearly done. Remove and allow to cool. Reserve stock. Pick off meat and cut in small pieces but do not chop. Brown shallots lightly in butter, from which 1 tablespoon is reserved, and blend in flour. Add chicken, wine, and milk and simmer gently for 10 minutes. Cook noodles in stock, adding as much additional water as may be necessary. Drain, place in casserole, and swirl with 1 tablespoon butter, then pour in chicken mixture. Mix together whipped cream, beaten egg yolks, and cheese and spread on top. Place in hot oven (450°) until delicately browned. Serves 6 to 8.

CHICKEN FRICASSEE FLORENTINE

½ cup dried Italian mushrooms
2 (1½-pound) broilers, disjointed
flour
2 tablespoons olive oil
2 tablespoons butter
1 medium-sized onion, chopped
1 clove garlic
¾ cup dry red wine
12 ripe olives cut in quarters
12 green olives, pimiento stuffed, cut in quarters
1 cup sour cream
salt and cayenne

Wash mushrooms well in warm water and allow to soak ½ hour. Dredge chicken sections in flour, and brown well in olive oil and butter. Remove chicken and sauté onions, garlic, and chopped mushrooms until tender but not brown. Add wine and simmer gently 20 minutes. Add chicken and cook, covered, about 20 minutes more or until chicken is tender. Add olives, sour cream, and seasonings and reheat. Serves 4.

CHICKEN FRICASSEE CHARLESTON STYLE

2 (2½-pound) frying chickens, disjointed
5 cups water
¼ teaspoon nutmeg
¼ teaspoon mace
salt and pepper
2 anchovies
1 cup sliced mushrooms
1 medium-sized onion, sliced
½ cup dry Sherry
1 cup cream
¼ cup butter
¼ cup flour
1 egg yolk
2 tablespoons lemon juice

Simmer the chicken until it is very tender with the seasonings, anchovies, onion, mushrooms, and wine. Remove the chicken, strain the cooking liquor, allow to cool slightly, and stir in the cream, butter, flour, and lightly beaten egg yolk, well blended. Bring to a simmer and add the lemon juice gradually. Pour over chicken and serve. Serves 6.

CHICKEN CROQUETTES

1 tablespoon butter
¼ cup sliced mushrooms
2 teaspoons chopped onions
1 teaspoon chopped parsley
3 cups chicken meat, cooked and ground
1 cup Thick White Sauce (p. 28)
1½ tablespoons lemon juice
dash mace or nutmeg
salt and pepper
2 tablespoons Sherry
flour
1 egg, slightly beaten
1 tablespoon milk
bread crumbs

Sauté mushrooms, onions, and parsley in butter until tender. Add chicken meat, White Sauce, seasonings, lemon juice, and Sherry. Chill thoroughly. Mold into any desired shape: cylinders, cones, balls, or cutlets. Roll in flour, dip in egg to which milk has been added, then roll in crumbs. Fry in hot deep fat (365-385°) until browned, 2-5 minutes. Drain on soft paper and serve at once. 8-12 croquettes.

CHICKEN WITH BURGUNDY

1 (5 pound) chicken, disjointed
flour
½ cup butter
12 button onions
2 cloves garlic, crushed and minced
1 cup lean uncooked ham, diced
¼ teaspoon thyme
1 bay leaf
½ teaspoon chopped parsley
½ cup sliced mushrooms
salt and pepper
¼ cup brandy
1½ cups Burgundy

Flour the pieces of chicken and brown well in butter; add onions, garlic, ham, thyme, bay leaf, mushrooms, and seasonings. Simmer gently, while stirring, for 3 minutes. Add brandy, ignite, and allow to burn out. Place in casserole, add wine, seal tightly with pastry dough, and cook in moderate oven (250-325°) for 2 hours. Reduce or thicken sauce if desired. Serves 6 to 8.

CHICKEN AVOCADO MOUSSE

4 tablespoons butter
1½ cups light cream
½ cup dry bread crumbs
¼ teaspoon salt
⅛ teaspoon mace (or nutmeg)
4 eggs, lightly beaten
½ cup Sherry
2 cups chopped cooked chicken
2 large or 3 small avocadoes, diced
1 cup mayonnaise

Melt butter over hot water, add cream, and stir in crumbs. Season and cook 10 minutes, stirring often. Blend eggs and Sherry, and mix thoroughly with chopped chicken and stir into the sauce. Put into a greased ring mold, cover with parchment paper, place mold in a pan of hot water, and bake in a moderate oven (350-375°) 30-35 minutes or until firm. Unmold; mix diced avocados with mayonnaise and fill center of mold. Serves 4.

CHICKEN LIVERS WINDSOR

12 chicken livers
6 tablespoons butter
2 tablespoons flour
2 cups chicken broth
1½ cups sliced mushrooms
2 shallots, chopped
½ cup heavy cream
4 cooked artichoke bottoms, chopped
½ cup Port
salt
pepper
2 cups cooked rice
½ cup grated Parmesan cheese

Sauté chicken livers in 4 tablespoons butter, turning once. Add flour, stir, and add broth gradually, stirring constantly until thickened. Season and keep hot. Sauté mushrooms and shallots in remaining butter until tender, add to chicken-liver mixture, and simmer gently 15 minutes. Add cream, artichoke bottoms, and wine. Reheat but do not allow to boil. Place rice in a mound on hot serving dish, make a deep hole in center, and fill with chicken liver mixture. Sprinkle rice with cheese. Serves 4 to 6.

DUCK BEAULIEU

1 (4-5 pound) duck
salt and pepper
15 ripe olives, pitted
4 medium-sized potatoes, quartered
2 cups water
5 ounces (½ can) chicken madrilene
½ cup Madeira or Sherry

Rub duck inside and out with salt and pepper; place in casserole with olives, potatoes, and water. Cover and place in hot oven (400-450°) allowing 20 to 25 minutes to the pound. About 5 minutes before duck is done, add madrilene and wine, and cover again. Serve with Sauce Bigarade (p. 44). Serves 4.

HOLLYWOOD DUCK

1 (5½-6 pound) duck, disjointed
1 cup dry red wine
½ cup brandy
3 medium-sized onions, sliced
1 clove garlic, crushed
1 tablespoon chopped parsley
½ teaspoon dried thyme
½ teaspoon dried marjoram
¼ teaspoon allspice
1 bay leaf
2 teaspoons salt
¼ teaspoon pepper
¼ pound chopped pork fat
1 tablespoon butter
½ pound mushrooms, sliced
6 slices whole wheat toast or rusks

Place duck pieces in bowl or small earthenware crock. Add wine, brandy, onions, garlic, parsley, thyme, marjoram, allspice, bay leaf, salt, and pepper. Marinate 4 to 6 hours at room temperature, turning pieces of duck occasionally. Fry chopped pork fat slowly in heavy frying pan, and when crisp add butter and duck. Brown duck on all sides, and add mushrooms and strained marinating mixture. Cover and simmer until duck is tender, about 1½ hours. Remove duck and keep warm. Reduce sauce slightly by vigorous boiling until somewhat thickened. Serve on toast or rusks, with sauce separately. Serves 6.

DUCK À L'ORANGE

1 (5½-6 pound) duck
salt and pepper
¼ cup butter
⅓ cup condensed consommé
½ teaspoon Angostura bitters
2 small navel oranges, peeled and quartered
1 tablespoon orange peel, sliced very fine
1 small unpeeled navel orange, sliced very thin
½ cup dry white wine
1 teaspoon cornstarch
2 tablespoons cold water
1½ tablespoons Curaçao (optional)

A saucepan, casserole, or Dutch oven with a tightly fitting cover is essential. Rub duck well inside and out with seasonings; brown very thoroughly in butter in covered dish, turning frequently. Add consommé and Angostura. Place quartered oranges around sides and sprinkle peel slivers on top. Cover tightly and simmer about 1½ hours or until tender. Do not uncover oftener than necessary. When done, place on platter surrounded by slices of unpeeled orange and keep hot.

Add wine to liquid in cooking vessel and simmer 1 minute. Dissolve cornstarch in cold water and stir in until sauce is slightly thickened. Add Curaçao. Pour over duck and serve. Serves 6.

SALMI OF DUCK WITH OLIVES

2 tablespoons butter
1 medium-sized onion, minced
4 cups cooked duck meat, cut up
2 teaspoons chopped thyme
1 teaspoon chopped parsley
1 bay leaf, crushed
2 tablespoons flour
2 cups condensed consommé
½ cup dry red wine
1½ cups green olives, pitted
salt and pepper

Brown onions lightly in butter. Add duck meat, thyme, parsley, and bay leaf; stir, cover, and cook gently for about 10 minutes, stirring frequently. Sift in flour and stir. Add consommé, wine, and olives, season, and simmer, covered, 20 minutes. Serves 4 to 6.

SALMI OF WILD DUCK

2 medium-sized onions, chopped
1 teaspoon minced thyme
1 teaspoon minced parsley
1 tablespoon chopped celery
1 clove garlic, crushed and minced
3 tablespoons butter
2 ducks, disjointed
salt and pepper
2 tablespoons chopped ham
1 bay leaf, crushed
½ cup dry red wine
1 cup condensed consommé

Brown vegetables and herbs lightly in butter. Rub pieces of duck well with salt and pepper, and brown well. Add chopped ham, bay leaf, and wine and simmer 10 minutes, stirring constantly. Add consommé, season to taste, cover, and simmer gently until ducks are tender, about 1 hour. Serves 4.

WILD DUCK CROQUETTES

(From leftovers)

4 cups duck meat (approximately)
1 hard-cooked egg, chopped
¼ cup stock
¼ cup dry red wine
¼ teaspoon thyme
¼ teaspoon marjoram

Put duck meat through food chopper using finest blade. Simmer carcasses for ½ hour in enough water to cover, strain and reduce to about ¼ cup. Add dry red wine. Mix well with chopped duck meat, make into croquettes, and fry in deep fat. Serves 6.

ROAST DUCK WITH RED WINE

1 (5½-6 pound) duck
1 cup dry red wine
1 cup water
½ teaspoon salt
⅛ teaspoon pepper
Any desired stuffing

Stuff duck and roast, breast down, in moderate oven (350-375°), basting with seasoned wine and water. Allow 25 minutes per pound. Turn breast up and turn oven on full for about 10 to 15 minutes more or until breast side is browned. Use more wine and water if necessary. Serves 6.

DUCK EN CASSEROLE NO. 1

1 (5½-6 pound) duck, disjointed
butter or vegetable oil
½ pound sliced mushrooms
6 carrots, julienne
4 medium-sized onions, sliced
1 teaspoon fines herbes (p. 9)
1 clove garlic, crushed and minced
12 pitted olives, sliced
dry red wine
salt and pepper

Brown the duck in as little butter or cooking oil as possible. Remove and brown the vegetables in the same pan. Add herbs in a small cheesecloth bag (an empty tea bag is perfect). Add garlic, cover with wine, season, and cook in a covered casserole slowly until duck is very tender. Add olives 10 minutes before removing. Remove spice bag, and skim. Serve with rice. The gravy can be slightly thickened or not as preferred. Serves 6.

PRESSED DUCK

1 wild duck
¼ cup butter
¼ cup water
¾ cup Burgundy
salt
black pepper
2 tablespoons brandy

Roast duck in very hot oven (450-500°) 15-20 minutes, basting with mixture of melted butter and hot water. Bring duck to table on hot serving platter. Remove thighs and slice breast very thin. Put slices of breast around sides of hot chafing dish plate; add liquid from baking pan with ½ cup Burgundy and a pinch of freshly ground black pepper. Place carcass in a duck press, pour over it remaining ¼ cup of wine, and turn screw until last possible drop of juice has been extracted. Add brandy and pour slowly in chafing dish, stirring constantly until sauce thickens. Season as desired. Bathe slices of breast well in sauce and serve on very hot plates. If desired the duck liver or a spoonful of paté de foie gras may be mashed into the duck juices before heating. Return thighs to kitchen, season, broil quickly, and serve separately. All operations except roasting of duck and broiling of legs are, of course, done at table. If you do not own a duck press, one may be rented from any good restaurant. Currant jelly is always served with this and wild rice is a natural accompaniment. Serves 1 to 2.

DUCK EN CASSEROLE NO. II

1 (5½-6 pound) duck, disjointed
4 tablespoons flour
salt
pepper
4 tablespoons butter
giblets, chopped
2 tablespoons chopped onion
1 tablespoon chopped parsley
¼ teaspoon thyme
¼ teaspoon marjoram
¼ teaspoon basil
¼ cup dry white wine
1 tablespoon brandy
½ cup cream

Dredge pieces of duck in well-seasoned flour and brown well in butter on all sides. Put in casserole with all other ingredients except cream and bake in moderate oven (350-375°) for 1 hour. Add cream and cook about 20-30 minutes longer or until tender. Serves 6.

DUCK WITH CHERRIES

1 (5½-6 pound) duck
1 carrot, sliced
3 medium-sized onions, sliced
1 bay leaf
6 sprigs parsley
salt
pepper
3 cups water
¼ cup dry white wine
2 tablespoons flour
1 cup sour cherries, fresh or canned

Place duck in Dutch oven, or kettle which can be covered tightly, with carrot, onion, bay leaf, parsley, salt and pepper, and hot water. Cover and simmer until duck is tender, 45 minutes to 1 hour. Remove duck and keep hot. Strain cooking liquid, blend in flour, add wine, and simmer 2 minutes, stirring constantly. Add cherries. Carve duck just before serving and pour sauce over. Serves 6.

DUCK IN WINE ASPIC

1 package aspic gelatin
1 cup dry red wine
4 cups cooked duck meat
½ teaspoon salt
4 sautéed mushrooms or truffles, sliced thin
red or black currant jelly

Follow directions on package for aspic, substituting the wine, which has been brought to simmering point, for 1 cup of water. Cut duck meat into fairly large pieces. Arrange mushroom or truffle slices over bottom of the mold and pour in the aspic. As soon as it starts to jell arrange the duck evenly. Chill until set. Serve garnished with jelly. Serves 4 to 6.

BRAISED DUCK WITH CHESTNUTS

1 pound chestnuts
1 large Bermuda onion, quartered
2 cups stock or strained chicken soup
1 egg
1 (4-5 pound) duck
¼ cup butter
1 cup small sliced onions
¼ cup sliced turnips
½ cup sliced carrots
½ cup chopped celery
2 tablespoons chopped parsley
½ teaspoon thyme
¼ teaspoon allspice
¼ teaspoon cloves
salt and pepper
1½ cups Espagnole Sauce (p. 35)
¼ cup Port
1 tablespoon red currant jelly

Boil chestnuts and skin. Cook Bermuda onion in stock, remove, and chop together with chestnuts, mix in egg, and use for stuffing duck. Melt butter in large covered dish, add sliced vegetables and seasonings, well mixed, and sauté gently, uncovered, for 20 minutes. Add enough stock to nearly cover vegetables. Place duck on top of vegetables. Cover tightly and simmer about 2 hours or until duck is tender, adding more stock as necessary. Heat Espagnole Sauce, and add wine and jelly. Serve duck surrounded by vegetables. Pour part of sauce over duck and serve rest separately. Serves 4.

DUCK WITH RED WINE

1 onion, chopped
2 tablespoons butter
2 tablespoons flour
2 cups condensed chicken consommé
juice of 1 orange
rind of 1 orange (white part removed), shredded
¼ cup dry red wine
1 cold roast duck, disjointed
salt and pepper

Sauté onion in butter, add flour, stir until brown, add consommé, and simmer 10 minutes. Add orange juice, orange rind, wine, and duck to sauce. Season and simmer very gently ½ hour. Serves 4 to 6.

PARTRIDGES WITH SAUERKRAUT

2 partridges
salt and pepper
4 slices bacon
5 tablespoons butter
4 shallots, chopped
2 medium-sized carrots, sliced
1 juniper berry, crushed
2 tablespoons water
⅓ cup sour cream
1 tablespoon flour
2 cups sauerkraut
1 cup Sauterne, not too dry

Rub birds inside with salt and pepper. Pin 2 strips of bacon with toothpicks firmly to each breast and fry in 3 tablespoons butter, turning until brown on all sides. Add shallots, carrots, juniper berry, and water; season and simmer gently, covered, until partridges are tender, 20-30 minutes, basting occasionally. Remove and keep hot. Blend flour with gravy, stir in sour cream, and boil gently about 2-3 minutes, or until well thickened. Season to taste and serve separately.

Meanwhile, wash and drain sauerkraut, put in covered pan with remaining butter and wine, and simmer gently for about 30 minutes or until sauerkraut is tender, adding a small amount of water if necessary to prevent burning. Cut partridges in half and pile sauerkraut around. Serves 2.

PARTRIDGES HUNTER STYLE

3 partridges, disjointed
3 tablespoons butter
1 medium-sized onion, chopped fine
1 carrot, chopped fine
1 teaspoon chopped thyme
1 teaspoon chopped parsley
3 tablespoons flour
1½ cups consommé
½ cup Sherry or Madeira
2 cups chopped mushrooms
salt and pepper

Brown pieces of partridge well in butter, add chopped onion, carrot, thyme, and parsley, and brown lightly. Stir in flour and gradually stir in consommé, wine, and chopped mushrooms. Season and simmer, covered, until partridge is tender, 15 to 30 minutes. Serve with croutons. Serves 3.

PARTRIDGES WITH CABBAGE

4 partridges
4 tablespoons vegetable oil
2 small heads cabbage
salt and pepper
4 slices bacon
1 pound small carrots, scraped
2 medium-sized onions, each stuck with a clove
1 bouquet garni (p. 9)
18 small sausages
2 cups chicken or veal stock
1 cup dry white wine
1 tablespoon flour
1 tablespoon butter

Brown partridges in oil in deep frying pan, turning frequently. Remove all outer leaves of cabbage which have any green color, shred white part, cover with boiling water, let stand 5 minutes, and drain thoroughly. Season. Place in bottom of a casserole with a tightly fitting lid; put birds on top with a slice of bacon on each. Add remaining ingredients with sausages on top. Cover, seal with flour paste, and put in moderate oven (350-375°) for 1½ hours. Thicken stock with roux of flour and butter. Serve with cabbage in center of platter, partridges on top, and sausages around sides. Pour sauce over. Serves 4.

GUINEA HEN WITH JUNIPER

6 juniper berries
6 tablespoons butter
1 (2-3 pound) guinea hen
salt and pepper
½ cup dry white wine

Make juniper butter as follows: Roast juniper berries in covered pan in oven until very dry, taking care not to scorch them. Pound in a mortar or grind to a powder and cream with 2 tablespoons butter. Spread mixture on inside cavity of bird as evenly as possible. Season and place in casserole with remaining butter and water. Put in hot oven (450-475°) uncovered about 20 minutes or until browned. Reduce heat quickly to slow (300-325°), turn bird over, and roast, covered, 25-30 minutes longer. Baste frequently. (Allow 18-20 minutes total roasting time per pound.) A few minutes before serving add wine and allow to heat thoroughly. Serves 2.

BREAST OF GUINEA HEN CUMBERLAND

(From Camil Virla, Chef, Hotel Mark Hopkins, San Francisco Calif.)

Breasts of 2 guinea hens, seasoned with salt and pepper
1 tablespoon butter
2 tablespoons vinegar
1 tablespoon currant jelly
1 teaspoon dry mustard
1 teaspoon chopped shallots
1 teaspoon lemon juice
1 orange peeling, shredded and parboiled
dash of tabasco
pinch of ground ginger
pinch of ground black pepper (freshly ground)
½ cup good Port Wine
¾ cup strong brown gravy

Place butter in a sauté-pan and when melted arrange breasts close together and cook them slowly about 25 minutes. Remove breasts from pan, add shallots, vinegar and half of the Port wine, boil down almost dry. Stir in currant jelly and ginger, then brown gravy and let simmer 10 minutes. Before serving add mustard, tabasco, pepper, orange peeling, and remainder of Port wine. Strain over breasts, bring to a boil, rectify seasoning. Serve with spiced cantaloupe circles, on croutons of fried hominy. Serves 4.

BREAST OF GUINEA HEN SAUCE GRENO

6 breasts of guinea hen, larded
4 tablespoons butter
⅓ cup sour cream
⅔ cup Brown Sauce (p. 28)
¼ cup dry white wine
½ teaspoon salt
dash cayenne
1 teaspoon lemon juice
¼ cup Sherry
3 cups croutons

Melt butter and pour over breasts in casserole, turning them so that they are evenly coated. Place them in moderately hot oven (375-400°) until they are well browned, turning occasionally. Remove and keep hot. Add sour cream, Brown Sauce, white wine, seasonings, and lemon juice to drippings in casserole and reduce by one third. Strain. Arrange breasts on bed of buttered croutons, stir Sherry into sauce, pour over breasts, and serve. Serves 6.

ROAST PHEASANT

1 pheasant (2-3 pounds)
1 medium-sized onion, chopped fine
1 teaspoon salt
⅛ teaspoon pepper
½ teaspoon poultry seasoning
2 cups fresh bread crumbs
1 cup hot water
1 cup Sherry
giblets (cooked and chopped)
1 small can mushrooms
1 teaspoon Maggi's seasoning
1 tablespoon flour

Stuff bird with mixture of onion, seasonings, and bread crumbs. Close opening and place breast down in shallow uncovered pan in moderately hot oven (375-400°). Baste with mixture of wine, hot water, and butter. Turn breast up after 25 minutes and continue roasting for 20 minutes longer. Remove pheasant to serving dish. Mix flour and a little of liquid in pan to a smooth paste and stir into remainder of liquid. Add giblets, Maggi's seasoning, and mushrooms and stir constantly over low heat about 5 minutes until gravy is well thickened. Serve separately. Serves 2.

GUINEA HEN FRICASSEE

6 slices bacon, diced
1 (3½-4 pound) guinea hen, disjointed
2 tablespoons flour
giblets, chopped
1 medium-sized onion, chopped
1 cup dry red wine
1 cup boiling water
salt
paprika

Fry bacon until crisp and remove. Dredge guinea hen pieces with flour and brown in bacon fat. Add giblets, onion, wine, and water and season. Be very liberal with the paprika. 1 level tablespoon of the common mild kind will not be too much. Cover and simmer gently for 2-2½ hours or until fowl is very tender. Serve with white or wild rice. Serves 4.

TURKEY EN GELÉE

1 (12-14 pound) turkey
pecan stuffing (p. 194)
salt and pepper
½ pound thinly sliced salt pork
1 tablespoon gelatin
1 cup water
1 large bouquet garni (p. 9)
2 medium-sized onions, sliced
2 medium-sized carrots, sliced
1 teaspoon ground cloves
2 cloves garlic, crushed and minced
1 teaspoon poultry seasoning
3 cups consommé
3 tablespoons brandy
2 cups dry white wine

Stuff turkey (pecan stuffing is preferred), and rub with salt and pepper. Cover bottom of a deep baking dish, preferably earthenware, with sliced salt pork. Dissolve gelatin in water, add together with all the other ingredients, and simmer, very slowly, for 5 to 6 hours. Turn turkey once when half cooked. Remove turkey and strain sauce. Pour sauce over turkey and place in refrigerator for 4 hours. Serves 12 to 14.

TURKEY RAGOUT

1½ cups turkey gravy, thickened, *or*
- 3 tablespoons butter
- 1 tablespoon flour
- 1½ cups clear gravy, stock, or consommé

salt and pepper
pinch of nutmeg
½ teaspoon Worcestershire sauce
1 teaspoon Angostura bitters
3 cups (approximately) cooked turkey, cut up
1 tablespoon cranberry jelly
¼ cup Sherry
6 slices toast

If you do not have thickened gravy left over, make a Brown Sauce (p. 28) with butter, flour, clear gravy, stock or consommé. Add seasonings, stir in turkey, and simmer 10 minutes. Stir in jelly and wine, bring just to a boil, and serve on toast. Serves 6.

PECAN STUFFING FOR TURKEY

4 cups bread crumbs, well browned
½ cup boiling water
½ cup butter
6 hard-cooked eggs
1 teaspoon salt
½ teaspoon pepper
1 teaspoon thyme
1 teaspoon mace
1 teaspoon powdered celery seed
2 tablespoons chopped parsley
2 cups chopped pecans
1 cup chopped mushrooms
2 medium-sized onions, chopped
1 turkey liver, boiled and chopped
½ cup Sherry

Mix bread crumbs to a paste with boiling water. Add egg yolks and 6 tablespoons of butter, and rub smooth. Dice egg whites very fine and mix all in the bread paste together with the seasonings, nuts, and mushrooms. Brown the onions and the turkey liver in 2 tablespoons butter, and add with the wine. Stuffing for 1 medium-sized turkey.

ROAST GOOSE WITH SAUERKRAUT

1 (10-12 pound) goose
3 teaspoons salt
½ teaspoon pepper
2 tablespoons goose fat
1 large onion, sliced
2 pounds sauerkraut
1 teaspoon caraway seeds
1 teaspoon paprika
2 medium-sized potatoes, grated
½ cup dry white wine

Remove nearly all fat from inside of goose, wipe inside with damp cloth, and rub in half the salt and pepper. Heat 2 tablespoons fat until grease is tried out and fry onion in fat to golden brown. Wash and drain sauerkraut. Mix in onion together with rest of salt and pepper, caraway and paprika and bring to a simmer. Add grated potato, stir until thickened, and add wine. If too moist, add more grated potato. Stuff goose and truss, and roast in moderately slow oven (325-350°) 20 to 25 minutes per pound. Serve with dumplings and unthickened goose gravy. Serves 10 to 12.

POULTRY STUFFING

giblets, cooked and chopped
giblet stock
1½ cups (approximately) browned bread crumbs
1 cup celery, chopped
1 small onion, chopped
1 cup Sauterne
⅓ cup evaporated milk
2 eggs, lightly beaten
1 teaspoon chopped parsley
2 tablespoons melted butter
1 tablespoon poultry seasoning
1 teaspoon Maggi's seasoning
salt
pepper

Cook giblets in small saucepan in just enough water to cover; reduce stock to about ¼ cup. Knead all ingredients together. If too dry add more milk. Stuffing enough for 1 large chicken or duck; double recipe for turkey or goose.

SAVORY OYSTER STUFFING

4 cups soft bread crumbs
1 teaspoon salt
½ teaspoon sage
¼ teaspoon thyme
⅛ teaspoon nutmeg
1 egg, slightly beaten
2 cups melted butter
2 cups oysters, very coarsely chopped
½ cup Sauterne

Combine all dry ingredients and mix thoroughly. Add egg, butter, chopped oysters, and wine and mix well. Stuffing for 1 small turkey

CAPER STUFFING

2 cups fresh bread crumbs
2 tablespoons chopped shallots or onions
2 tablespoons crushed capers
1 tablespoon minced parsley
2 tablespoons melted butter
salt and pepper
2 tablespoons dry white wine

Mix all ingredients together. This makes a fairly dry dressing. If you prefer it a bit more moist, add 1 to 2 tablespoons of milk or cream.

GROUSE EN CASSEROLE

2 grouse
6 tablespoons butter
grated peel ½ orange
grated peel ½ lemon
12 juniper berries
¼ cup dry white wine (Chablis preferred)
2 tablespoons brandy

Sauté birds in 3 tablespoons butter about 20 minutes or until golden brown. Place in casserole with fat from pan and remaining butter, melted, orange and lemon peel, and juniper berries, and pour in wine. Cook in moderate oven (350-375°) 15 minutes, basting occasionally. Remove birds to serving dish, skim fat from gravy, and strain. Light brandy and when flames begin to die down add to sauce, pour over birds, and serve. Serves 2 to 4.

SQUAB EN CASSEROLE

4 small or 2 jumbo squabs
Parsley Dressing
4 slices bacon
4 tablespoons butter
2 cups tiny canned peas
1 chopped onion, sautéed
1 cup sliced mushrooms
2 tablespoons Sherry
salt and pepper

Stuff squabs with your favorite dressing, to which 4 tablespoons chopped parsley have been added. Put breast down in baking dish with a strip of bacon on top of each. Dot with butter and put in moderate oven (350-375°) for 35 minutes. Add more butter from time to time and baste frequently. Put peas and onions in casserole. Remove squabs from baking pan and put in casserole. Add mushrooms and Sherry to liquid left in baking pan, and simmer until mushrooms are tender. Pour over squabs and return to oven for 10 minutes. Serves 2 to 4.

SQUAB PIE BURGUNDY

4 medium-sized squabs split in half
4 tablespoons butter
3 tablespoons brandy
8 very small onions
½ cup diced cooked ham
livers and gizzards, chopped
½ cup Burgundy
½ cup chicken broth
salt
pepper
½ recipe plain pastry

Brown squab lightly in butter on both sides, cover, and cook over low heat 10-15 minutes. Pour in brandy, light it, and when flames have died add onions, ham, giblets, and wine and simmer slowly about 5 minutes more. Put all in casserole and add chicken broth. Roll pastry about ¼ inch thick, moisten edges of casserole, and put on like top crust of pie, but do not make any incisions, as steam must do most of cooking. Bake in moderate oven (350-375°) for 45 minutes or until crust is brown. Serves 4.

ROASTED SQUAB CREOLE STYLE

6 shallots, chopped
1 tablespoon butter
1½ cups cooked wild rice
¾ cup piñon or pistachio nuts
salt and pepper
4 small squabs or 2 jumbo squabs
bacon slices
½ cup Port

Sauté shallots in butter until tender but not brown. Mix with rice and nuts, and stuff squabs. Wrap 2 slices of bacon over breast of each squab, holding in place with toothpicks. Bake in hot oven (400-450°), uncovered, until brown, about 20-30 minutes. Add Port about 10 minutes before they are done and baste frequently. Serves 2 to 4.

SQUAB ROYALE

4 jumbo squab split in half
4 tablespoons olive oil or vegetable oil
4 tablespoons butter
½ cup dry white wine
salt and pepper
3 shallots, minced
4 squab livers, chopped
2 chicken livers, chopped
4 whole cloves
2 small cans button mushrooms

Brown squab halves in hot fat on both sides. Add wine, season, and simmer, covered, for 25 minutes. Add shallots, livers, cloves, and mushrooms and simmer about 10 minutes longer or until sauce is almost entirely reduced. Serves 4.

Excellent with wild rice.

SQUAB VERMOUTH

½ cup finely chopped mushrooms
3 tablespoons butter
1 cup dry bread crumbs
¼ cup finely chopped pecans
milk
salt and pepper
1 cup dry Vermouth
4 jumbo squab
4 slices bacon, cut in half

Sauté mushrooms lightly in butter, add bread crumbs, and salt to taste; add 1 tablespoon Vermouth and enough milk to just bind all together, and stuff squabs. Place in roasting pan with 2 half-slices of bacon on breast of each squab. Roast in very hot oven (450-500°), basting frequently and generously with Vermouth for about 20 minutes or until tender. Serve individually on hot buttered toast with sauce poured over. Serves 4.

KYCKLING LEFVER

(Swedish)

8 chicken livers
2 tablespoons butter
¼ cup chopped lean beef
1 tablespoon flour
1 cup water
½ pound mushrooms, sliced
½ cup Sherry
salt and pepper

Cut livers in two, sauté 2-3 minutes in butter, and remove. Put in beef and brown. Blend in flour and stir in water gradually. Simmer 3 minutes, stirring constantly. Put in livers and mushrooms, wine and seasonings. Cover and simmer 20 minutes. Serves 4.

RABBIT POT PIE

¼ pound cream cheese
4 hard-cooked eggs
4 slices bacon, fried and chopped
1 teaspoon salt
⅛ teaspoon pepper
4 cups cooked rabbit meat, cut up
2 cups consommé
juice of ½ lemon
½ cup Sherry
½ recipe plain pastry

Mash cream cheese and eggs to a paste, and mix in chopped bacon and seasonings. Place ⅓ of rabbit meat in bottom of large greased casserole, cover with ⅓ of cream cheese and egg mixture; repeat until all is used. Mix consommé, lemon juice, and Sherry and pour over all. Cover with pastry. Bake for 10 minutes in very hot oven (450-500°), then reduce heat to moderate (350-375°) until top is well browned, about 20 minutes. Serves 6.

RABBIT STEW NO. I

½ pound salt pork, diced
3 tablespoons butter
10 or 12 very small white onions, quartered
1 (2½-3 pound) rabbit, cut in small pieces
1 tablespoon flour
2 cups bouillon
1 cup dry white wine
1 bouquet garni (p. 9)
salt
pepper

Fry salt pork until golden, add butter and onions, and sauté until tender. Put in pieces of meat and brown. Stir in flour and gradually add bouillon and wine. Add bouquet garni and simmer 1½ to 2 hours or until rabbit is tender. Serves 4.

RABBIT STEW NO. II

2 (2½-3 pound) young rabbits, disjointed
4 cups water
½ cup vinegar
flour
salt and pepper
¼ pound bacon, diced
¼ pound fat salt pork, sliced thin
rabbit livers
1 bay leaf
½ cup Port
¼ cup browned flour
2 tablespoons butter

Put rabbit pieces in crock, cover with water and vinegar, and marinate 4 to 8 hours, or longer if possible. Remove, drain well, and dredge with seasoned flour. Fry bacon until crisp and remove. Sauté rabbit in bacon fat until well browned. Fasten a thin strip of salt pork about 1 inch wide with a toothpick to each piece of rabbit; place in pot with rabbit livers, fried bacon, and bay leaf. Cover with cold water, add salt and pepper, bring to a boil, and simmer until very tender, about 1½ to 2 hours. Remove livers, mash thoroughly, mix to a paste with a little wine, and add together with rest of wine. Mix butter and browned flour to a paste and stir in gradually. Cook gently, stirring constantly, 10 minutes. Remove bay leaf and serve in tureen, garnished with parsley. Serves 6.

CIVET OF RABBIT

¾ pound salt pork
3 tablespoons butter
¾ pound very small white onions
2 (2½-3 pound) young rabbits, cut up for frying
1½ tablespoons flour
3 cups beef bouillon
¾ cup dry white wine
1 bay leaf
2 teaspoons chopped parsley
2 teaspoons chopped thyme
salt and pepper

Pour boiling water over salt pork, let stand 5 minutes, drain, and dice. Try out in frying pan until golden, then discard. Add butter. Add onions and sauté slowly, covered, stirring occasionally, until brown, or about 15 minutes. Remove onions and keep hot. Put in rabbit pieces and fry slowly until golden on all sides. Remove. Blend in flour and add bouillon, wine, herbs, and seasonings. Add rabbits and simmer gently, covered, until tender, about 1½ to 2 hours. Serve with sauce poured over and surrounded by browned onions. Serves 6.

ROAST HARE ENGLISH STYLE

2 hare, hindquarters only, larded
20 whole cloves
30 whole allspice
6 whole peppercorns
8 bay leaves
1 medium-sized onion, sliced
2 teaspoons salt
dry white wine
cider or wine vinegar
¼ cup vegetable oil
12-18 gingersnaps, crushed
1 cup sour cream

Marinate hare in spices and onion with enough wine and vinegar in equal proportions to cover, for 24 hours, turning several times. Brown well in hot oil in heavy covered vessel. Add strained marinating liquor and simmer, covered, about 1½ hours or until hare is tender. Add water if necessary. Remove hare to hot serving dish, add sour cream to liquid, and thicken with crushed gingersnaps, reducing if necessary. Pour over hare and serve. Serves 4.

LAPINO (HARE ITALIAN STYLE)

1 young Belgian hare
5 cloves
3 bay leaves
4 chili peppers
dry white wine
salt and pepper
1 teaspoon poultry seasoning
1 teaspoon paprika
flour
½ cup olive oil
4 medium-sized onions
2 carrots, sliced
½ pound mushrooms, sliced
12 olives, pitted and sliced

Have hare cut up as for frying. Put in a crock and add all the spices except the poultry seasoning and paprika. Add enough wine to just cover and marinate two to four days.

Remove, wipe dry, and dust with salt, pepper, poultry seasoning, and paprika. Flour well and brown in olive oil. Put in casserole with onions, carrots, mushrooms, and olives and add enough of the wine in which the hare was marinated to half cover. Cover and simmer until hare is tender, about 1¼ hours. Serves 6.

ROAST LEG OF VENISON WITH SOUR CREAM

4 medium-sized onions, sliced
4 medium-sized carrots, sliced
6 stalks celery, sliced
6 bay leaves
1 cup water
1 (6-7 pound) leg of venison
½ pound fat salt pork, sliced
salt and pepper
½ cup butter
1 cup flour
3 cups sour cream
1½ cups dry red wine
1½ cups currant jelly

Put vegetables and bay leaf in baking pan, and add water. Put in meat, skin side up. Place in very hot oven (450-500°) until browned, 20-30 minutes. Turn and cover with strips of salt pork and season. Reduce oven temperature to moderate (350-375°) and roast, approximately 30 minutes to the pound or until meat thermometer shows 180°. Remove meat, strain liquid, and skim. Melt butter, add flour, then add to strained liquid. Gradually add sour cream, jelly, and wine and simmer until thick. Serves 10 to 14. (Leg of lamb may be substituted for venison.)

ROAST LEG OF VENISON DANISH STYLE

1 (6-7 pound) leg of venison
½ pound fat salt pork
1½ teaspoons salt
¼ teaspoon pepper
⅛ teaspoon ginger
1 cup butter or vegetable oil
3 cups condensed beef consommé
3 tablespoons flour
2½ tablespoons butter
2 tablespoons currant jelly
⅓ cup dry white wine
½ teaspoon grated orange rind
¼ cup Sherry
¾ cup sour cream
2 tablespoons currant jelly

Cut fat pork in strips about ¼ inch by 2 inches and lard venison. Place venison in roaster and pour over melted butter or oil. Roast in moderate oven (350-375°) until done, about 30 minutes per pound, or until a meat thermometer shows 180°. Baste frequently but do not add water. When done remove from pan. Skim off as much fat as possible. Blend flour and butter, and mix to a smooth paste with drippings. Stir in white wine and bring to a simmer. Add Sherry and currant jelly, and simmer 3 minutes. Garnish roast with small pieces of jelly and serve gravy separately. Serves 10 to 14.

CHAPTER EIGHT

Eggs and Cheese

Someone once remarked that if eggs cost a dollar apiece they would be the greatest delicacy in the world. Certainly they are as nearly indispensable in cooking as any item we can think of.

And because of their delicate flavor there is not one single egg dish with which wine cannot be combined. This may seem at first like a sweeping statement and you may be inclined to question it. "How about soft boiled or coddled eggs?" Try stirring them up with a spoonful of Port or Sherry, especially when serving them to an invalid or convalescent. Or poach them in Burgundy, and serve with the well-reduced wine poured over for an epicurean masterpiece; or hard-cooked and pickled in red wine for a relish or a glowing garnish, or in white wine for an indescribably delicious new flavor; or scrambled with a hint, no more, of wine, any kind. Omelets, soufflés of all kinds, can be lifted to a higher plane by the judicious use of wine.

For the benefit of those to whom the kitchen is still a bit strange, may we say just a word about egg cookery. Of course, you have often heard the phrase, "she can't even boil an egg." Well, she shouldn't. Really good cooks *never* boil eggs. In fact, eggs in any form should always be cooked at low heat. That's why modern cook books always refer to "hard-cooked" or "soft-cooked" eggs, never "hard-boiled" or "soft-boiled." For soft-cooked eggs, put them in a quart of *cold* water and bring to a boil—for more than four or six, increase the amount of water correspondingly. If you want them really soft, take them out at once; for medium, remove from heat, cover, and leave from two to four minutes. To coddle, bring a quart or more of water to a vigorous boil, remove from heat, slip in the eggs with a spoon, and cover. Allow them four minutes for soft, six for medium, and eight to ten for slightly hard. Puncture the large end with a pin and they won't crack when they hit the hot water. Either method insures a perfect, even texture all the way through. Tough whites and runny yolks are out of the question.

Even when you want eggs really hard you don't actually boil them. The secret is in having the water just below simmering, or, as the French say, "trembling," and leave them for 15 to 20 minutes. Then cover with cold water. Eggs cooked this way will be delicate and firm in texture, easy to peel; and you'll find that the usual dark ring around the yolks will be almost wholly absent.

There's a bit of a knack about poaching eggs. Use the largest frying pan you can find and a skimmer or large slotted spoon. Put in one inch of water, about one tablespoon vinegar, and one teaspoon salt per quart of water and bring to a boil. Break the eggs, one by one into cups—yes, cups, it saves time in the end—one for each egg, and slip carefully in the water to avoid breaking the yolk. Reduce the heat immediately until the water is just simmering and cover. When the yolk is covered with a white film, remove from heat and lift them out with skimmer or spoon. Don't try to do more than four at once.

Is there more than one way to fry an egg? Yes, and if you'll try this one just once you won't ever go back to the old-fashioned way again. Use a tablespoon of butter or bacon fat for each egg and *two teaspoonfuls of water*. When the butter or fat is melted, put in an egg and tilt the frying pan until the egg begins to firm. Do that with each egg, and they'll keep their individuality and be easy to remove whole. Turn down the heat very low, cover, and let them cook in steam. When they're done to your taste, remove with a pancake turner. No frizzled, tough edges, just the best eggs you'll want to taste.

To many people, soufflés and omelets are the higher mathematics of egg cookery. Certainly some grim messes are too often served under these names. In reality, they are extremely easy, and there are just a few simple rules which must be rigidly followed to guarantee invariable success. Here they are:

For soufflés, first make a White Sauce (p. 27); second, allow to cool slightly before adding the well-beaten egg yolks; third, fold in whites, beaten until they stand up in peaks. Do this gently. Set the baking dish in a pan of hot water and bake in a medium oven. They are done when a cake straw comes out dry from the center. Take the same precautions to avoid falling that you would with a cake. Serve at once. No more than a pampered debutante will they tolerate being kept waiting.

There are two basic types of omelets which are generally recognized, fluffy and French.

First, the foundation recipe for fluffy omelet:

4 eggs, separated
½ teaspoon salt
pinch of white pepper
¼ cup milk
1 tablespoon butter

First, beat yolks until very thick. Five minutes is not too much. This is vital. Mix with milk and seasonings. Second, beat whites until stiff, not dry, and fold yolk and milk mixture into them. Third, melt butter in the thickest 9-inch frying pan you have, pour in mixture, and cook over *low* heat, not less than three minutes or more than five. After it puffs up well, lift edge gently with a spatula and, as soon as it is *slightly* browned, put it in a moderate oven (350-375°) until a cake straw comes out clean, 10 to 15 minutes. Fourth, score across center with spatula and fold.

French omelets use the same ingredients in the same proportions. The difference in preparation is that yolks and whites are beaten together and added to milk and seasonings. Melt butter over low heat and, when it just begins to sizzle, pour in egg mixture. Now comes the part which is so seldom clearly explained and which is the only secret of a perfect French omelet. As soon as the mixture begins to thicken lift the edge away from you with a spatula and tilt the pan so that some of the uncooked mixture can run underneath. Repeat on the side nearest you and on the other two sides. When bottom is browned, fold or roll it as you prefer. French omelets should be quite moist.

Cheese and wine have always been inseparably connected. *Au naturel*, they form the perfect ending for any meal from the simplest to the most elaborate. To develop the fullest possibilities of cheese cookery, wine is essential. And don't forget that every time you use a different type of wine you produce a different dish.

When war resulted in the virtual disappearance of imported varieties, cheese lovers mourned and demanded that something be done about it. Something was. American cheese makers discovered they could exactly duplicate many of the most famous imported types and approximate many of the rest so closely that only an expert can tell the difference.

One of the most favored imported delicacies, whose cost, unfortunately, put it in the luxury class, was cheese in wine. Now, by the use of our own products, you can make them yourself and serve them as freely as you will. Here is the easiest way: with an ordinary table knife, cut four evenly spaced cylindrical plugs from the cheese. Cut off about one inch from the top and bottom of each plug. Replace four of the short pieces in the bottom, turn the cheese over, and with the handle of the knife ram down the plug until it fits tightly. Fill the holes with wine—for instance, Port for Stilton, Sherry for Gorgonzola, Sauterne for Cheddar and Edam—and put in the top plugs. Every day or two change the position of the cheese so the wine has a chance to permeate every part. It will take about two weeks to complete the process, but the result is well worth while.

Another method is to cream the cheese with the wine and pack it in jars. The texture is not the same but the flavor is, and it is especially recommended for small quantities.

Try wrapping a piece of the milder types in a cloth saturated with one of the milder dry wines, covering tightly, and leaving in a cool place for a week or two. The result will surprise you.

Remember, any cheese dish can be completely ruined by too much heat. Chewy rarebits, for example, are an indigestible abomination, yet, how often do you get a perfect one? In any cheese dish, make it a rule to use the lowest heat for the shortest time.

MATELOTE OF EGGS

3 tablespoons chopped onion
2 tablespoons minced celery
1 clove garlic, crushed and minced
3 tablespoons butter
1 sprig thyme
1 small bay leaf
⅓ cup water
1 cup dry red wine
1 tablespoon flour
salt and pepper
4 eggs
1 tablespoon minced parsley

Sauté onion, celery, and garlic in 2 tablespoons butter until tender but not brown. Add thyme, bay leaf, water, and wine and simmer 20 minutes. Strain. Make Beurre Manié by kneading together remaining butter and flour, add, and stir 5 minutes over low heat. Put in baking dish, break in eggs, season, and put in moderate oven (350-375°) until eggs are set, about 10 minutes. Sprinkle with parsley. Serves 4.

EGGS MALAGAÑA

4 eggs
¾ cup canned peas
¾ cup sliced and sautéed mushrooms
12 cooked shrimp, cut up
4 small sausages, fried and cut up
4 tablespoons Sherry
salt and pepper

Break one egg in each of four custard cups or large individual ramekins, taking care not to break yolk. Add to each 3 tablespoons peas, 3 tablespoons mushrooms, 3 shrimp, 1 sausage, and 1 tablespoon Sherry. Season and put in moderate oven (350-375°) for about 15 minutes or until the white of the egg is set. Serves 4.

TIPSY EGGS

3 cups Chestnut Sauce (p. 33)
8 slices bacon, fried
4 eggs
salt
pepper
dash of cayenne
3 tablespoons melted butter
3 tablespoons dry red wine

Place chestnut sauce in layer in bottom of buttered casserole, lay crisp bacon slices on top, break in eggs, and season. Beat melted butter and wine together, and add. Bake in moderate oven (350-375°) until eggs are set. Sprinkle with paprika. Serves 4.

EGGS BELGIAN

3 tablespoons butter
6 hard-cooked eggs, coarsely chopped
½ cup shrimp
½ teaspoon dry mustard
1 tablespoon chopped parsley
1 cup cream
2 tablespoons dry Sherry
½ teaspoon salt
dash of cayenne
paprika

Melt butter, add other ingredients, and stir gently over low heat until it just begins to simmer. Serve on toast and dust with paprika. Serves 4.

EGGS IN TOMATO NESTS

4 very large tomatoes
4 eggs
2 tablespoons butter
4 tablespoons dry white wine
salt and pepper

Peel tomatoes, cut out 1-inch section from stem ends, and scoop out centers. Break 1 egg in each, and add ½ tablespoon butter and 1 tablespoon wine. Season and bake in moderate oven (350-375°) 15 to 20 minutes or until eggs are firm but not hard. Serves 4.

SHIRRED EGGS BERCY AU GRATIN

Butter ramekins, line with thin slices cooked sausage, add 1 tablespoon Sauce Bercy (p. 40), break in egg, top with buttered bread crumbs. Put on baking sheet or shallow pan and bake in moderate oven (350-375°) until eggs are set, about 15-20 minutes.

KIDNEY OMELET

1 tablespoon chopped onion
2 tablespoons butter
½ bay leaf
6 whole peppers
1 teaspoon flour
4 bouillon cubes
2 tablespoons boiling water
3 tablespoons Sherry
½ teaspoon salt
¼ teaspoon pepper
3 lamb kidneys or equivalent (p. 111)
3 eggs, separated

Cook onion in 1 tablespoon butter with bay leaf and peppers for 5 minutes without browning. Add flour and stir about 1 minute. Dissolve bouillon cubes in boiling water and add together with Sherry, salt, and pepper. Cut prepared kidneys in small slices and cook 5 minutes in sauce. Beat egg whites stiff but not dry. Add 2 tablespoons cold water and ½ teaspoon salt to yolks, and beat until lemon colored. Fold into whites. Melt remaining 1 tablespoon butter in omelet pan or medium-sized frying pan, put in kidney mixture, and when it begins to boil add eggs. Do not stir but, when eggs begin to set, slip a spatula or knife under the omelet to prevent sticking and shake pan to and fro occasionally. When light brown on bottom place under broiler to brown the top. Serves 4 to 6.

OMELET GLACÉ

6 eggs
3 tablespoons powdered sugar
½ teaspoon salt
½ cup Wine Chaudeau (p. 266)

Beat eggs with 1 tablespoon sugar and salt until creamy. Make omelet (p. 206), fold, sprinkle with remaining sugar, and place close to broiler until sugar is slightly caramelized. Pour Chaudeau around. Serves 4.

MUSHROOM OMELET

3 tablespoons butter
½ cup chopped mushrooms
2 tablespoons lemon juice
½ cup dry white wine
6 eggs
salt and pepper

Sauté mushrooms in 2 tablespoons butter over high heat until butter is slightly brown. Add lemon juice and wine, reduce heat, and simmer until mushrooms are tender. Make omelet (p. 206). When done place part of mushrooms in center and fold. Place on serving dish, and pour rest of mushrooms and sauce on top. Serves 4.

EGGS BENEDICT

8 ⅛-inch slices broiled ham, about 4 inches square
8 slices thin buttered toast, crusts removed, *or*
4 English muffins, split, toasted, and buttered
8 poached eggs
2 cups Hollandaise Sauce with Sauterne (p. 48)

Place 1 slice boiled ham on each slice toast or muffin; lay on poached egg. Pour Hollandaise Sauce over. Serves 4.

POACHED EGGS ESPAGNOLE

4 poached eggs
4 slices buttered toast
1 cup Sauce Espagnole (p. 35)
salt and paprika
minced parsley

Place a poached egg on each slice of toast, pour on ¼ cup Sauce Espagnole, season, and sprinkle with chopped parsley. Serves 4.

OMELET SAUTERNE

(from Gretchen Green—The Whole World & Co.)

Make a flat French omelet. Fold it over orange marmalade or any type of marmalade. Pour over it a dry Sauterne.

SHERRY CHEESE SOUFFLÉ

4 tablespoons butter
4 tablespoons flour
½ teaspoon salt
¾ cup milk
¼ cup Sherry
½ cup grated American cheese
4 eggs, separated

Blend flour with butter, add salt, and gradually stir in milk and Sherry. Add cheese and cook until thick, about 2 to 3 minutes, stirring constantly. Remove from heat and allow to cool 10 to 15 minutes. Add well-beaten egg yolks gradually. Beat whites until they are stiff but not dry and fold in gently. Pour into greased baking dish, place in pan of hot water, and bake in moderate oven (350-375°) 50-60 minutes or until a toothpick stuck in the center comes out dry and the edges pull away slightly from the baking dish. Serves 6.

SOUFFLÉ ROLAND

4 tablespoons butter
4 tablespoons flour
¾ cup milk
¼ cup Sherry
½ teaspoon salt
½ cup black olives, pitted and coarsely chopped
½ cup mushrooms, sliced and sautéed lightly
3 tablespoons sliced almonds
4 eggs, separated

Blend flour with butter, add salt and gradually stir in milk and Sherry; cook until thick, about 2 to 3 minutes, stirring constantly. Remove from heat and stir in olives, mushrooms, and nuts. Cool. Add well-beaten egg yolks gradually. Beat whites until they are stiff but not dry and fold in gently. Pour into greased baking dish, place in pan of hot water, and bake in moderate oven (350-375°) 50-60 minutes or until a toothpick stuck in the center comes out dry and the edges pull away slightly from the baking dish. Serves 6.

CHEESE PIE

½ recipe pastry
¾ cup minced onions
1 4-ounce box Swiss cheese (processed)
4 medium-sized tomatoes, peeled and sliced
flour
1 cup cream
½ cup Sauterne, not too dry
1 3-ounce can anchovies, chopped fine
3 tablespoons butter

Line 9-inch pie tin with crust and spread in minced onions; crumble cheese and arrange over onions. Dip tomato slices in flour and use for next layer. Sprinkle in chopped anchovies, pour in cream, add wine, and dot with butter. Bake in slow oven (300-325°) for 40-50 minutes. Do not serve until ½ hour after removing from oven. Serves 6 to 8.

NEUFCHATEL FONDUE

1 pound Swiss cheese, grated
3 tablespoons flour
1 cup Chablis or Riesling
1 clove garlic, crushed
salt and pepper
dash of nutmeg
¼ cup Kirsch
French bread

Stir grated cheese and flour together until thoroughly mixed. Rub small cooking dish or top of chafing dish with garlic and heat wine until it just begins to simmer. Add cheese and flour mixture, and stir constantly until cheese is melted. Season to taste, omitting nutmeg if preferred. As soon as fondue starts to bubble, stir in Kirsch and serve immediately, preferably in chafing dish or over electric plate. Serve with French bread, which each guest tears in small pieces and "dunks" in fondue with a fork. Serves 6.

RAREBIT WITH SHERRY

1 cup Medium White Sauce (p. 27)
¼ cup Sherry
2 cups grated soft cheese
salt and pepper
dash of Worcestershire sauce

Place White Sauce, wine, cheese, and seasonings in top of double boiler and stir constantly in one direction until smooth. Serve at once on buttered toast. Do not overcook. Serves 4.

MONKEY

1 cup grated Cheddar cheese
¾ cup light cream
¼ cup Sherry
1 cup bread crumbs, toasted
½ teaspoon salt
¼ teaspoon paprika
½ teaspoon English mustard
1 egg, lightly beaten
4 slices buttered toast

Cook cheese, cream, Sherry, and toasted crumbs in double boiler until cheese is melted. Add seasonings and egg, and cook, stirring constantly, about 1 minute. Pour over toast (or toasted, buttered English muffins). Serves 4.

CHEESE PUDDING

3 cups cottage cheese
3 tablespoons melted butter
¾ cup cream
¾ cup dry white wine
¾ cup sugar
3 eggs, separated
1 tablespoon lemon juice
½ teaspoon salt

Blend cheese, butter, cream, and wine in order and beat until smooth. Beat egg yolks with sugar and add. Beat egg whites with salt until stiff but not dry and fold in. Bake in casserole or individual ramekins in slow oven (250-325°) until set, about 35-45 minutes. Serves 6.

CHEESE CURLS

2½ cups sifted flour
¾ teaspoon salt
1 teaspoon baking powder
1½ cups grated cheese
¾ cup shortening
⅓ cup Sherry, iced

Sift flour, salt, and baking powder. Mix grated cheese and shortening, and mix into flour mixture with fingertips until like coarse sand. Add wine, a spoonful at a time. Place on floured board and roll out ¼ inch thick. Cut in 4-inch strips, ½ inch wide, and curl up like a watch spring. Bake in hot oven (400-450°) until lightly browned, about 15 minutes. Approximately 20 curls.

GENEVA CHEESE PUDDING

1 pound Swiss cheese, sliced ¼ inch thick
2 tablespoons butter
8-10 slices white bread, crusts removed
3 eggs
2½ cups milk
½ cup dry white wine
1 teaspoon salt
⅛ teaspoon mace or nutmeg

Butter a deep baking dish, using 2 tablespoons butter. Cover bottom with sliced bread, add layer of cheese, and repeat until all cheese is used. More or less bread may be needed according to size of slices. Beat eggs with milk, wine, salt, and mace or nutmeg and pour over top. Let stand for 15 minutes to allow bread to become thoroughly soaked. Put in pan of hot water and bake in moderate oven (350-375°) for 30 minutes. Serves 4 to 6.

CHAPTER NINE

Vegetables, Salads, and Salad Dressings

One who has never become really acquainted with the kitchen of a great hotel or restaurant has missed an extremely interesting experience. Here you will find the strictest kind of class system and the relative status of each member is gauged by the importance of his work as well as the ability of the individual. Overlord of all, of course, is the chef. His authority is absolute. His chieftains are the heads of departments, and here you will find specialization carried to the *n*th degree. Perhaps you would expect to find the vegetable chef near the bottom of the list, but, on the contrary, he is well up in the hierarchy. The reason is that every chef knows an indifferently prepared vegetable dish can mar the finest meal, while a really fine one can raise it to the heights. Perhaps we can learn something from their experience.

First, see how seldom vegetables are actually boiled. Waterless cooking had its origin here, and the small amount of liquid left is almost invariably used in soups or sauces. Steaming is in favor too, and pressure cookers are increasingly in use, especially the smaller two- and four-quart sizes for the quick preparation of small quantities. You may be surprised to notice that baking temperatures are as carefully watched here as in every other part of the kitchen. Also, see how low they are. Overcooking of vegetables, they will tell you, is a cardinal sin and one of the commonest.

Wine, of course, is used in endless variations and what subtleties of flavor it evokes! No vegetable is too lowly to resist its transformation. Perhaps you are one of those who can't see any place for turnips among civilized people. Try Gloire Turnips on page 230. Kraut—no? See Sauerkraut with White Wine on page 231.

The possible vegetable and sauce combinations are endless. Those given in this chapter are intended only to give you a conception of what may be done. Each one will give you ideas for a dozen others.

What can we learn from these experts about salads? That the ingredients must be fresh, well washed, crisp? We know that. Selection of ingredients? The only problem here is where to stop. Practically everything edible that grows above or below the ground is a possibility. It has been appropriately remarked that "age can wither but custom cannot stale their infinite variety."

Just a hint. When freshening leafy vegetables or cucumbers, a little lemon juice added to the water does wonders.

All authorities agree that cider or malt vinegar is too harsh for salads and is apt to overpower the more delicate flavors unless used with extreme caution. Wine vinegars we may consider too expensive for everyday use. Ready-made ones do come high, but you can make as fine a vinegar as money will buy simply by leaving a bottle of unfortified wine uncorked at room temperature, and this at a cost very little more than you pay for the best cider or malt vinegar. (You will quickly learn never to throw away wine leftovers.) A scum will form on top, and a cloudy, jellylike substance will appear and grow. Don't worry—these are essential. When the vinegar is done, strain it and throw away the scum, but put back a spoonful or two of the gelatinous "mother" in some more wine or a bit of vinegar as a starter for the next batch. You will find your white-wine vinegar a bit more delicate than the red, and there is a definite field for each.

Once start making herb vinegars, and your pantry shelves will be filled with them. The most commonly used are tarragon, thyme, marjoram, basil, chervil, mint, and parsley. There is hardly any salad dressing that can't be improved by one or more of these, and, remember, for a full complement, you'll want each type in both white- and red-wine vinegars. The making of them is simplicity itself. Use an earthenware crock, one third filled with fresh herbs, or one quarter full of dry herbs, pour in the wine vinegar of your choice to the top, and cover. Tarragon will take two weeks to mature, the rest will be ready for use in ten days. Then, strain once, twice if necessary, and bottle. But don't throw away the herb. Put it in a jar covered with vinegar to chop and use when you need its help in salads and sauces.

Many porous vegetables such as carrots, celery, etc. achieve an extra touch of distinction by being marinated in wine or wine vinegar for half an hour or so before using.

Comparatively few salad recipes are given in this chapter because few people ever make exactly the same salad twice and a recipe is only a temptation to experiment. And that's as it should be.

ARTICHOKES IN WHITE WINE

6 small artichokes
1 onion, minced
1 clove garlic, crushed and minced
2 teaspoons salt
1 tablespoon vegetable oil
1 cup Sauterne

Cut off tops and stems of artichokes and remove outside leaves. Place upright in pot. Add onions, garlic, and salt. Pour oil and wine over all, cover tightly, and allow to simmer slowly. Add more wine if necessary. Cook 45 minutes or until hearts are tender. Serves 6.

ARTICHOKES SPANISH STYLE

4 medium-sized artichokes
4 teaspoons saffron
2 shallots, chopped
½ small clove garlic, crushed and minced
1 tablespoon olive oil or vegetable oil
1 tablespoon lemon juice
1½ cups Sauce Espagnole (p. 35)
salt

Cut off tops and stems of artichokes and remove outside leaves. Cook in rapidly boiling salted water to which saffron has been added until bottoms can easily be pierced with a fork, about 30-40 minutes. Remove, turn upside down, and drain. Sauté shallots and garlic in oil until golden, add to Sauce Espagnole together with lemon juice, and season to taste. Quarter artichokes, pour sauce over them, and place in oven to reheat. Serves 4.

KIDNEY BEANS BURGUNDY STYLE

2 tablespoons butter
1 medium-sized onion, chopped
pinch of ground cloves
1 bouquet garni (p. 9)
½ cup dry red wine
salt and pepper
3 cups canned red kidney beans

Brown onion lightly in butter. Add all other ingredients except beans, season to taste, and simmer gently about 10 minutes. Remove bouquet garni, add beans, and stir until they begin to simmer. Serves 6.

CALIFORNIA BEANS

2 tablespoons olive oil or vegetable oil
1 medium-sized onion, chopped
1 teaspoon chopped parsley
¼ cup Sauterne, not dry
1 can kidney beans

Sauté onion in oil until just tender, add parsley, wine, and beans, and simmer gently over low heat, stirring occasionally, until wine is absorbed. Serves 4.

BOSTON BAKED BEANS WITH SHERRY

1 pound white pea beans
¼ teaspoon soda
1 small onion
¾ pound fat salt pork
5 tablespoons molasses
1 scant teaspoon dry mustard
1½ teaspoons salt
1 cup boiling water
1 cup Sherry

Wash and soak beans in plenty of water overnight. Drain, cover with fresh water, add soda, heat slowly, and cook just below the boiling point until the skins burst. This may be determined by taking a few on the tip of a spoon and blowing on them. Drain. Put the onion and a small piece of salt pork in bottom of a bean pot and pour the beans over it. Scald remaining pork and score the rind in several places 1 inch deep. Mix together molasses, salt, mustard, and boiling water. Pour over beans with enough more water to cover. Cover bean pot and bake in slow oven (250-325°) 7 to 8 hours, adding more water if beans become too dry. During last hour of baking add Sherry and leave cover off so pork rind may become crisp.

HARVARD BEETS

3 cups diced cooked beets
½ cup sugar
½ tablespoon cornstarch
½ cup dry red wine
¼ cup vinegar
½ teaspoon salt
2 tablespoons butter

Mix the sugar and cornstarch, and add wine, vinegar, and salt. Cook until thick. Add beets. Let stand on back of stove to keep warm ½ hour. Just before serving add the butter. Serves 6.

SCALLOPED BEETS WITH WINE

3 tablespoons butter
3 tablespoons flour
½ cup water
½ cup dry red wine
½ teaspoon salt
⅔ cup red-wine vinegar
4 teaspoons sugar
2 cups sliced cooked beets
12 half-slices bacon

Make a roux of butter and flour, and gradually stir in water, wine, vinegar, salt, and sugar. Cook, stirring constantly, until thick. Put beets in buttered casserole, pour over sauce, place bacon strips on top, and bake in hot oven (400-450°) until bacon is crisp, 15 to 20 minutes. Serves 6.

CALIFORNIA CARROTS

8 medium-sized carrots
1 onion, minced
½ clove garlic, crushed and minced
1 tablespoon butter
1 tablespoon flour
½ cup canned condensed consommé
½ cup Sauterne
salt and pepper

Scrape and slice or dice carrots, and parboil 10 minutes in boiling salted water. Drain. Sauté onion and garlic in butter until yellow. Add flour, blend well, then stir in consommé and wine. Season, put in carrots, and let simmer until carrots are tender, adding a little more consommé if sauce gets too thick. Serves 6.

GLAZED CARROTS

24 baby carrots
½ cup light brown or maple sugar
¼ cup butter
2 tablespoons water
2 tablespoons Sherry

Put carrots in cold salted water, bring to a boil, and cook until just tender. Drain. Make sirup of sugar, water, and Sherry and simmer 5 minutes. Put carrots in single layer close together in small shallow baking dish. Brush with part of sirup and put in moderately hot oven (375-400°) basting occasionally with remaining sirup until browned, about 15-20 minutes. Serves 4 to 6.

CARROTS SAUTÉ CREOLE STYLE

1 tablespoon butter
3 scallions, with tops, chopped
1 medium-sized onion, chopped
2 tablespoons minced ham
6 medium-sized pork sausages
1 teaspoon minced thyme
1 teaspoon minced parsley
1 clove garlic, crushed and minced
1 chopped tomato
1 cup condensed consommé
½ cup dry white wine
3 cups cooked and diced carrots
salt and pepper

Lightly brown chopped scallions and onion in butter. Prick sausages with fork and add together with minced ham. Cook until sausages are well browned. Add minced herbs and tomato, and bring to a simmer. Add consommé, wine, and carrots, season to taste, cover, and simmer about 15 minutes, stirring frequently. Serves 6.

SPANISH CARROTS

6 medium-sized carrots, sliced
1 medium-sized onion, sliced
1 clove garlic, crushed and minced
2 tablespoons butter
1 tablespoon flour
¾ cup condensed chicken consommé
¼ cup Chestnut Pureé (p. 34)
⅓ cup dry white wine
salt
pepper
paprika
1 egg yolk, lightly beaten

Parboil sliced carrots 5 to 10 minutes, according to age, until they just begin to get tender. Drain. Sauté onion and garlic in butter until tender, blend in flour, and add consommé gradually, stirring constantly. Stir in wine and Chestnut Purée (which may be purchased already prepared). Season. Add carrots and simmer gently until tender. If more liquid is required add ½ consommé and ½ hot water. Remove from heat, stir in slightly beaten egg yolk, and serve hot. Serves 4.

RED CABBAGE TYROLEAN STYLE

1 medium-sized head red cabbage
¼ pound salt pork, diced
1 cup beef bouillon or stock
2 tablespoons vinegar
¼ cup dry red wine
3 medium-sized tart apples, peeled, cored, and sliced
½ tablespoon flour
1 teaspoon sugar
salt
pepper
¼ teaspoon ground caraway seed (optional)

Remove outer leaves and cut away hard center of cabbage, and shred finely. Cover with boiling water and cook briskly for 10 minutes. Drain. Place diced pork in casserole, add cabbage, pour over bouillon or stock, cover, and cook in moderate oven (350-375°) for ½ hour. Mix flour and sugar into vinegar and wine. Add together with apples, caraway seed, salt, and pepper and cook about 20 minutes or until apples are tender. Serve with goose, duck, rabbit, roast pork, pork chops, or sausage. Serves 4 to 6.

STUFFED CABBAGE

1 large cabbage
3 sprigs fresh dill
¾ pound ground veal
½ cup sour cream
¼ cup minced onion
1 cup chicken stock
1 cup Sherry
salt
pepper

Remove toughest outer leaves of cabbage and cut out heart. Boil dill in 1 quart salted water 10 minutes. Remove dill and discard. Add cabbage heart and cook 10 minutes. Remove, chop coarsely, and mix with veal, sour cream, and onion. Spread out leaves of cabbage head and put a little of the mixture between each, stuffing center with the rest. Tie cabbage in shape with strips of cheesecloth and bake in casserole in moderately slow oven (325-350°) until cabbage is tender, about 2 hours. Baste frequently with a mixture of wine and chicken broth to which seasonings have been added. Serves 6 to 8.

BAVARIAN CABBAGE

1 medium-sized head red cabbage
3 medium-sized tart apples, sliced
3 tablespoons butter
¼ cup vinegar
⅓ cup brown sugar
1 cup dry red wine
½ teaspoon salt
dash of cayenne

Shred cabbage after removing outer leaves. Put cabbage and apples in heavy pottery, stainless steel, or enamel saucepan; add rest of ingredients. Cover tightly and cook over slow fire about 30 minutes or until cabbage is tender. Serves 4 to 6.

KNOB CELERY WITH WINE

8 medium-sized knob celery
4 tablespoons butter
1 cup condensed beef bouillon
½ cup dry white wine
salt and pepper

Peel roots, cover with cold salted water, bring to a boil, and simmer about 10 minutes. Drain and rinse with cold water. Melt butter, add bouillon and wine and celery, and simmer until tender. Season to taste. Excellent as a garnish. Serves 4.

CAULIFLOWER DIPLOMATIQUE

2-pound head cauliflower
1 teaspoon dried thyme
2 cups dry white wine
2 tablespoons melted butter
½ cup grated mild cheese
½ cup bread crumbs
salt
pepper

Remove leaves and stalks, separate into flowerets, and cook uncovered in boiling salted water, to which thyme has been added, 5 to 8 minutes. Drain. Cover with wine and allow to stand for 1 hour. Drain, place in saucepan with melted butter, and shake with grated cheese and bread crumbs until each piece is well coated. Reduce wine to ½ cup. Place cauliflower in casserole, pour over reduced wine, season, and put in hot oven (400-450°) until lightly browned. Serves 4 to 6.

CAULIFLOWER AND CHICKEN IN CASSEROLE

3 cups cooked cauliflower
1½ cups cooked chicken, cut up
1 cup Medium Cream Sauce (p. 28)
3 tablespoons Sauterne or Sherry
3 tablespoons grated cheese

Put a layer of cauliflower in buttered casserole, add a thin layer of chicken, and repeat until all are used. Pour over Cream Sauce mixed with wine, top with grated cheese, and bake in moderate oven (350-375°) until cheese is browned, about 15 minutes. Serves 6.

Broccoli or asparagus may be used in place of cauliflower, but with asparagus use only white wine.

CUCUMBERS REINE

2 medium-sized cucumbers, peeled and quartered lengthwise
1 tablespoon butter
1 tablespoon flour
¾ cup milk or light cream
¼ cup Sherry
salt
pinch of mace or nutmeg

Boil cucumbers in salted water until transparent. Make a roux of butter and flour. Gradually add milk or cream and Sherry mixed together. Cook over low heat 2-3 minutes, stirring constantly. Cut cucumbers into ½-inch pieces and add. Season to taste and reheat. Serves 4.

BOMBAY CUCUMBERS

6 medium-sized cucumbers
2 tablespoons butter
1 medium-sized onion, chopped
1 medium-sized green pepper, chopped
1 teaspoon salt
1 teaspoon curry powder
1½ cups dry white wine
2 tablespoons chopped parsley

Peel cucumbers and cut lengthwise in sections. Sauté onion and pepper in butter until tender but not brown. Add cucumbers, salt, curry powder, and wine. Stir and bake in moderate oven (350-375°) 40 minutes, basting occasionally. Sprinkle with chopped parsley. Serves 6.

EGGPLANT ESPAGNOLE

1 medium-sized eggplant
salt and pepper
flour
⅓ cup butter
1¼ cups grated cheese
1¼ cups bread crumbs
½ cup chopped nuts
1½ cups Sauce Espagnole (p. 35)

Pare eggplant, cut in ¼ inch slices, sprinkle with salt and pepper, dredge with flour, and sauté in butter until delicately browned, about 15 minutes. Mix cheese and nuts with 1 cup bread crumbs. Arrange eggplant slices in casserole with crumb mixture and sauce between each layer. Top with rest of bread crumbs soaked in the butter in which eggplant was sautéed. Bake, covered, in moderate oven (350-375°) 25 minutes. Uncover and bake about 20 minutes more or until crumbs are brown. Serves 6.

STUFFED EGGPLANT ORIENTALE

2 small eggplants
2 cups soft bread crumbs
1 small onion, minced
1 small cucumber, minced
1 tomato, peeled and chopped
1 cup cooked, chopped shrimp
½ cup Sauterne, not dry
salt and pepper
paprika

Cut eggplants in half and put in boiling salted water until fairly tender, 15 to 20 minutes. Scoop out meat to within ½ inch of shell. Mix with 1½ cups bread crumbs, add all other ingredients, and season. Fill eggplant shells, top with rest of crumbs, and bake 30 minutes in moderate oven (350-375°). Serves 4.

HOMINY IN CREAM WITH WINE

2½ cups cooked hominy
1 cup cream
3 tablespoons Sherry
salt
pepper

Heat and drain hominy (canned may be used); stir in cream, Sherry and seasonings. Reheat and serve. Serves 4.

MACARONI NEAPOLITAN

1 package (8 oz.) macaroni
2 quarts boiling water
2 teaspoons salt
1 tablespoon butter or olive oil
1 cup tomato sauce
1 cup Sauce Espagnole (p. 35)
½ cup grated Parmesan or other sharp cheese
1 cup diced mushrooms
¼ cup diced smoked beef tongue
¼ cup diced carrots
¼ cup chopped celery
1 bouquet garni (p. 9)
1 cup dry red wine
salt and pepper

Cook macaroni, according to maker's directions, in boiling salted water. Drain and rinse in cold water. Melt butter in saucepan, add all other ingredients except macaroni, season to taste, and simmer gently about 15 to 20 minutes, stirring frequently. Add a little water if necessary to keep from burning. Remove bouquet garni. Stir in cooked macaroni and simmer 5 minutes, tossing two or three times. Serves 6 to 8.

MACARONI WITH WINE

4 cups cooked macaroni
1 medium-sized onion, minced
2 medium-sized tomatoes, sliced
2 tablespoons minced green pepper
2 tablespoons butter
2 hard-cooked eggs
½ pound mild yellow cheese
¼ cup Sherry

Sauté onion, green pepper, and tomatoes in butter until tender but not browned. Combine with macaroni and sliced hard-cooked egg, and place in baking dish. Melt cheese in double boiler; when soft add wine and mix well. Pour wine-cheese sauce over macaroni mixture. Bake in moderate oven (350-375°) ½ hour. (If you care for a more pronounced cheese flavor, prepare additional wine-cheese sauce and serve as an accompaniment to the macaroni.) Serves 4 to 6.

MACARONI WITH WINE AND TOMATO SAUCE

1 package (8 oz.) macaroni
2 quarts boiling water
2 teaspoons salt
3 tablespoons butter
1 large onion
4 cloves
⅔ cup tomato sauce
⅔ cup Sherry or Madeira
salt, pepper, and a dash of cayenne
1½ cups grated Parmesan or other sharp cheese

Cook macaroni, according to maker's directions, in boiling salted water, adding 1 tablespoon butter and onion stuck with cloves. Discard onion, drain macaroni, and rinse with cold water. Put in saucepan with tomato sauce, 2 tablespoons butter, wine, and ½ cup grated cheese. Season to taste. Simmer slowly for 10 minutes, stirring frequently. Serve remaining cheese separately. Spaghetti may be used if preferred. Serves 6 to 8.

CREAMED MUSHROOMS, FLAMBÉ

1 pound mushrooms, sliced
1 medium-sized onion, minced
½ cup butter
⅓ cup Sherry
⅓ cup brandy
1 cup cream
salt and pepper

Sauté mushrooms and onion in butter until tender, about 10 minutes. Add Sherry and simmer 3 minutes. Pour in brandy, light it, and stir constantly until flames have died out. Simmer very gently until only a small quantity of liquid remains. Add cream, season, and simmer, stirring occasionally, until thickened. Serve on toast. Serves 4.

MUSHROOMS IN SAUTERNE

1 pound mushrooms
¼ cup butter
1 cup Sauterne
salt

Sauté mushrooms in butter until tender. Add Sauterne and simmer until wine is reduced by half. Season to taste 5 minutes before removing from heat. Serves 4.

SHERRIED MUSHROOMS AU GRATIN

20 medium-sized mushrooms
¼ cup melted butter
½ cup Sherry
2 teaspoons beef extract *or*
4 bouillon cubes dissolved in wine
salt
grated mild cheese

Sauté mushrooms in butter 1 minute on each side. Add beef extract or bouillon cubes and wine, season, and simmer, covered, until mushrooms are tender. Remove mushrooms to heat-proof dish and reduce sauce until quite thick. Put small amount of sauce in each. Add 1 teaspoon grated cheese to each and brown under broiler. Serves 4.

SHERRIED MUSHROOMS AND OYSTERS

1¼ cups (1 can) Newburg Sauce
⅓ cup cream
1 cup button mushrooms
1 tablespoon butter
½ pint oysters
1 tablespoon Sherry
salt

Heat Newburg Sauce (which may be bought prepared) in double boiler with cream. Sauté mushroom in butter and add to sauce. Add oysters and cook until plump and edges curled. Stir in Sherry and serve on toast immediately. Serves 4 to 6.

SCALLOPED MUSHROOMS

3 pounds mushrooms, sliced
1 cup butter
1 cup veal or chicken broth
1 tablespoon lemon juice
salt and pepper
2 egg yolks
2 tablespoons Sherry

Drop mushrooms into boiling water for about 1 minute. Drain and cover with cold water to blanch. Drain and sauté in butter in double boiler. When almost done, add broth and simmer 10 minutes. Add lemon juice and seasonings. Place over boiling water, stir in egg yolks, add Sherry, and cook until thickened. Serve in individual ramekins or timbales. Serves 6 to 8.

MUSHROOMS CECIL

1 pound mushrooms, sliced
¼ cup butter
1 cup dry white wine
½ cup grated Swiss cheese
salt

Sauté mushrooms in butter 3 minutes. Add wine and simmer until tender, about 10 minutes. Stir in grated cheese, season, and stir until cheese is just melted. Serve on toast. Serves 4 to 6.

SPINACH DE LUXE

(From Gretchen Green—The Whole World & Co.)

Stick a small onion with whole cloves and boil in ½ peck of spinach. When tender rub through sieve and season. Put into mold and shape before serving with slices of tongue and the following sauce: Melt a glass of currant jelly with 1 cup of Claret or any dry red wine. Add 1 tablespoon Sultana raisins and thicken slightly with a little browned flour. Season with a beef bouillon cube. Serve hot. Serves 4 to 6.

OFFICERS' MESS SPINACH

1 can cooked spinach
1 cup heavy cream
½ cup Sauterne (not dry)
1 tablespoon butter
salt and pepper

Drain and chop spinach, add all other ingredients, mix well, and simmer 2 minutes. Serves 6.

WHITE SQUASH WITH WHITE WINE

1 white squash (about 1 pound)
2½ cups dry white wine
1 cup grapefruit juice
1 teaspoon chopped parsley
⅛ teaspoon mace or nutmeg
1 tablespoon grated cheese
2 tablespoons butter
salt and pepper

Peel and quarter squash; remove seeds and white pith. Slice ¼ inch thick. Place in saucepan with all other ingredients and simmer until squash is very tender, about 1 hour. Stir frequently, especially during last part of cooking. Sauce should be very thick, but water may be added if necessary to prevent burning. Serves 4.

SWEET POTATO CECILIA

3 pounds sweet potatoes
½ cup butter
½ cup Sherry
¼ teaspoon nutmeg
¼ teaspoon cinnamon
milk
salt and pepper

Boil potatoes in their jackets until soft, peel, and put through ricer. Add butter, Sherry, nutmeg, cinnamon, salt and pepper to taste, and enough milk to moisten. Mix well. Put in buttered baking dish, dot top with butter, and sprinkle with cinnamon. Bake in moderate oven (350-375°) until top is browned. Serves 6.

YAMS IN SHELLS

6 medium-sized yams or sweet potatoes, baked
4 tablespoons butter
3 tablespoons cream or evaporated milk
salt and pepper
dash of mace or nutmeg
2 tablespoons Sherry or Madeira

Grease potatoes before baking. Cut in two lengthwise and remove pulp, being careful not to break shells. Mash, add all other ingredients and beat until very light. More cream and butter may be necessary if potatoes are very dry. Refill shells, sprinkle with brown sugar or maple sugar, and put into hot oven (400-450°) until lightly browned. Serves 6.

AUNT JEMIMA'S SWEET POTATOES

4 medium-sized sweet potatoes, boiled and mashed
2 tablespoons butter
2 tablespoons brown sugar
½ teaspoon cinnamon
2 tablespoons seedless or seeded raisins
2 tablespoons chopped walnuts
¼-⅓ cup cream
¼ cup Sherry
salt and pepper

Mix all ingredients together and beat until creamy. Season to taste and bake in moderate oven (350-375°) until brown, about 30 minutes. Serves 4.

BAKED LENTILS

1 pound lentils
1 pound bulk pork sausage
1 medium-sized onion, chopped
1 clove garlic, crushed and minced
1 can condensed tomato soup
⅔ cup Sherry
1½ teaspoons salt
⅛ teaspoon pepper

Wash and pick over lentils. Cover with cold water and let soak at least 8 hours. Drain, cover with boiling salted water, and simmer until skins break. Mix together sausage, chopped onion, and garlic. Put lentils in covered dish, make a cake of sausage to fit, and put on top of lentils. Add soup and wine, and water if necessary, to cover lentils. Cover and bake in slow oven (250-300°) 6-8 hours. Add more water from time to time to keep lentils just covered. Remove cover and increase heat to moderate (350-375°) to brown sausage.

Red kidney beans may be used instead of lentils, in which case red wine may be substituted for Sherry.

GLOIRE TURNIPS

2 pounds turnips
3 tablespoons butter
¼ cup heavy cream, whipped
1 teaspoon rum (optional)
4 tablespoons Sherry
salt
pepper

Boil turnips. Peel and mash. Stir in all other ingredients, reheat and serve. Serves 4 to 6.

TURNIPS OR CARROTS WITH WINE

2 pounds turnips or carrots, scraped and sliced
boiling salt water
2 cups (approximately) broth or consommé
2 tablespoons butter
¼ cup dry white wine

Parboil vegetable i enough boiling salted water to cover. Drain off water, add broth t cover, and boil until tender. Drain off broth, add butter to vegetable, and stir until melted. Boil broth to ¼ cup, add wine and vegetable, and simmer until most of the liquid is absorbed. Serve very hot. Serves 4 to 6.

SAUERKRAUT WITH WHITE WINE

1 pound sauerkraut, canned or bulk
3 tablespoons butter
½ cup Riesling or Chablis
½ cup water

Heat sauerkraut in saucepan with butter, wine, and water and cook until liquid is reduced by half. A sprinkling of celery seed or caraway seed may be added if desired. Serves 4.

ZUCCINI VERMOUTH

2 pounds zuccini, sliced
¼ cup butter
¼ cup Vermouth
salt and pepper

Sauté zuccini in very hot butter until tender and slightly brown. Add Vermouth, season, reduce heat, and simmer 5 minutes. Serves 4.

SWEETBREAD SALAD

4 pairs sweetbreads
1 carrot, diced
¼ cup pearl onions
1 teaspoon chopped parsley
2 cups Sherry or Madeira
salt and pepper
French dressing

Put prepared sweetbreads (p. 110) in casserole with vegetables, wine, and seasoning. Cook in moderate oven (350-375°) 30 minutes. Cool, slice, and serve very cold with French dressing. Serves 8 to 10.

HOLLYWOOD SALAD

2 cantaloupes
½ cup Tokay or Muscatel
⅛ teaspoon allspice
2 tablespoons lemon juice
½ cup canned shredded pineapple
1 head lettuce
½ cup French dressing

Peel melons, cut in half, remove seeds, and slice flesh into pieces about 2 inches long by ⅛ inch thick. Mix wine, allspice, and lemon juice and pour over melon. Mix thoroughly and chill. Serve in cups of lettuce with French dressing and sprinkled with shredded pineapple. Serves 4 to 6.

FRIDAY'S SALAD

1 pound flaked, cooked fish
¼ cup dry white wine
½ cup sliced radishes
2 teaspoons minced parsley
2 very small cucumbers, diced but not peeled
2 chopped green onions, including tops
salt and pepper
mayonnaise
paprika

Pour wine over flaked fish and allow to stand 1 hour, stirring occasionally. Mix with other salad ingredients, season, and serve on lettuce or romaine, dusted with paprika. Serves 4.

JELLIED EEL SALAD

1 4-pound eel
2 cups dry white wine
1 bay leaf
4 slices lemon, including rind, cut in quarters
1 teaspoon salt
⅛ teaspoon pepper
1 tablespoon gelatin
½ cup cold water

Clean and skin eel. Cut in 2-inch pieces; add wine, seasonings, and cold water to cover. Cook until very tender, about 1 to 1½ hours. Remove from heat and allow to cool in stock. Take out eel and flake. Strain broth and reduce to 1½ cups. Soften gelatin in ½ cup cold water, add to stock, and cool. When fairly well thickened, add flaked eel and chill until set. Serve with Wine French Dressing (below). Serves 6.

WINE FRENCH DRESSING

1 tablespoon sugar
1 teaspoon salt
½ teaspoon dry mustard
1 teaspoon Worcestershire sauce
4 tablespoons catsup
4 tablespoons Claret or Burgundy
4 tablespoons red-wine vinegar
¾ cup salad oil
1 clove garlic, crushed slightly

Combine ingredients in a pint or quart jar and shake until well mixed. Approximately 1½ cups dressing.

PENTHOUSE FISH SALAD

1 cup Burgundy
1 pound flaked, cooked fish
½ cup chopped celery
2 tablespoons finely chopped onion
1 tablespoon finely chopped parsley
2 tablespoons mashed pimiento
salt and pepper
1 tablespoon gelatin
½ cup cold water

Bring wine just to a simmer and allow to cool. Pour ¼ cup wine over fish and let stand 1 hour, stirring occasionally. Mix fish, celery, onion, parsley, and pimiento, making sure that the mashed pimiento is thoroughly distributed. Soften gelatin in cold water, add to rest of wine, and add to other ingredients, mixing thoroughly. Place in mold and chill 4 hours or until set. Unmold on lettuce bed and garnish with mayonnaise and slices of tomato. Serves 6.

WHITE-WINE SALAD DRESSING

¼ cup white-wine vinegar or lemon juice
¼ cup Riesling
1 cup salad oil
salt, pepper, and paprika

Mix all ingredients thoroughly. 1½ cups dressing.

AMBROSIA CHICKEN SALAD

2 cups cooked chicken, coarsely chopped
1 cup seeded white grapes
2 cups orange slices
1 cup Sauterne, not too dry
1 cup chopped celery
¼ cup almonds, blanched and sliced
lettuce
French dressing

Place chicken and grapes in a dish about 1½ quarts capacity and pack slightly. Arrange the orange slices on top and add wine. Chill in refrigerator for at least 2 hours. A short time before serving, pour off wine and simmer it until reduced to about 3 tablespoons. Make French dressing, using lemon juice and reduced wine in place of vinegar. Brown almonds lightly in a little butter. Mix all together and put back in refrigerator for a few minutes as it must be served very cold. Serve on lettuce leaf. Serves 4.

POTATO SALAD WITH RED WINE

6 medium-sized potatoes
2 medium-sized onions, sliced
6 hard-cooked eggs, sliced
1 clove garlic, crushed and minced
½-1 teaspoon curry powder
4 anchovies, chopped, *or*
2 tablespoons anchovy paste
¼ cup dry red wine
6 tablespoons olive oil
2 tablespoons red-wine vinegar
salt and pepper

Boil potatoes in their jackets, peel, and while still warm tear apart with two forks into convenient-sized pieces. Add all other ingredients, mix well, and chill at least 1 hour before serving. Serves 8.

LOBSTER AVOCADO SALAD

2 medium-sized avocados, diced
2 tablespoons Sauterne
1 teaspoon lemon juice
1 cup flaked cooked lobster meat
1 cup diced celery
½ cup Wine French Dressing (p. 232)
mayonnaise

Sprinkle avocados with Sauterne and lemon juice, mix lightly, and put in refrigerator for 1 hour. Mix lobster and celery, add French dressing, and chill 1 hour. Drain lobster mixture, place on plates, add avocado, and top with mayonnaise dusted with paprika. Serves 4.

ROQUEFORT DRESSING

½ cup grated Roquefort cheese
1 cup olive oil or vegetable oil
⅓ cup vinegar
1 cup dry Sherry
¼ cup grated onion
½ clove garlic, crushed and minced
salt
paprika
cayenne

Make a paste of cheese and oil. Add other ingredients and beat until very smooth. 2 cups dressing (approximately).

POTATO SALAD WITH WHITE WINE

4 large or 6 medium-sized potatoes
½ cup dry white wine
¼ cup salad oil
3 tablespoons white-wine vinegar
1 tablespoon sugar
¼ cup chopped onion
salt and pepper

Boil potatoes in jackets until just done (do not overcook). Peel and while still warm tear apart with two forks (do not slice). Add wine and stir until potatoes have soaked it all up. Add all the other ingredients and stir. Place in refrigerator at least one hour before serving. Serves 6.

Variations: add chopped fried bacon, slivers of Brazil nuts, sliced hard-cooked eggs, green or ripe olives, chopped celery, green peppers, or pimiento.

WINE MAYONNAISE

Add 3 tablespoons dry white wine and ½ tablespoon lemon juice to 1 cup mayonnaise and mix thoroughly.

DRESSING FOR FRUIT OR FISH SALADS

Thin 1 cup of mayonnaise or salad dressing with 4 tablespoons Sherry and stir well.

CHAPTER TEN

Fruits, Desserts, and Dessert Sauces

One hostess, famed for the excellence of her meals, was asked for her secret. "Desserts," was the laconic reply. It was her theory that, if the end of the meal provides an unforgettable memory, any hint of mediocrity in what has gone before will be forgotten. While not wholly subscribing to this theory, there is more than a bit of truth in it. Certainly there is no reason why the last course should not wind up the meal on a high plane when wine offers such limitless opportunities.

For example: Plain ice cream is good but add a wine sauce and proudly serve it to your most distinguished and critical guests. Or a plain rice pudding served with a wine sauce is something that will long be remembered. Baked Alaska, one of the most expensive desserts in restaurants (and one of the easiest to make at home), is simply glorified by soaking the foundation cake in wine.

There is no fruit which does not combine well with wine, either fresh or cooked, and canning and preserving with wine is a comparatively untouched field. The recipes given in the following pages by no means cover the subject. To do so would require a book of its own. But each has been chosen with the idea of giving you a starting point from which you can branch out on your own.

One point is especially well worth remembering—replacing part or all of the sugar with honey in any dessert gives delightful effects.

There is one comforting thought. You will have practically no outright failures, but you will develop some outstanding successes.

HOLLYWOOD GRAPEFRUIT

1 cup pineapple or grapefruit juice
½ cup sugar
¼ cup dry red wine
2 grapefruit

Boil fruit juice and sugar to a medium-thick sirup. Cool and pour over grapefruit, which have been halved, cored, and sectioned. Chopped mint leaves make an excellent addition. Serves 4.

GRAPEFRUIT WITH TOKAY

2 large grapefruit
½ pound Tokay grapes, halved and seeded
2 cups Tokay

Core and section grapefruit. Fill centers with grapes and wine. Chill several hours. Serves 4.

GRAPEFRUIT AND ALMOND ASPIC

2 grapefruit
5 tablespoons almonds, blanched and chopped
1 tablespoon gelatin
¾ cup hot water
2 tablespoons sugar
1 cup grapefruit juice
1 tablespoon lemon juice
grated rind of 1 lemon
¼ cup Tokay or Malaga wine

Remove the pulp of the grapefruit, break into small pieces, and drain. Add the chopped almonds. Dissolve gelatin in hot water; add sugar, grapefruit juice, lemon juice, lemon rind, and wine. When it begins to harden add grapefruit pulp and almonds and put in refrigerator. Allow twice the usual time to harden on account of the fruit acids. Serves 4 to 6.

SHERRIED GRAPEFRUIT

2 grapefruit
4 tablespoons maple sugar, honey, or brown sugar
½ cup Sherry

Core and section halved grapefruit. Fill centers with sugar or honey and add wine. Place about 4 inches under broiler until grapefruit is lightly browned. Serves 4. May be served hot or cold, and as a first or last course.

SHERRY-ORANGE CUP

6 medium-sized navel oranges, peeled and diced
3 tablespoons powdered sugar
3 tablespoons finely chopped mint
1 tablespoon lemon juice
½ cup Sherry

Stir all ingredients together, mixing thoroughly. Chill and serve in sherbet glasses. Serves 6.

AMBROSIA

4 navel oranges
1 can sliced pineapple
½ cup shredded coconut
½ cup powdered sugar
½ cup Sherry or Madeira

Peel oranges, remove all white outer membrane, and slice thin. Cut pineapple slices into quarters. Make a layer of orange slices in bottom of serving dish, sprinkle with sugar, another layer of pineapple, sprinkle with coconut, and repeat until you have 4 layers. Add wine. Let stand 1 hour. Serve chilled or not as desired. Serves 6 to 8.

Shredded pineapple may be substituted for sliced, or peaches, fresh or canned, for oranges.

SHERRIED ORANGES (with duck and game)

3 large navel oranges
¼ cup Sherry
2 tablespoons brandy
3 tablespoons powdered sugar

Peel oranges and slice thin. Add wine, brandy, and sugar. Stir very gently to avoid breaking slices. Chill for at least an hour before serving. Serve separately. Serves 4 to 6.

FROSTED PEACH CUP

1 cup quick-frozen peaches
1½ tablespoons lemon juice
1 tablespoon powdered sugar
⅔ cup Port (approximately), chilled

Allow peaches to thaw slightly in refrigerator, place in sherbet cups or fruit dishes, sprinkle on lemon juice and sugar, and pour on enough well-chilled wine to nearly fill serving dishes. Serve at once. Serves 4.

STUFFED BAKED PEACHES

6 freestone peaches
6 macaroons, crumbled
¼ cup maple sirup or honey
½ cup Sherry

Select peaches which are ripe but firm. Peel as directed in following recipe. Remove pits carefully to keep fruit whole. Fill centers with crumbled macaroons and pour in sirup or honey. Bake in moderate oven (350-375°) about 20 minutes, basting frequently with Sherry. Serves 6.

PEACHES BAKED IN WINE

6 whole peaches
6 tablespoons dry white wine
1 cup sugar
½ teaspoon mace or nutmeg
2 tablespoons butter
grated rind of 1 lemon

Select peaches which are ripe but firm. Cover with boiling water for 15-30 seconds, drain, and cover with cold water. Skins will slip off easily. Place in baking dish and add wine, sugar, and mace or nutmeg. Dot with butter and sprinkle grated lemon peel on top. Bake, covered, in hot oven (400-450°) until tender, about 20-30 minutes. Serves 6.

PEACHES OR PEARS IN SHERRY

6 pounds fruit
12 cups sugar
6 cups water
6 2-inch pieces stick cinnamon
12 cloves
1½ cups Sherry

Choose fruit which is ripe but firm and free from bruises or blemishes. Peel peaches by dipping in boiling water. Skins will then slip off easily. Halve and remove pits.

Pears should be peeled, quartered, and cored.

Boil sugar, water, cinnamon, and cloves 3 minutes. Add fruit and simmer gently until fruit is tender. Remove from heat and place fruit in jars which, together with tops, have been sterilized in boiling water for 15 minutes. Add Sherry to sirup, bring to a boil, and fill jars to overflowing. Partially seal and process in boiling water to cover for 25 minutes. Tighten caps and let stand overnight. 6 pints.

PEARS JUBILEE

4 pears
1 cup Sherry
1 teaspoon grated orange peel
½ teaspoon grated lemon peel
2 whole cloves
1 ½-inch stick cinnamon

Peel pears carefully, quarter, and core. Simmer gently in wine, to which seasonings have been added, until just tender. Remove to serving dish. Cook wine until thick, strain over pears, and chill. Serves 4.

PEARS BAKED IN PORT

4 firm pears, peeled, cored, and halved
1 cup Port
1/4 cup sugar

Choose pears which are a trifle under rather than over-ripe. Bake in moderately slow oven (325-350°) until tender, about 1-1½ hours, basting frequently with the wine, in which sugar has been dissolved. Serve either hot or cold, topping with whipped cream. Serves 4.

PEARS IN PORT

1 can pears
Port

Drain pears, measure sirup, and add half as much Port. Pour over pears and chill in refrigerator for 2 to 3 hours. Serve garnished with maraschino cherries. Serves 4 to 6.

BAKED RHUBARB WITH HONEY

2 pounds young rhubarb, cut in ¾-inch sections
1/2 cup honey
1/2 cup sugar
3 egg whites, stiffly beaten
3 tablespoons powdered sugar
2 tablespoons Sherry

Use only the tender pink portion of the rhubarb stalks. Put in casserole, add sugar and honey, cover, and bake in moderate oven (350-375°) until tender. Beat powdered sugar into beaten egg whites, mix in Sherry, cover top of rhubarb, and place in oven until meringue is lightly browned, about 15 minutes. Serve either hot or cold. Serves 6.

MAINE CRUNCH

8 firm apples, sliced thin
1/4 cup butter
1/2 cup flour
3/4 cup sugar
3/4 teaspoon cinnamon
1/2 cup dry white wine

Put apples in greased casserole. Mix butter, flour, sugar, and cinnamon thoroughly and sprinkle on top. Pour over wine and bake in moderate oven (350-375°) about 30-40 minutes or until apples are done. Serves 6 to 8.

APPLE SAUCE VERMOUTH

4 tart apples, peeled, cored, and sliced
½ cup water (approximately)
½ cup sugar
juice of ½ lemon
grated rind of ½ lemon
1 tablespoon butter
¼ teaspoon salt
⅓ cup Vermouth

Add all ingredients except Vermouth to apples and cook until apples are tender, then stir in Vermouth and continue cooking until sauce reaches desired consistency. Serves 4.

STUFFED APPLES

6 large firm apples
½ cup chopped almonds
⅔ cup chopped figs
1 tablespoon butter
1 cup honey
½ cup wine*

Remove stems from apples and cut a very thin slice from stem end if necessary to make them stand evenly. Peel from blossom end ⅓ down. Core about ⅔ down. Knead almonds and figs together with well-moistened hands until thoroughly blended or put through food chopper. Arrange apples in baking dish. Stuff with almond and fig mixture. Heat butter, honey, and wine together until butter is melted and pour over apples. Bake in moderately hot oven (375-400°) 30-40 minutes or until just tender, basting frequently. Remove apples carefully with pancake turner or spatula to sauce dishes and cook sirup a few minutes longer, if necessary, until thickened. Pour over apples and cool. Serve at room temperature covered with sweetened whipped cream. Serves 6.

*Choose any wine you desire. Port or any of the red wines give a beautiful color. Tokay, Muscatel, or Angelica are excellent, while the white wines are most commonly used.

APRICOT SAUCE WITH SHERRY

1 pint apricot marmalade
½ cup sugar
½ cup Sherry
¼ teaspoon salt

Mix ingredients in saucepan and bring to boiling point. Serve on sponge cake or pudding. Serves 6 to 8.

ANGEL FINGERS

4 large bananas
1 ½ tablespoons butter
½ cup honey
¼-⅓ cup wine*

Select bananas of as nearly equal size as possible, ripe but firm. Peel and quarter, lengthwise and crosswise, into 2-inch pieces. Sauté in butter over low heat until light brown. Add honey and tip frying pan from side to side, holding well above heat, until honey is melted and mixed with butter. Cook over very low heat for 2 or 3 minutes. Remove bananas carefully and place in individual sauce dishes. Add wine to honey, reheat and pour over bananas. Serves 4.

*Choose any wine to suit your taste except the lighter dry white wines, whose delicate flavor will be overpowered by the bananas. Port, Sherry, or the heavy dry red wines are excellent.

BANANAS IN RED WINE

4 small bananas (green-tipped)
2 tablespoons butter
1 cup dry red wine
1 cup sugar
½ tablespoon cornstarch
dash of nutmeg
⅛ teaspoon salt

Peel bananas and brown lightly in butter. Heat wine, add sugar mixed with cornstarch, and cook, stirring, until clear and slightly thickened. Add nutmeg and salt, and pour over bananas. Simmer slowly 15 minutes. Serves 4.

BANANAS NEWBURG

4 large bananas
1 tablespoon lemon juice
flour
salt
2 tablespoons butter
3 tablespoons honey
¼ cup Sherry

Select bananas which are slightly speckled with brown and without green tips. Peel and cut in half, lengthwise and crosswise. Moisten with lemon juice. Dredge with flour and salt mixed, and sauté in butter until light brown. Remove bananas, add Sherry and honey, and simmer until thick. Pour sauce over bananas. Serves 4.

CANTALOUPE COUPE

3 cantaloupes
3 cups strawberries
2 cups diced pineapple, fresh or canned
½ cup lemon juice
¼ teaspoon salt
½ cup sugar
¼ cup Sherry

Cut melons in half crosswise and remove seeds. Cut ½-inch slice from small end of each piece and peel. Slice 2 cups strawberries, mix with pineapple, and put in centers of melon cups. Stir together lemon juice, salt, sugar, and Sherry until sugar is dissolved and pour over fruit. Chill thoroughly and serve on bed of grape leaves garnished with remaining whole strawberries. Serves 6.

CANTALOUPE EDOUARDO

1 large cantaloupe
peaches
Sauterne (not dry)
sugar

Cut a 3-inch circular piece from top of cantaloupe and a small slice from stem end to enable it to stand upright. Scoop out seeds with spoon, fill cavity with sliced peaches, and pour in wine until full. Add sugar according to sweetness of peaches. Replace cap and secure with two toothpicks. Place in refrigerator for at least four hours. Serves 2 to 4.

CANTALOUPE SLICES IN PORT

2 medium-sized cantaloupe
1 cup Port

Peel cantaloupe, cut in half, remove seeds, and cut in ¼-inch slices. Place in bowl and pour on wine. Chill in refrigerator at least 2 hours. Serve in sauce dishes garnished with any fruit in season. Serves 4.

MELON COCKTAIL

4 cups cubed melon
2 tablespoons powdered sugar
1 cup Sherry

The melon may be cut into balls by means of a potato scoop if desired. Combine the melon, sugar, and wine and put in a covered dish. Chill at least 3 hours. Honeydew, muskmelon, and watermelon make an attractive combination topped with mint leaves. Other fruits may be used if desired. Serves 6.

PRUNES IN RED WINE

1 pound prunes
dry red wine
½ cup sugar
1 bay leaf
½ stick cinnamon
rind of ½ lemon

Soak prunes at least 8 hours in half again as much wine as is necessary to cover them. It may require overnight if prunes are very dry, in any case, the longer the better. When they are thoroughly soft, add sugar, bayleaf, cinnamon, and lemon rind and more wine if necessary to cover them completely. Simmer until well done, remove them carefully, and continue boiling the wine until it is a thin sirup. Strain and pour over prunes. Serve with cream. Serves 6.

BAKED QUINCE WITH RED WINE

4 medium-sized quinces
1½ cups dry red wine
4 tablespoons sugar
½ cup stale cake crumbs or macaroon crumbs
2 tablespoons butter

Select quinces which are fully ripe, deep yellow, and of uniform size. Wash, peel, cut in two, and core. Simmer peelings and cores in wine and sugar for 20 minutes. Strain. Put quince halves in buttered baking dish, pour sirup over and bake, covered, in slow oven (250-325°) until tender, about 2 hours, basting 3 or 4 times. Remove cover, sprinkle with cake or macaroon crumbs, dot with butter, and brown under broiler. Serves 4.

CRANBERRIES CABERNET

4 cups cranberries
2 cups honey
2 cups Cabernet (or any dry red wine)
pinch of salt

Wash and pick over cranberries. Put honey, wine, berries, and salt in saucepan and bring to a boil. Simmer, *without stirring,* until skins are broken, about 10 minutes. Skim and cool. Approximately 5 cups sauce.

SPICED FRUIT IN WINE

2 cups dry red wine
$3/4$ cup sugar
2 2-inch sticks cinnamon
4 firm pears, peeled, cored, and halved

Put wine, sugar, and cinnamon in small saucepan, bring to a boil, and simmer 3 minutes. Add pears and cook until tender, about 15 minutes. Remove pears, boil sirup until fairly thick, and pour over pears. Chill 2 to 3 hours. Serves 4.

Fresh peaches or apricots may be used instead of pears or in combination with them. For berries, seeded grapes, or cherries, simmer sirup 5 minutes or until thick and pour over uncooked fruit. Prepare canned fruit in the same way after draining off sirup.

COUPE ST. JACQUES

2 cups fresh fruits
$1/2$ cup dry white wine
sugar or honey
1 cup fruit ice

Any desired assortment of fresh fruits may be used. The larger ones such as peaches, pears, and pineapple should be cubed. Green almonds, if obtainable, are an excellent addition. Add wine and a generous amount of sugar or honey to the fruits. Place in refrigerator for 4 to 5 hours. The mixture should be nearly frozen. Place a spoonful of any desired flavor of fruit ice in a well-chilled sherbet glass. Heap on some strained fruit and top with more fruit ice. Serves 6.

FRUIT COMPOTES

Fruit compotes are usually combinations of several fruits in very heavy sirup but may be made from any one fruit, canned or fresh.

For canned fruit, drain and add to juice $1/2$ the amount of water and 1 cup of sugar to each cup. Bring to a boil and add $1/4$ cup of any desired wine to each cup of sirup, cool, and pour over fruit.

For fresh fruits make heavy sirup of 2 parts sugar to 1 part water, add $1/4$ part wine, and pour over fruit. It is best to allow an hour or more for the wine flavor to develop.

Don't be afraid to use red wines, either sweet or dry. Compotes may be served either chilled or not as desired, and may be topped with sweetened whipped cream.

FRUIT MÉLANGE

½ cup sugar
1 cup Sherry
3 cups mixed fruits, fresh or canned

Dissolve sugar thoroughly in wine, pour over fruit, and chill in refrigerator for at least two hours. Serves 4 to 6.

WATERMELON À LA ROMERO

1 large ripe watermelon
1 bottle champagne

Have both melon and champagne icy cold. Cut 2-inch plug from melon to center. Pour champagne in gradually. When it is all absorbed replace plug and return melon to refrigerator for at least 6 hours. Serves 6 to 10.

CUBAN COCONUT PUDDING

¾ cup coconut liquid
1¾ cups sugar
1 1-inch stick cinnamon
½ teaspoon salt
1¾ cups shredded fresh coconut
2 tablespoons Sherry
2 egg yolks, well beaten

Boil coconut liquid, sugar, cinnamon, and salt to a sirup which will spin a heavy thread (228-230°). Reduce heat, add coconut, and stir until it begins to leave side of pan. Add 1 tablespoon wine and cook dry, stirring constantly. Cool thoroughly, and stir in egg yolks and remaining wine. Bake in buttered casserole, uncovered, in moderate oven (350-375°) about 1 hour or until golden brown. Serves 4 to 6.

ALMOND PUDDING

1½ cups Thick White Sauce (p. 28)
4 eggs, separated
½ cup sugar
3 tablespoons Sherry
¾ cup shredded and toasted almonds
½ teaspoon salt

Beat egg yolks until very thick, add sugar, and add to slightly cooled White Sauce. Stir in nuts (which should be very finely shredded and only lightly toasted), Sherry, and salt. Fold in stiffly beaten whites of eggs and pour into a greased baking dish, which should not be filled more than two-thirds full. Set baking dish in pan of hot water and bake in moderate oven (350-375°) until firm, about 1 hour. Serves 6.

CABINET PUDDING

½ cup seeded raisins, cut up
flour
¼ loaf stale bread, grated
peel of ½ lemon, white removed and sliced thin
½ teaspoon cinnamon
1½ cups sugar
1 cup milk
4 eggs, well beaten
½ cup Sherry or Madeira
½ cup brandy

Flour raisins and cut up with scissors. Mix with bread crumbs. (Do not use prepared bread crumbs in cartons as they are too dry.) Bread should be about 3 or 4 days old.

Cook lemon peel, cinnamon, sugar, and milk in double boiler for 15 minutes; strain, and add to bread crumbs and raisins. Mix in wine and brandy, and stir in beaten eggs. Line a 2-quart mold with well-buttered paper, or use a buttered spring form. Pour in mixture and steam for 1½ hours. Serves 4 to 6.

APRICOT FRITTERS

1 dozen apricots
grated peel of 1 lemon
1 cup sugar
1 cup Sherry or Madeira (approximately)
1 cup sifted flour
1 teaspoon baking powder
½ teaspoon salt
2 tablespoons sugar
1 egg, lightly beaten
¾ cup milk
1 tablespoon melted butter

Peel apricots by first dipping them in boiling water until skins slip off easily. Cut in half and stone. Stir grated lemon peel and sugar well together and pour over fruit. Cover with wine and place in refrigerator for two hours.

Mix and sift flour, baking powder, salt, and sugar. Combine milk, egg, and melted butter and mix well with dry ingredients.

Drain apricots and dip in batter. Drop from spoon into hot deep fat (375°) until golden brown, about 3 to 4 minutes. Drain on unglazed paper and dust with powdered sugar. Boil sugar and wine down to a thick sirup and serve over fritters. Serves 4 to 6.

CREOLE PUDDING

1 cup dark New Orleans molasses
1½ cups heavy cream
3 cups flour
1 teaspoon baking powder
½ teaspoon allspice
½ teaspoon cinnamon
½ teaspoon cloves
1 teaspoon mace
1 teaspoon salt
¼ cup brandy
¼ cup rum
⅓ cup Sherry

Mix molasses and cream. Sift together flour, baking powder, spices, and salt. Stir in gradually to molasses and cream. Mix in brandy, rum, and wine. Pour into buttered baking dish, set in pan of hot water, and bake in moderate oven (350-375°) 2 hours. Serve with Sea Foam (p. 273). Serves 4 to 6.

PLUM DUMPLINGS

¾ cup milk, scalded
4 cakes compressed yeast
2 eggs, lightly beaten
4 egg yolks, lightly beaten
grated peel of 1 lemon
1 cup sugar
4 cups flour
1 cup melted butter
¾ cup dry white wine
2 pounds plums

Allow milk to cool until it is barely lukewarm. Place ½ cup in mixing bowl, crumble in yeast cakes and stir until thoroughly dissolved. Add eggs and egg yolks, lemon peel, two tablespoons sugar, and ½ cup melted butter. Mix in flour a little at a time and beat well. Brush with butter, cover, and let rise in a warm place until doubled in bulk. Knead well and let rise again. Make a sirup of remaining sugar and wine, put in plums, and simmer until just tender. Time will depend on ripeness of plums. Remove plums carefully with a spoon and keep warm. Form dough with the hands on a floured board into a roll about 2 inches thick. Pinch off lumps and form into 1-inch balls. Add remaining butter to plum sirup, put in dumplings, and cook without uncovering for 10 minutes. Put dumplings in casserole with remaining milk and place in moderate oven (350-375°) for 20 minutes, until most or all of the milk has been absorbed. Place dumplings in middle of serving dish, arrange plums around, and pour sirup over dumplings. Serves 6.

MOCHA PUDDING

5 eggs, separated
¾ cup powdered sugar
grated rind of 1 orange
grated rind of 1 lemon
1 teaspoon baking powder
1 cup very dry bread crumbs
2 cups coffee, triple strength
⅓ cup granulated sugar
3 tablespoons Sherry

Beat egg yolks until very thick, add grated lemon and orange, and beat in powdered sugar a little at a time. Mix baking powder with bread crumbs and add. Beat egg whites until stiff and fold in. Bake in pan lined with well-buttered paper, or in a spring form, in a moderately slow oven (325-350°) for 30 minutes. Invert pan and turn out pudding on serving dish. Dissolve sugar in cold coffee, add Sherry, and pour over pudding. Place in refrigerator at least 24 hours before serving. Serves 6 to 8.

SHEROFFEE

5 tablespoons coffee
2 cups water
5 tablespoons sugar
5 eggs, separated
¾ cup powdered sugar
grated rind of 1 lemon
grated rind of 1 orange
1 cup very dry bread crumbs
1 teaspoon baking powder
3 tablespoons Sherry

Make a strong infusion of coffee, add sugar, and cool. Beat egg yolks until light, add powdered sugar gradually, and then grated lemon and orange rind. Mix crumbs and baking powder well. Beat egg whites until stiff but not dry. Mix egg-yolk mixture and crumbs, and fold in beaten whites. Bake in moderately slow oven (325-350°) 30 minutes. Remove from pan to serving dish at once. Mix coffee and Sherry, pour over top, and let stand 24 hours. May be served with sweetened whipped cream if desired. Serves 4-6.

ALMOND TART

½ cup dry rye bread crumbs
¼ cup dry red wine
10 eggs, separated
1 cup powdered sugar
1 cup ground, blanched almonds
1 square bitter chocolate, grated
1 teaspoon candied citron, chopped fine
1 teaspoon candied orange peel, chopped fine
1 teaspoon candied lemon peel, chopped fine
Wine Chaudeau (p. 266)

Bake thin slices of rye bread in slow oven (250-275°) until light brown. Crush into very fine powder with rolling pin. Add wine. Mix sugar with egg yolks, which should be beaten until very thick, about 20 minutes. This is essential. Stir in ground almonds, grated chocolate, and candied fruits. Fold in stiffly beaten egg whites and bake in greased mold in moderate oven (350-375°) 30-45 minutes. Serve with Wine Chaudeau. Serves 6 to 8.

ORANGE FRITTERS

2 large navel oranges
wine
1 cup sifted flour
1 teaspoon baking powder
½ teaspoon salt
2 tablespoons sugar
1 egg, lightly beaten
¾ cup milk
1 tablespoon melted butter

Peel oranges and cut in ¼-inch slices. Cover with any type of wine you choose. If very dry, add a couple of tablespoons of sugar. Let stand at least 4 hours. Mix flour, baking powder, salt, and sugar. Stir together egg, milk, and shortening and mix with dry ingredients, beating until smooth. Dip slices of orange in this cover batter, fry in deep fat to a light golden brown, and dust with powdered sugar. Serves 4 to 6.

Canned pineapple sticks, drained and cut in half, may be used instead of orange slices, in which case a fairly sweet white wine should be used.

WHITE NUT CAKE

1 cup butter
1½ cups sugar
4 eggs, separated
3 tablespoons cream
2¼ cups cake flour
2 teaspoons baking powder
¼ cup Sherry
2 tablespoons lemon juice
1 tablespoon grated lemon rind
1 cup shaved blanched almonds

Cream shortening, add sugar gradually, and cream thoroughly. Blend in egg yolks, one at a time, beating well after each addition. Blend in cream. Sift flour once before measuring. Sift flour and baking powder together, and add to cream mixture alternately with Sherry and lemon juice. Add grated lemon rind and almonds. Fold in stiffly beaten egg whites. Pour into greased and floured tube pan (9-inch). Bake 1 hour and 25 minutes in moderate oven (350-375°). Frost with Sherry Icing.

SHERRY ICING

2 egg whites
1½ cups white sugar
⅓ cup Sherry
2 teaspoons light corn sirup

Beat ingredients together in top of double boiler. Place over boiling water and beat with rotary beater about 7 minutes or until it holds its shape when dropped from beater. Remove from boiling water and continue beating until stiff enough to spread.

PORT CAKE FILLING

¾ cup sugar
2 tablespoons cornstarch
pinch of salt
1 egg yolk, lightly beaten
3 tablespoons milk
¾ cup Port
1 tablespoon butter

Mix sugar, cornstarch, and salt. Stir in egg yolk, milk, and wine and cook 15 minutes in double boiler, or until mixture is thick. Stir constantly for first five minutes and frequently until done. Remove from heat, add butter, and cool. Filling for 2 9-inch layers.

WINE CAKE

½ cup butter or vegetable shortening
1 cup sugar
1½ (scant) cups cake flour
½ teaspoon salt
1½ teaspoons baking powder
juice of 1 lemon
grated rind of 1 lemon
6 tablespoons sweet wine
7 egg whites

Cream shortening and sugar, and beat until fluffy. Sift flour, measure, add salt and baking powder, and sift again. Mix wine, lemon juice, and grated lemon peel and add alternately with flour to sugar and butter. Beat smooth. Beat egg whites until stiff but not dry and fold in. Bake in moderately slow oven (325-350°) about 1 hour.

HOLIDAY FRUIT CAKE

2 cups seeded raisins
2 cups currants
1 cup shredded candied lemon peel
1 cup shredded candied orange peel
1 cup quartered candied cherries
½ cup chopped candied pineapple
1 cup shredded citron
1 cup chopped nuts—almonds or pecans

1 cup butter
1 cup sugar
5 eggs
¼ cup molasses
1 cup Sherry
2 cups cake flour
1 teaspoon mace
1 teaspoon cinnamon
½ teaspoon nutmeg
½ teaspoon cloves
½ teaspoon ginger
¾ teaspoon soda
¼ teaspoon salt

First prepare fruit. Then cream butter and beat in sugar gradually. Add egg yolks, molasses, and wine. Mix and sift flour, soda, spices, and salt together. Add the fruit and nuts to the flour mixture, making sure the fruit is well separated and well floured. Gradually add this to the butter mixture. Stir. Fold in stiffly beaten egg whites. Transfer to a round pan 10 inches in diameter, or a pyrex baking dish of the same size, which has been oiled and lined twice with heavy oiled paper. Bake for 5 hours in a slow oven (250-325°). Cover the cake during the first hour of baking. Cool thoroughly. Remove from the dish and remove the paper.

Cover with a clean cloth which has been slightly dampened with Sherry. Keep in a cool dry place, preferably a stone jar. Keep well covered and dampen cloth around cake once each week with Sherry. Store one month before using. Makes 6½ pounds.

PORK CAKE

¾ pound very fat salt pork, chopped
1 cup Sherry
¼ cup light molasses
1 cup light brown sugar
1 teaspoon cinnamon
1 teaspoon cloves
½ teaspoon allspice
4 cups sifted flour
1 teaspoon baking soda
1 teaspoon salt
¼ cup chopped candied orange peel
¼ cup chopped candied lemon peel
¼ cup chopped citron
½ cup chopped seeded raisins
½ cup currants
½ cup chopped English walnuts or almonds
4 egg yolks, lightly beaten

Pour boiling water over pork and let stand 10 minutes. Drain and *chop by hand* not too finely, about ⅛-inch pieces. (Do not put through food chopper.) Mix with wine, spices, molasses, and sugar. Sift flour, salt, and baking soda together, add candied fruits and nuts, and stir well. Add to first mixture, then add egg yolks and stir until thoroughly mixed. Pour into greased 8 x 4 x 4-inch loaf pan lined with parchment or waxed paper greased on both sides. Bake in moderately slow oven (325-350°) until well browned, about 2 hours.

FRENCH TOAST WITH WINE

1 cup milk
¼ cup Port or Sherry
2 eggs, lightly beaten
½ teaspoon salt
8 slices bread
4 tablespoons butter or vegetable shortening

Whip milk, wine, eggs, and salt together. Dip in bread and sauté in butter or fry in deep hot fat to a rich golden brown. Sprinkle with maple sugar or serve with sirup or honey. Serves 4.

SHERRY CHIFFON PIE

1 9-inch pastry shell
1 tablespoon gelatin
⅓ cup cold water
4 eggs, separated
1 cup sugar
⅔ cup Sherry
⅓ teaspoon salt
1 cup heavy cream, whipped
¼ cup powdered sugar

Prepare, bake, and cool pastry shell. Soften gelatin in cold water 5 minutes. Beat egg yolks with ½ cup sugar until light. Add wine. Cook in a double boiler, stirring constantly, until the mixture is the consistency of a custard. Stir in gelatin and cool. Beat egg whites stiff and add remaining sugar and salt. Combine with custard. Pour into pastry shell. Chill in refrigerator until firm, allowing 2 to 3 hours. When ready to serve cover with sweetened whipped cream. This pie is best served immediately after it is firm.

MAM' MANDY'S PUMPKIN PIE

2 cups canned pumpkin
1 tablespoon butter
3 eggs, lightly beaten
1½ cups milk
½ cup cream
⅓ cup brown sugar, firmly packed
3 tablespoons honey
¼ teaspoon ginger
½ teaspoon cinnamon
½ teaspoon allspice
pinch nutmeg
1 teaspoon salt
1 tablespoon Bourbon
2 tablespoons Sherry
½ recipe pie pastry

Melt butter in saucepan, add pumpkin, and cook, stirring constantly, 10 minutes after pumpkin begins to bubble. Cool. Mix all other ingredients, add pumpkin, and beat until perfectly smooth and creamy. Line 9-inch pie plate with pastry, making a high fluted rim. Pour in pumpkin mixture over a tablespoon to avoid making hole in pastry. Bake in hot oven (400-450°) 10 minutes. Reduce heat to moderate (350-375°) and bake until silver knife inserted in center of pie comes out dry, about 20-25 minutes longer.

YAM PIE NO. I

2 cups boiled mashed yams
1 cup butter
1 cup sugar
6 eggs, well beaten
2 tablespoons lemon juice
1 tablespoon grated lemon rind
2 tablespoons brandy
½ cup Sherry
1 tablespoon Bourbon
½ teaspoon salt
½ recipe plain pastry

Mash or rice yams while still hot, and stir in butter and sugar creamed together. Add eggs, lemon juice and rind, brandy, Sherry, whisky, and salt and beat until creamy. Line 9-inch pie plate with plain pastry, fill, and bake in a hot oven (400-450°) 10 minutes, then reduce heat to moderate (350-375°) and bake for about 25 minutes longer, or until silver knife comes out dry when inserted in center. Sweet potatoes may be used instead of yams in which case increase sugar to 1½ cups or add ½ cup honey.

YAM PIE NO. II

1½ cups cooked, mashed yams
2 eggs, beaten
⅓ cup dark brown sugar, firmly packed
1 teaspoon cinnamon
¼ teaspoon mace or nutmeg
¼ teaspoon allspice
½ teaspoon salt
⅔ cup milk
3 tablespoons melted butter
2 tablespoons Sherry
1 8-inch pastry shell, unbaked
½ cup heavy cream, whipped

Mix yams and beaten eggs, and stir in sugar, spices, and salt. Add milk, melted butter, and Sherry and beat until smooth. Fill pastry shell and bake 10 minutes in hot oven (450°), then reduce to moderate (350-375°) and bake until firm, about 25-30 minutes longer. Cool and top with whipped cream. Sprinkle with cinnamon or nutmeg if desired.

If yams are not obtainable, sweet potatoes may be substituted, using ½ cup of sugar instead of ⅓ cup.

COLONIAL CREAM

4 egg yolks
½ cup sugar
2 cups Sherry, Port, or Madeira
Heavy cream, whipped
1 tablespoon grated bitter chocolate

Beat egg yolks until very thick. Beat in sugar and add wine gradually. Put in double boiler over cold water and let water come to a boil. Allow mixture to simmer until it coats a spoon thickly. Pour in serving dishes and chill. Serve topped with whipped cream sprinkled with grated chocolate. Serves 4.

CHOCOLATE-SHERRY BAVARIAN CREAM

1 tablespoon gelatin
¼ cup Sherry
1 square chocolate
1 cup milk
3 eggs, separated
⅓ cup sugar
½ cup heavy cream, whipped

Soften gelatin in Sherry. Add chocolate to milk and heat in double boiler, beating with egg beater until thoroughly mixed. Stir together slightly beaten egg yolks, sugar, and gelatin mixture. Add to chocolate and milk, and cook, stirring constantly, until sugar is dissolved, about 5 minutes. Cool until slightly thickened. Fold in whipped cream. Beat egg whites until dry and fold in. Pour into mold or individual dishes and chill. Serves 4 to 6.

CHOCOLATE-SHERRY SOUFFLÉ

2 tablespoons butter
2 tablespoons flour
¾ cup milk
¼ cup Sherry
1 cup dry cake crumbs
2 squares unsweetened chocolate, melted
⅓ cup sugar
⅛ teaspoon salt
3 eggs, separated

Make a roux of butter and flour, add milk and Sherry, and cook until thickened. Stir in cake crumbs, melted chocolate, sugar, and salt. Cool slightly and add beaten egg yolks. Fold in egg whites beaten stiff but not dry. Pour into buttered 8-inch casserole, place in pan of hot water, and bake in moderate oven (350-375°) about 45 minutes. Serves 4 to 6.

QUEEN'S CREAM

¼ cup Sherry
1 tablespoon gelatin
½ cup hot water
¼ cup triple-strength coffee
¾ cup cream cheese
2 tablespoons powdered sugar
pinch of salt
2 egg whites, beaten dry

Heat wine just to a simmer. Cool. Add gelatin and when softened dissolve in hot water. Beat coffee and cheese together until creamy, and add to gelatin and wine. Add sugar and salt, and beat thoroughly. Chill. When about half set, fold in egg whites, beaten very dry, and chill at least 2 hours. Serves 4 to 6.

CATAWBA CREAM

½ cup sugar
3 tablespoons cornstarch
⅛ teaspoon salt
1 cup grape juice
1 cup sweet Catawba wine
½ cup heavy cream, whipped
2 tablespoons powdered sugar

Mix sugar, cornstarch, and salt and gradually stir in grape juice and wine. Cook in double boiler 5 minutes after simmering point is reached, stirring constantly. Turn into sauce dishes and chill. Top with whipped cream sweetened with powdered sugar. Serves 4 to 6.

RASPBERRY SPONGE

2 cups powdered sugar
¾ cup butter
¼ cup brandy
⅓ cup Sherry
1 cup raspberries, black or red, cooked
6 eggs, separated
1 stale sponge or pound cake

Cream butter and sugar together, and stir in wine, brandy, and berries. Beat egg yolks well and stir in, then fold in stiffly beaten whites. Pour over cake in pan and put in moderately hot oven (375-400°) for about ½ hour. May be baked in a rich pie crust instead of with cake, if desired, and topped with meringue. Serves 6.

WINE CREAM

6 egg yolks, well beaten
2½ tablespoons sugar
1⅓ cups Sauterne or Chablis
salt
vanilla
1 tablespoon gelatin
½ cup cold water
1 cup heavy cream, whipped
2 tablespoons powdered sugar

Make a Chaudeau of egg yolks, sugar, wine, and seasonings (p. 266). Soften gelatin in cold water, add to Chaudeau, and cool. Add sugar to whipped cream and stir well into wine mixture. Put in mold or individual glasses and chill in refrigerator 4 to 5 hours. Serves 6 to 8.

PORT TUTTI FRUTTI

2 tablespoons gelatin
½ cup cold water
2 cups heavy cream, whipped
⅔ cup confectioner's sugar
2 cups cooked rice
1 cup Port
¼ cup chopped dates
¼ cup chopped figs
2 tablespoons candied ginger
1 tablespoon candied orange peel

Soften gelatin in cold water. Add whipped cream, sugar, rice, and wine, which has been heated just to a simmer. Chill. When it begins to set, add chopped fruit. Stir occasionally, if necessary, to prevent fruits from settling. Chill 4 hours. Serves 6.

TIPSY CHARLOTTE RUSSE

1 cup Port or Sherry
1 tablespoon gelatin
2 cups heavy cream
½ cup powdered sugar
1 cup chopped almonds
1 tablespoon butter
¼ pound lady fingers

Heat wine just to simmering. Cool. Soften gelatin in ½ cup of wine for 5 minutes and dissolve in remaining wine. Whip cream, add sugar, and stir in gelatin. Brown chopped almonds lightly. Line serving dish with lady fingers, pour in mixture, sprinkle toasted almonds on top, and chill 2 to 3 hours. Serves 10 to 12.

SAUTERNE SPONGE

1 tablespoon gelatin
2 tablespoons cold water
1 1/2 cups Sauterne
3 tablespoons sugar
3 egg whites, beaten

Soften gelatin in cold water. Bring wine to a simmer, and stir in gelatin and sugar. Chill until it begins to thicken, then beat to a foam and fold in egg whites. Chill 2 to 3 hours and serve heaped up in sherbet glasses. Serves 4.

MACAROON AMBROSIA

20 stale macaroons
1/2 cup Port or Sherry
1 cup heavy cream, whipped, *or*
1 cup custard sauce

If macaroons are fresh and moist, dry them out in the oven. Break them (do not crumble) into individual dessert dishes, allowing 5 to a portion. Moisten each portion with 2 tablespoons wine and place in refrigerator for several hours or overnight. Serve topped with whipped cream or custard sauce. Serves 4.

ENGLISH TRIFLE

1 sponge cake, 2-3 inches thick
1 cup jam (apricot, currant, raspberry, or peach)
1 1/4 cups Port or Sherry
1 1/2 cups milk
3 tablespoons flour
2 egg yolks, beaten
1/3 cup sugar
1/2 teaspoon salt
1/2 teaspoon vanilla
1 cup heavy cream, whipped
3/4 cup almonds, blanched and cut in slivers

Divide cake lengthwise into two layers, spread half of jam on one layer, place other layer on top, and spread with remaining jam. Place in serving dish and pour 3/4 cup wine over and around cake. Bring 1 cup milk to a boil. Make paste of remaining cold milk and flour, stir into hot milk, and let boil 3 minutes. Add sugar and salt to beaten egg yolks in double boiler. Stir in hot milk slowly and continue cooking until mixture coats spoon. Cool, add vanilla and remaining wine, and pour over cake. Spread with whipped cream and stick in almond slivers. Chill well before serving. Serves 6 to 8.

FROZEN TRIFLE

1 slice plain butter cake, 1 inch thick, cut to fit refrigerator tray
½ cup Sherry
½ cup toasted almonds, chopped
½ cup strawberry or raspberry jam
2 egg yolks
6 tablespoons sugar
pinch of salt
1 cup milk
1 cup heavy cream, whipped

Put cake in refrigerator tray. Pour Sherry over cake slowly so that it will absorb the wine. Add ¼ cup chopped almonds and cover with the jam. Beat the eggs, sugar, and salt together. Cook in double boiler, stirring constantly, until it coats a spoon. Chill and add whipped cream. Pour this over cake, nuts, and jam, cover with remaining almonds, and freeze so that it may be cut. Serves 4 to 6.

FRUIT-NUT TRIFLE

24 macaroons
½ cup Sherry
3 egg yolks, beaten
1 cup sugar
⅛ teaspoon salt
3 cups sliced strawberries (or raspberries, peaches, or any fresh fruit)
1 cup heavy cream, whipped
¼ cup powdered sugar
½ cup almonds, blanched and sliced

Soak macaroons in wine until about half the wine is absorbed and arrange in serving dish. Beat egg yolks until very thick, then beat in sugar. Thorough beating is important. Stir in remaining Sherry and salt, and cook in double boiler until thick. Pour on macaroons and chill. Add chilled fruit and whipped cream, dust with powdered sugar, and top with sliced almonds just before serving. Serves 4.

WINE SUNDAE

1 cup sugar
½ cup water
⅓ cup Port or Burgundy

Cook sugar and water until it makes a heavy sirup. Cool and add wine. Pour over vanilla ice cream.

Thomas Jefferson was one of the most famous gourmets of his age and an ardent recipe collector. This was one of his favorites.

FLOATING ISLAND NO. I

(Thomas Jefferson's Recipe)

2 cups milk
1 cup light cream
1 cup Sauterne
4 egg whites, beaten *dry*
2 tablespoons strawberry or raspberry jam or jelly
6 slices pound or sponge cake, about 3 x 4 inches

Mix milk and cream and wine together. Beat egg whites as stiffly as possible and beat in jam or jelly (more jam or jelly may be added if desired). Place slices of cake in serving dishes, pour on syllabub (wine and cream mixture), heap on egg froth, and serve very cold. Serves 6.

FLOATING ISLAND NO II

4 eggs, separated
¼ cup confectioner's sugar
2 cups milk
½ teaspoon salt
¼ cup granulated sugar
3 tablespoons Sherry

Beat whites of eggs until dry, then beat in confectioner's sugar. Heat milk to boiling in heavy frying pan, drop in beaten egg whites a spoonful at a time, and keep moving until cooked firm. Remove and place on cloth or absorbent paper. Beat egg yolks and add granulated sugar, milk, and Sherry gradually. Cook as custard in double boiler. Cool, pour in serving dish, arrange poached whites on top, and chill. Serves 4.

FLOATING ISLAND NO. III

2 eggs, separated
¼ cup sugar
⅛ teaspoon salt
1½ cups scalded milk
2⅓ tablespoons Sherry

Beat egg yolks with sugar and salt. Add milk and cook until spoon is coated. Add 2 tablespoons Sherry. Beat egg whites stiff. Add 2 tablespoons sugar and 1 teaspoon Sherry. Pour custard in glasses and top with egg whites. Serves 4.

PINEAPPLE-SHERRY MOUSSE

- ⅔ cup milk
- ½ pound marshmallows (about 20)
- ½ cup canned pineapple, drained and crushed
- ⅛ teaspoon salt
- ½ cup Sherry
- ½ pint heavy cream, whipped

Melt marshmallows in the milk in double boiler. Chill until thickened. Add pineapple, salt, and Sherry. Add the whipped cream and stir until well blended. Pour into refrigerator tray and freeze without stirring. Serves 4 to 6.

FROZEN EGGNOG

- 4 egg yolks
- 1 cup sugar
- ½ teaspoon salt
- 1 quart heavy cream
- ⅓ cup Sherry
- ⅓ cup brandy
- ⅓ cup rum

Beat egg yolks until thick. Beat in sugar and salt until fluffy. Mix in cream and freeze in freezer until very firm. Add Sherry and liquors, and mix well for 2 or 3 minutes. Serves 10 to 12.

MISS MUFFET ICE CREAM

- 2 eggs, slightly beaten
- 1¾ cups sugar
- ½ teaspoon salt
- 3 tablespoons flour
- 2 cups milk
- 1 tablespoon whisky
- 3 tablespoons Jamaica rum
- 6 tablespoons Sherry
- ⅓ cup hot water
- 2 tablespoons gelatin
- 4 cups cream
- 1 cup chopped candied cherries

Add sugar, salt, and flour to beaten eggs. Stir in milk and cook in double boiler to a thick custard. Add liquors, wine, and gelatin dissolved in hot water. Allow to cool thoroughly. Dust cherries well with confectioner's sugar before chopping. Add together with cream and freeze in automatic refrigerator or in ice-cream freezer. Serves 6.

MACAROON ICE CREAM

24 macaroons
1 cup sugar
1 cup Sherry
1 quart heavy cream, whipped
1 cup almonds, blanched and shredded

Put macaroons in slow oven until very dry and roll to fine crumbs. Dissolve sugar in wine and blend with whipped cream. Mix shredded almonds with macaroon crumbs and add to whipped-cream mixture. Freeze in freezer or in automatic refrigerator. If the latter, remove and stir three or four times after it begins to harden. Best if left to ripen for 3 or 4 hours. Serves 10 to 12.

SHERIMEL ICE CREAM

1 can (1¼ cups) sweetened condensed milk
½ cup Sherry
1 cup heavy cream, whipped

Caramelize the condensed milk by immersing the unopened can in boiling water for 3 hours. Be sure to keep can covered with water. Or place in pressure cooker with ½ cup water and keep at 15 pounds pressure 35 to 40 minutes. Cool, remove from can, and beat until perfectly smooth. Heat Sherry in fairly large saucepan until it steams (150°). Do not allow it to simmer. Stir into caramelized milk and add whipped cream. Freeze in automatic refrigerator. Does not require stirring and will not become grainy. Serves 4 to 6.

BAKED ALASKA

1 slice stale plain cake, approximately
  8 x 6 x 1 inches
½ cup sweet wine
1 quart ice cream
5 egg whites
¾ cup powdered sugar

Place cake on steak plank or on 3 or 4 thicknesses of cardboard on a baking sheet. Moisten with any desired sweet wine. (The amount of wine used depends upon the staleness of the cake, which should be quite dry. Do not use enough to make it mushy.) Cut ice cream into slices and cover cake to within ¾ inch of edges. Beat egg whites until dry and add ½ cup sugar gradually, beating after each addition. Spread over ice cream and edges of cake. Dust remaining sugar over meringue. Bake in very hot oven (450-500°) until gently browned. Serve at once. Serves 6.

GUAVA ICE CREAM

(From Gretchen Green—The Whole World & Co.)

Melt a small glass (6 ounces) of guava jelly in a double boiler with 1 sherry glass of dry Sherry and ½ cup sugar. Add this to 3 pints of double cream. Stir well and flavor with the juice of a lime. Freeze. This can be colored pink if desired. Serves 8.

CLARET SHERBET

2 tablespoons gelatin
2 cups Claret
1 cup water
1 cup sugar
2 tablespoons lemon juice
2 egg whites

Soften gelatin in ¼ cup Claret. Boil the sugar and water for 10 minutes. Add gelatin, the remaining 1¾ cups Claret, and lemon juice to the sirup and stir. Put in refrigerator tray and freeze to a mushy consistency. Place in chilled bowl and beat. Fold in stiffly beaten egg whites and finish freezing. Makes 1½ quarts.

CARDINAL PUNCH

6 medium-sized oranges
4 cups sugar
2 cups water
2 tablespoons whole cloves
2 cups Burgundy or Claret
2 cups Port
10 egg whites, beaten dry
4 tablespoons raspberry juice
red vegetable coloring (if necessary, to give the proper color)

Bake oranges in a moderate oven (350-375°) for 1 hour, or less if juice begins to exude. Boil sugar, water, and cloves for 3 minutes. Add wine, bring to a simmer, and put in oranges. Cool. Cut oranges in half and extract juice, bruise skins, and add with juice to sirup. Let stand 2 hours or more and strain. Fold in beaten egg whites and raspberry juice or enough red vegetable coloring to give a bright red color. Place in freezer and cover. Stir every four or five minutes until it has become of sherbet consistency. Serve in sherbet glasses. Serves 12 to 16.

ZABAGLIONE

There are many spellings of Zabaglione. The one just used is preferred by Italians while Sabayon is the choice of the French.

Of the many recipes, the following have been chosen as the best. In each, vigorous and long beating is essential in securing professional results.

ZABAGLIONE

6 egg yolks
¼ cup sugar
dash of salt
½ cup Marsala or Sherry

Put enough water in bottom of small double boiler to come within about an inch of bottom of top portion. Put egg yolks in top of double boiler, and beat until very thick and light. Gradually add sugar and salt, beating until sugar is dissolved. Add wine, beating constantly until mixture is thick and frothy. Serve in sherbet glasses either hot or iced. Dust with cinnamon or nutmeg. Serves 4.

ZABAGLIONE TRIFLE

Pour 1½ cups macaroon crumbs into Zabaglione. Mix, stirring as lightly as possible. Serves 4 to 6.

SABAYON (FRENCH)

8 eggs, separated
1 cup powdered sugar
½ cup sweet Sherry

Beat egg yolks and sugar together in top of double boiler very thoroughly. Add Sherry and continue beating until mixture thickens. Pour into beaten whites and serve at once. Serves 4 to 6.

SAUCE SABAYON

(from Lucien Toucās, chef, Hotel Astor, New York City)

2 ounces sugar
4 egg yolks
3 ounces Madeira, Marsala, or Sherry
juice of ½ orange

Mix sugar and egg yolks in a mixing bowl, and beat until it becomes a light color. Add wine and orange juice, pour in a double boiler, and cook until it binds. Serve hot with lady fingers or sponge cake. Serves 3 to 4.

WINE CHAUDEAU

5 egg yolks
2 tablespoons sugar
pinch of salt
½ cup dry white wine
1 egg white, stiffly beaten
¼ teaspoon vanilla or almond extract

Beat egg yolks until thick and lemon-colored. This step is important: 5 minutes beating by hand is not too much. Beat in sugar and salt, and put in top of double boiler with wine. Cook, beating constantly, until very smooth and well thickened. Remove from heat, and fold in egg white and flavoring. Serve hot or cold as a sauce or a light dessert. Approximately 3 cups sauce.

WINE FOAM

3 eggs, separated
3 egg yolks
3 tablespoons lemon juice
1 cup sugar
2 cups dry white wine
½ teaspoon grated lemon peel
pinch of salt

Beat egg whites until stiff and yolks until lemon-colored. Put all ingredients in top of double boiler over rapidly boiling water, and beat with rotary beater until stiff and frothy. Serve at once.

FRENCH PANCAKES WITH SHERRY JELLY

1½ cups flour
½ teaspoon baking powder
¼ teaspoon salt
1 tablespoon sugar
2 eggs, separated
1 cup milk
2½ tablespoons melted butter
Sherry Jelly (p. 274)

Sift flour, baking powder, salt, and sugar together. Beat egg yolks until light, add milk and melted butter, and combine with sifted dry ingredients. Fold in stiffly beaten egg whites. Drop by tablespoonfuls onto a hot well-oiled griddle. Fry until brown, first on one side, then on the other. Place on board which has been sprinkled with powdered sugar and spread first with butter, then with Sherry Jelly and roll. Place on plate and sprinkle with powdered sugar. Approximately 1½ dozen small pancakes.

MARRONS GLACÉ IN SHERRY

large chestnuts
lemon juice
sugar
water
Sherry

Cover chestnuts with boiling water and cook rapidly until tender enough to be pierced easily with fork, about 20 to 30 minutes. When just cold enough to handle, remove shells and brown skin. Cover chestnuts with cold water to which 2 tablespoons lemon juice per quart has been added and let stand in refrigerator for at least 12 hours so they will not break up in cooking.

Measure and prepare sirup of 4 cups sugar to 2 cups water to each pint of nuts. Pour over nuts and cook in heavy sauce over asbestos mat, *without boiling*, until chestnuts are clear, about 2 to 3 hours. Watch heat carefully at start, when sirup begins to simmer, and reduce very slightly until it is exactly adjusted. This, together with the soaking in acidulated water, is the secret. Drain off sirup and boil it rapidly until reduced to ⅓. Add ¼ cup Sherry to each cup sirup, bring to a simmer, and pour over chestnuts. Can in ½-pint jars or glasses.

SHERRY COOKIES

2 cups sifted flour
3 teaspoons baking powder
½ teaspoon salt
½ cup butter
1¼ cups sugar
1 cup water
2 tablespoons sliced orange peel, white part removed
¼ cup Sherry

Sift together flour, baking powder, and salt. Cream butter and add 1 cup sugar and beat until smooth. Cut orange peel in strips the thickness of toothpicks and ½ inch long; cook in sirup of ¼ cup sugar and 1 cup water until transparent and the sirup is thick. Add to creamed butter and sugar together with sirup. Stir in flour and wine alternately. Drop by teaspoonfuls on greased baking sheet. Bake in medium-hot oven (375-400°) 10 to 12 minutes. Approximately 4 dozen cookies.

Two tablespoons sliced Brazil nuts or chopped almonds may be added if desired.

SHERRIED ALMONDS

½ cup butter
4½ cups confectioner's sugar
¼ cup Sherry
¼ cup brandy
4 cups blanched almonds
½ cup chopped pistachio nuts

Cream butter and sugar, and beat in wine and brandy. Beat until very smooth. Put almonds in shallow pan in moderate oven (350-375°) until golden, about 15-20 minutes, stirring frequently. While hot stir into sugar mixture until each is well coated. Roll each almond in chopped pistachio nuts and lay on absorbent paper until cool.

LEMON SHERRY SAUCE

⅔ cup sugar
1 teaspoon cornstarch
1 cup water
½ cup Sherry
grated rind of ½ lemon
juice of ½ lemon
½ inch stick cinnamon
¼ teaspoon salt

Mix sugar and cornstarch, add to all other ingredients, and bring slowly to a simmer. Stir constantly over low heat until creamy. Strain. Approximately 1⅔ cups sauce.

HARD SAUCE

½ cup butter
1¼ cups powdered sugar
⅛ teaspoon salt
dash of nutmeg
juice of ½ lemon
⅓ cup dry white wine

Cream butter, then blend in sugar, salt, and nutmeg. Add lemon juice and wine, and beat until completely blended. 2¼ cups sauce.

SHERRY HARD SAUCE

⅓ cup butter
1 egg yolk
2 cups sifted confectioner's sugar
¼ cup Sherry

Beat all ingredients together thoroughly. 2½ cups sauce.

CHOCOLATE SAUCE

2 squares unsweetened chocolate, melted
3 eggs, separated
⅔ cup sugar
¼ cup Sherry
¾ cup heavy cream, whipped

Cook chocolate, beaten egg yolks, and sugar in double boiler, beating constantly with egg beater until creamy. Add Sherry and beat 2 minutes. Remove from heat, and fold in whipped cream and stiffly beaten egg whites. Approximately 3 cups sauce.

CREAMY CHOCOLATE SAUCE WITH SHERRY

(for desserts, especially ice cream)

2 squares unsweetened chocolate
1¼ cups light cream
½ cup sugar
1 tablespoon arrowroot or cornstarch
½ teaspoon salt
½ teaspoon cinnamon
3 tablespoons honey
¼ cup Sherry
½ teaspoon vanilla

Melt chocolate in double boiler, add cream, and beat until smooth. Mix together sugar, arrowroot or cornstarch, salt, and cinnamon and stir in gradually. Add honey and stir until thickened, about 5 minutes. Remove from heat, add Sherry and vanilla, and beat 2 minutes with rotary beater. Serve hot or cold. Approximately 1½ cups sauce.

CLARET SAUCE

2 eggs, separated
⅔ cup powdered sugar
1 cup heavy cream, whipped
2 tablespoons Claret

Beat egg whites until stiff but not dry. Beat in sugar gradually. Beat egg yolks thoroughly. Mix with cream and wine, and fold into egg whites and sugar. Best with steamed puddings, especially chocolate. Approximately 3 cups sauce.

GINGER SHERRY SAUCE

1 cup chopped preserved ginger
¼ cup Sherry

Simmer ginger and Sherry together for 5 minutes over very low heat, stirring constantly. Excellent over devil's food cake. 1¼ cups sauce.

CLEAR RED WINE SAUCE

3 tablespoons arrowroot or cornstarch
⅓ cup sugar
2 cups water
¼ cup honey
1 1-inch stick cinnamon
4 whole cloves
2 tablespoons butter
1 tablespoon lemon juice
½ teaspoon salt
½ cup dry red wine

Mix arrowroot or cornstarch and sugar, add water, and stir until dissolved. Add all other ingredients except wine and simmer gently, stirring constantly, over low heat until perfectly clear and thickened. Stir in wine and strain. May be served either hot or cold. Approximately 3 cups sauce.

Grated lemon rind may be added if desired. If a thinner sauce is desired, more water or wine may be added.

CATAWBA SYLLABUB

⅓ cup sugar
juice of 1 lemon
grated rind of 1 lemon
2 tablespoons brandy
¼ cup sweet Catawba
2 cups heavy cream, whipped

Mix together sugar, lemon juice, rind, brandy, and wine. Stir into whipped cream. Chill. Approximately 3 cups sauce.

WHITE WINE SAUCE, SWEET

¾ cup butter
3 cups powdered sugar
¾ cup boiling water
⅔ cup dry white wine
1 teaspoon grated nutmeg

Cream butter and sugar in double boiler, and mix in boiling water and nutmeg. Have water in lower part simmering, not boiling. Add wine gradually, stirring constantly, until sauce is quite thick. Serve hot or cold. Approximately 4½ cups sauce.

PINEAPPLE-PORT SAUCE

Combine 1 cup each of sugar, crushed pineapple, and Port and cook to a heavy sirup. Serve on ice cream or pudding.

WINE SAUCE FOR PUDDING

⅔ cup dry red wine
⅓ cup water
½ cup sugar
1 tablespoon cornstarch
pinch of salt
2 tablespoons butter
dash of nutmeg

Bring wine and water to a boil. Mix sugar, cornstarch, and salt and add to hot liquid. Let boil 3 to 4 minutes, stirring constantly. Remove from fire, add butter and nutmeg, and serve hot over individual portions of bread pudding, tapioca cream, or other simple pudding. Approximately 1 cup sauce.

CARAMEL SAUCE

1 cup sugar
1 cup boiling water
pinch of salt
2 tablespoons Sherry

Melt 1 tablespoon sugar slowly in heavy saucepan over low heat until it takes on a light mahogany color. Remove from heat, and slowly add boiling water; return to heat, add remaining sugar and salt, and boil until caramel is dissolved, about 10 minutes. Add Sherry. Approximately 1 cup sauce.

WINE SIRUP

(for waffles, pancakes, and desserts)

4½ cups any sweet wine
3 cups sugar
¾ cup water

Put all ingredients in saucepan, bring to a boil, stirring until sugar is dissolved, and boil 10 minutes. Cool and bottle. It will keep indefinitely. 5 cups.

TOKAY SIRUP

(for pancakes, waffles, or French toast)

1½ cups sugar
2¼ cups white Tokay
3 tablespoons water

Mix ingredients and stir until sugar is dissolved. Boil for 10 minutes. Serve hot or cold. This can be made up ahead, put in bottles, and kept indefinitely.

WHITE APRON SAUCE (for cakes and puddings)

3 egg whites
9 tablespoons powdered sugar
1½ tablespoons melted butter
2 tablespoons Sherry

Beat egg whites very dry. Add powdered sugar, melted butter, and Sherry. Mix thoroughly.

WINE CUSTARD SAUCE

3 eggs, lightly beaten
½ cup sugar
pinch salt
2 cups milk, scalded
¼ cup Sherry or any sweet wine

Mix eggs, sugar, and salt thoroughly. Stir in ¼ cup hot milk slowly. Add to rest of hot milk in double boiler and cook until mixture coats spoon. Cool, stir in wine, and chill. Approximately 2½ cups sauce.

WINE SAUCE FOR ICE CREAM

1 cup sugar
½ cup water
⅓ cup Port or Burgundy

Cook sugar and water to a heavy sirup. Cool and add wine. For fruit ice creams use Tokay, Muscatel, or Angelica. Approximately 1 cup sirup.

HONEY WINE SAUCE

1 cup honey
¼ cup boiling water
3 tablespoons Port or Sherry

Mix honey with boiling water and add wine, stirring well.

SHERRY BUTTER

1 cup butter
1 cup sugar
½ cup Sherry

Cream butter and sugar, add wine, and beat well. Chill.

SHERRY RUM BUTTER

As above, using ¼ cup rum and ¼ cup Sherry.

SHERRY BRANDY BUTTER

As above, using brandy in place of rum.

WINE BUTTER SAUCE

1 cup butter
2/3 cup wine

Use any sweet wine desired. Heat together until it just begins to simmer. Sugar may be added if a sweet sauce is desired. Approximately 1 2/3 cups sauce.

SEA FOAM (for fruits, puddings, etc.)

4 egg whites
1 1/2 cups honey
1/2 cup Port or Sherry

Beat egg whites until very dry. They should remain in bowl when it is inverted. Place dish containing honey in hot water until it can be very easily poured. Add wine to honey and stir thoroughly into the beaten egg whites. Chill well before serving. Approximately 4 cups sauce.

MINT JELLY

1 cup mint leaves
1/4 cup vinegar
1 cup Rhine wine
1/4 cup water
3 1/2 cups sugar
1/2 bottle liquid pectin
1/4 teaspoon green coloring

Wash mint leaves. Do not remove the leaves from the stems. Press with a wooden spoon; add vinegar, wine, water, and sugar and bring to a boil. Add coloring. Let mixture boil and add pectin, stirring constantly. Then bring to a full rolling boil and boil hard for 1/2 minute. Remove from fire, strain off mint leaves, and put into sterilized jars. Seal with paraffin.

SPICED CLARET JELLY

3 cups sugar
2 cups Claret
1/2 teaspoon whole allspice
1/4 teaspoon whole cloves
3 2-inch sticks cinnamon
2 tablespoons vinegar
1/2 bottle liquid pectin

Measure sugar, wine, spices, and vinegar into cooking pan. Bring to a boil. Add pectin, stirring constantly. Bring to a hard boil and boil for 1/2 minute. Remove from fire and put into sterilized jars. Seal with paraffin.

PORT JELLY

1 package raspberry-flavored gelatin
1¼ cups hot water
¾ cup Port
1 cup diced fruit

Dissolve gelatin in hot water. Pour wine over fruit and let stand until gelatin is cool, then combine. When it begins to harden, turn into mold and chill until firm. Oranges, bananas, canned or fresh peaches, and pears may be used. For plain wine jelly omit fruit. Serve with chilled custard sauce or whipped cream. Serves 6.

WINE JELLY

2 cups any wine
3 cups sugar
½ bottle fruit pectin

Measure sugar and wine into a saucepan. Bring to a boil and add fruit pectin, stirring constantly. Then bring to a hard boil and let boil for ½ minute. Remove from fire and pour into jelly glasses. Keeps indefinitely.

STRAWBERRY JAM

2 cups strawberries
2 cups sugar
⅔ cup sweet Catawba
½ bottle liquid pectin

Place cleaned, whole berries in saucepan. Mix ½ cup of sugar with fruit. Heat gently and bring to the simmering point. Add remaining sugar and let come to a boil. Boil 3 minutes. Add wine and bring to a boil again. Add pectin and stir. Let stand 1 minute before pouring into sterilized glasses.

CHAPTER ELEVEN

Wine Service, Wine Drinks, Appetizers, and Canapés

To many people the use of wine at the table is surrounded by so many complications of tradition and ritual with which they are unfamiliar that they fear to attempt it. This is a genuine pity.

The facts are that there are no unbreakable rules about wine service except those which your own good taste would naturally dictate.

Under no circumstances should you even think of serving a different wine with every course except at the most formal and elaborate dinners, and it is most emphatically not necessary even then. On the other hand, even when entertaining, it is perfectly "correct" to serve one wine throughout the meal. Of course, you would not want to choose a sweet wine for the same reason that you would not put sugar on oysters, fish, or a steak. For "one wine" meals select a dry wine. Which one? That is wholly and entirely up to you. One good way to decide is to use the one which will be happiest with your principal dish. For example, if it is a casserole of sea food or a roast of veal a dry white wine would be preferable. With a roast of beef or venison, Claret or Burgundy would be the obvious thing.

The old rule of "white wine with white meat and red wine with red meat" is a good one to remember—and to break whenever you feel like it. For example, some amateur experts profess to be shocked at the use of red wine to accompany any poultry except duck and wild fowl, yet any roast turkey is a nobler bird with a good upstanding Burgundy or Claret than with the best white wine that money can buy.

When only a single wine is used, don't overlook the possibilities of a good dry Sherry. Serve it before the meal in place of cocktails if you like and all the way through. For a more festive occasion, the palate-cleansing freshness of Champagne is perfection, and your judgment would be applauded by any real gourmet.

Sweet wines, if used, come with dessert, cheese, and nuts. Never should they precede a dry wine for exactly the same reason you would never serve a sweet before a salad.

For bridge or afternoon teas, fit the wine to the food, if any. For the casual caller a glass of wine is a traditional gesture of hospitality.

The proper temperature at which to serve wine is the one at which its flavor and bouquet are most pronounced. As a general rough guide, sparkling wines should be chilled (that, by the way, does not mean iced); Sherry, if sweet, at room temperature; very dry Sherry, quite cool; dry white wines, cold; dry red and sweet wines at room temperature. The chart opposite is all the guide you'll need. "Slightly chilled" means about half an hour in the refrigerator; "chilled," about an hour; "iced" at least three hours.

"Shall I use a decanter?" At the table, no—except perhaps for Port. On a sideboard, yes, if you have an unusually fine one or two you want to display, and then only for Port and Sherry.

The illustration (p. 279) shows the shape of glass for every wine, but under no circumstances should more than three glasses be used at one meal. The water goblet is placed at the right, slightly away from the tip of the knife, and the wine glass or glasses next to it. If more than one is used they are arranged in the order in which the wine is served.

Choose your wine glasses with these requirements in mind: They should be clear, thin and, as a rule, colorless so that the color of the beverage may be enjoyed. Slightly green-tinted glasses are permissible for Sauterne, Chablis and Riesling. The best all-purpose glass is tulip-shaped, of four- or five-ounce capacity. Even for Champagne a special glass is not necessary, but if it is used the tulip shape is slightly preferable as it enables the user better to enjoy the bouquet. Hollow-stemmed, saucer, or flute-shaped glasses do emphasize the sparkle and are a bit more festive. Fortified wines and Vermouth are generally served in flared glasses holding about two or three ounces, which may also be used for cocktails.

A point to remember: never fill a wine glass more than one-half to two-thirds full. The true wine lover wants to swirl it around and sniff the bouquet. The nose plays almost as important a part in the enjoyment of wine as the palate. The perfect host or hostess tries to avoid empty glasses except when a toast is drunk and at a formal dinner will carefully instruct the servant or servants on this point.

A wine bottle should never be surrounded by a napkin except in the case of Champagne when it is first removed from the ice bucket,

WINE SERVICE GUIDE

Type	*When*	*How*
Vermouth	As an aperitif	Cold
Dry or medium-sweet Sherry or dry or medium-sweet Madeira	As an aperitif With clear soups Throughout the meal	Slightly chilled
Sweet Sherry or sweet Madeira	With dessert	Room temperature
Dry Sauterne	With shellfish and fish Throughout the meal	Cold
Medium-sweet Sauterne	With fruit or dessert	Cold
Sweet Sauterne	With fruit or dessert	Cold
Chablis	With shellfish and fish Throughout the meal	Cold
Riesling, Rhine, Moselle, Hock	With seafood or delicate meat Throughout the meal	Chilled
Claret	With red meats Throughout the meal	Room temperature
Chianti (Red)	With red meats Throughout the meal	Room temperature
Chianti (White)	With seafood Throughout the meal	Slightly chilled
Burgundy, Catawba, Zinfandel, Barbera, Barberona	Roast, Entree, Game Throughout the meal	Room temperature
Malaga, Muscatel, Marsala, Angelica, Tokay	With dessert	Room temperature
Port	After dessert — with nuts or cheese	Room temperature
Champagne	With seafood Throughout the meal	Very well chilled

to avoid slipping. Properly chilled Champagne will open with only a slight pop as the cork is carefully worked out and with no effervescing.

It is an old custom to pour a few drops of wine in the host's glass first, so that he may see that it is in perfect condition. A nice touch perhaps, but not at all obligatory. Wine for the first course is not poured until after the food is served. If more than one wine is served, the glasses used for the previous one are removed, and the wine is poured after the next course is served.

If wines are to be stored for any length of time, remember that they must be placed on their sides so that the corks are always moist. The ideal storage place is dark, dry, and with a uniform temperature of about 55°. This, of course, presupposes a cellar, which the average city dweller does not have. Failing this, it is better to buy your wines in comparatively small quantities and let the wholesaler worry about the storage problem.

Sparkling wines obviously must never be recorked. Once opened they must be drunk or put aside for cooking purposes. Unfortified wines may be corked and put back in the refrigerator where they will keep for several days without too great impairment of flavor. Fortified wines will keep indefinitely at room temperature.

Careless opening of wine is unforgivable. Every bit of foil and covering should be removed, the cork extracted unbroken, and the lip of the bottle wiped clean before a drop is poured. A broken cork is, to say the least, embarrassing. A really good corkscrew, the kind used in bars and restaurants, is a sound investment. Start in the exact center of the cork and pull straight up. Be sure that it is large enough. A corkscrew that is too small will usually mutilate the cork.

WINE DRINKS

The coming of repeal brought forth a hideous crop of the most frightful combinations of wines and liquors that the mind of man could imagine. One, chosen at random, calls for 1/3 Port, 1/3 gin, and 1/3 kümmel! Try it at your own risk.

Of course, not even a purist would claim that wine should not be drunk otherwise than unmixed. There are too many utterly delightful combinations to permit that. In summer there is nothing more grateful than a long icy wine cooler.

Of course, you can make a punch without wine, but who wants to unless with the sole purpose of administering a quick knockout to the party. Don't take that to mean that every recipe that follows

Claret or All Purpose
Port
Sherry
Tulip Champagne
Hollow Stem Champagne
Flute Champagne
White Wine
Rhine Wine

is innocuous. Some are amazingly deceptive, but you will learn to distinguish them by experience. However, with drinks as with salad dressings, sooner or later you will hit upon a combination that, if pressed, you will modestly admit is the best ever compounded. Once there was a man who did just that but couldn't remember what he had used, and finally committed suicide in despair. The moral is plain.

RHINE WINE SOUR

3 teaspoons bar sugar
juice of 1 lemon
3 jiggers Rhine wine or Riesling
2 ice cubes

Mix in a cocktail shaker. Shake until sugar is dissolved. Strain and serve in a 4-ounce whisky-sour glass. Decorate with a thin slice of lemon or with mint leaves.

WINE MARTINI

2 parts white Tokay
1 part gin
dash of orange bitters

Mix and serve in a cocktail glass. Decorate with an olive.

CLARET FLOAT

1 tablespoon sugar
½ jigger lemon juice
4 jiggers Sauterne
1 jigger Claret

Mix sugar, lemon juice, and Sauterne in a 10-ounce glass. Stir until sugar is dissolved. Add crushed ice. Pour Claret slowly over the top so it will float. Serve with a straw.

GYPSY HIGHBALL

2 ounces white Tokay
2 ounces sparkling water

Add 2 lumps ice. Use 6-ounce glass.

CLARET LEMONADE

2 tablespoons sugar
1 jigger lemon juice
2 jiggers Claret

Mix sugar, lemon juice, and Claret in a 10-ounce glass. Stir until sugar is dissolved. Fill glass with crushed ice. Decorate with a slice of orange and a cocktail cherry. Serve with a straw.

CHAMPAGNE COCKTAIL NO. I

1 lump sugar
1 or 2 dashes Angostura bitters
Fill glass with chilled Champagne

Stir and serve with a thin piece of twisted lemon peel. (One split of Champagne makes about three cocktails.)

CHAMPAGNE COCKTAIL NO. II

1 cube sugar
1 dash Angostura bitters
1 slice orange peel
1 teaspoon brandy
Champagne

Moisten sugar with Angostura, twist orange peel, add brandy, and muddle. Add 1 ice cube and fill glass with Champagne.

TED'S SPECIAL

1/3 sweet Vermouth
1/3 dry Sherry
1/3 whisky

Mix ingredients with ice, strain, and serve in cocktail glass with twist of orange peel.

FRENCH "75"

1 jigger gin
1 jigger lemon juice
1 teaspoon powdered sugar
3 ice cubes

Use an 8-ounce glass. Stir the above ingredients and fill glass with Champagne. (One split bottle makes two drinks.)

CATAWBA COCKTAIL

2 jiggers Catawba
1 jigger Rhine wine
juice of 1 slice of lemon
1 slice of orange

Mix Catawba, Rhine wine, and lemon juice in a glass and stir. Serve in a cocktail glass. Decorate with a slice of orange.

PORT COCKTAIL

2 jiggers Port
1/2 jigger brandy
1 bar spoon Grenadine
1/2 jigger lemon juice

Stir with ice and serve in a cocktail glass.

SAUTERNE COCKTAIL

2 jiggers Sauterne
1 jigger orange juice
2 teaspoons Grenadine
2 ice cubes

Mix in cocktail shaker. Shake and strain into a cocktail glass. Serve with a maraschino cherry.

SHERRY BLOSSOM

1 part Sherry
2 parts orange juice

Add 2 ice cubes and shake. Strain into a cocktail glass.

SHERRY OLD FASHIONED

½ teaspoon sugar
3 dashes bitters
twist of lemon peel
2 jiggers Sherry
orange slice
maraschino cherry

Place sugar, bitters, lemon peel, and a little Sherry in Old Fashioned glass and muddle until sugar is dissolved and peel well bruised. Add rest of Sherry and ice cube. Garnish with cherry and orange slice.

VERMOUTH COCKTAIL

4 tablespoons sweet Vermouth
1 teaspoon Amer Picon
½ teaspoon Curaçao
1 dash Angostura bitters
½ teaspoon sugar
1 strip lemon peel
1 sprig mint, bruised
maraschino cherry

Shake with cracked ice. Add twisted lemon peel, mint, and cherry.

PORT OR SHERRY FLIP

1 egg
½ teaspoon powdered sugar
2 jiggers Port or Sherry
1 jigger brandy

Break egg into shaker glass, add sugar, brandy, wine, and 2 ice cubes. Shake well and strain. Sprinkle top with nutmeg.

RHINE AND SELTZER

Fill glass ½ full with Rhine wine. Add 2 ice cubes. Fill remainder of glass with sparkling water.

WINE COOLER

Add crushed ice to ½ glass of any type dry red or white wine. Decorate with fruit. Serve with straw.

BLACK VELVET

½ Champagne
½ Porter or Stout

Have both Champagne and Porter or Stout well chilled and pour both together into a glass pitcher. Serve in 10-ounce Collins glasses or 4-ounce wine glasses. Tastes so innocent!

CHAMPAGNE CUP

juice of ½ lemon
1 tablespoon powdered sugar
½ cup Curaçao
1 bottle sparkling water
2 4-inch slices cucumber rind
3 pints Champagne, well iced
sliced pineapple
sliced orange
strawberries
mint
ice cubes

Mix thoroughly all ingredients except fruits, mint, and ice cubes. Remove cucumber rind after approximately 15 minutes. Add ice cubes and garnish with fruits and a little mint, which must not be crushed. Serves 8 to 10.

HALLOWEEN CUP

4 quarts Claret
1 cup brandy
juice of 4 lemons
juice of 4 oranges
2 thinly sliced navel oranges
4 cored and baked apples
½ cup sugar
4 quarts sparkling water

Mix and pour over large cake of ice in punch bowl. Add sparkling water just before serving. Serves 50.

RHINE WINE COBBLER

1 tablespoon sugar
½ jigger lemon juice
4 ounces Rhine wine

Mix sugar, lemon juice, and wine in a 10-ounce glass. Stir until sugar is dissolved. Fill glass with crushed ice. Decorate the top with slice of lemon and mint leaves or a green cherry.

PEACH CUP

18 ripe peaches
½ cup sugar
2 bottles very dry white wine
1 bottle Champagne

Peel and halve 10 peaches, cover with sugar and wine, and add 6 peach-pit kernels, which have been blanched and skinned. Wash and wipe 8 perfect peaches, pierce them well with a fork, and add. Chill in refrigerator for at least 3 to 4 hours to allow flavor of pits to become absorbed. Place 1 whole peach in each of 8 high narrow glasses. Pour wine into punch bowl over block of ice and add Champagne just before filling glasses. Serves 8.

SAUTERNE CUP

1 bottle Sauterne
2 tablespoons Curaçao
juice 1 lemon
2 peaches, sliced thin
sugar
1 quart sparkling water

Mix wine, Curaçao, lemon juice, sliced peaches, and sugar to taste and let stand at least 1 hour. When ready to serve add sparkling water and ice. Serves 4 to 6.

VICHY CUP

1 pint Port
1 quart Burgundy
½ pint cherry brandy
½ cup orange juice
2 tablespoons lemon juice
1 slice cucumber
3 quarts sparkling water
sugar

Mix all ingredients except sparkling water and let stand ½ hour. Sweeten to taste, and add sparkling water and ice just before serving. Serves 50.

BRAZILIAN PUNCH

2 cups strong maté infusion
1 cup lemon juice
4 cups orange juice
2 cups brandy
2 quarts Sauterne or Chablis
2 quarts sparkling water
sugar

Make maté infusion by adding 4 tablespoons maté to 2 cups boiling water and allowing to stand 10 minutes. Strain and add all other ingredients except sparkling water. Chill until ready to serve. Pour over block of ice in punch bowl, and add sparkling water and sugar to taste. Serves 50.

CHAMPAGNE JULEP

¼ cup sugar
2 tablespoons boiling water
¼ cup fresh mint leaves, bruised
1 split Champagne, chilled
1 pint chilled sparkling water

Make sirup of sugar and water. Add mint leaves. Fill 10-ounce glasses with finely crushed ice, tightly packed. Add 1 teaspoon mint sirup to each glass. Half fill with champagne and fill up with sparkling water. Stir briskly. Glasses will frost if not held in hand while stirring. Add 1 sprig of mint before serving. Serves 6.

CHAMPAGNE COBBLER

1 bottle Champagne
6 slices lemon
6 slices orange
6 tablespoons sugar

Half fill 6 tumblers with chopped ice. Place a slice of lemon and orange and a tablespoon of sugar in each. Stir thoroughly and fill with Champagne.

Any other light wine may be used in place of Champagne.

KING'S COBBLER

½ ounce dry Sherry
½ ounce brandy
½ ounce applejack
½ ounce Bourbon
1 teaspoon sugar

Mix all ingredients and pour into 10-ounce glass half filled with finely cracked ice. Decorate with ½ slice unpeeled orange, stick of fresh pineapple, and maraschino cherry.

ARTILLERY PUNCH

½ pound sugar
juice 6 lemons
2 tablespoons Angostura bitters
1 quart dry red wine
1 quart Sherry
1 quart Scotch whisky
1 quart brandy
1 quart sparkling water

Mix thoroughly and ice well. Add sparkling water just before serving. Serves 50. This is well named.

CATAWBA PUNCH

1 bottle Catawba
½ bottle Rhine wine
juice of 1 lemon
½ cup fresh or frozen strawberries

Mix, chill, and pour in punch bowl just before serving. Decorate with orange slices. Serves 8.

CHAMPAGNE PUNCH

¼ cup sugar
juice of 2 lemons
1 lemon, sliced very thin
½ orange, sliced very thin
2 slices pineapple, cut in small pieces
2 large bottles Champagne

Dissolve sugar in lemon juice. Add the fruit and pour over a large piece of ice. Just before serving add the Champagne and stir. More Champagne may be added as needed. Serves 8.

CLARET PUNCH

1 bottle Claret
juice of 1 lemon
2 tablespoons sugar
2 tablespoons Maraschino
½ orange, sliced
½ lemon, sliced
1 slice pineapple, cut in small pieces
1 pint sparkling water

Place a large piece of ice in punch bowl. Mix lemon juice, sugar, maraschino, fruit, and Claret together. Pour over ice. Add sparkling water and serve at once. Serves 8.

SAUTERNE PUNCH

1 bottle Sauterne
½ cup Sherry
1 slice pineapple, cut in pieces
1 lemon, sliced
1 pint sparkling water
mint leaves

Mix Sauterne, Sherry, and fruit and chill well. Add sparkling water and serve very cold. Decorate with mint leaves. Serves 8.

BOMBARDIER PUNCH

2 cups double-strength black tea
3 quarts Burgundy or Claret
½ pint dark rum
1 quart Bourbon
½ pint brandy
1 cup Maraschino
juice of 12 lemons
1 tablespoon whole allspice
1 tablespoon whole cloves
sugar

Mix all liquid ingredients and sweeten to taste. Tie spices loosely in small bag and add. Let stand 1 to 3 days. Serve over block of ice. Serves 50.

NEW YEAR'S PUNCH

1 cup triple-strength black tea
4 cups sugar
grated rind 1 orange
grated rind 1 lemon
1 cup Burgundy
¾ cup brandy
¾ cup dark rum
¼ cup Bourbon
juice 4 oranges
juice 4 lemons
2 cups maraschino cherries
1 cup shredded pineapple
1 quart Champagne

Mix all ingredients except Champagne and chill 2 to 3 hours. Add chilled Champagne and 12 ice cubes just before serving. Serves 20.

TEA PUNCH

2 quarts boiling water
6 tablespoons black tea
12 sprigs mint, bruised
grated rind 2 lemons
8 slices cucumber
2 quarts Sauterne or Chablis
½ cup lemon juice
sugar

Add tea, mint, and lemon rind to boiling water and drop in cucumber slices. Let stand 4 minutes, then strain. Pour into punch bowl over large piece of ice, add wine and lemon juice, and sweeten to taste. Serves 30.

DUKE'S BRUNCH

1½ cups heavy cream
1 cup dark rum
1 cup Bourbon
1 cup Sherry
3 eggs, lightly beaten
1 cup sugar
juice of 1 lemon
nutmeg

Mix all together and beat until frothy. Chill several hours in refrigerator. Beat again before serving. Fill 10-ounce glasses with shaved ice, pour mixture over, and sprinkle with nutmeg. Serves 12.

FISHERMAN'S PUNCH

1 quart rye whisky
1 pint sweet Vermouth
1 pint Sherry
½ pint Jamaica rum
½ cup lemon juice
4 teaspoons orange bitters
4 teaspoons grenadine
1 pint sparkling water

Mix all ingredients except sparkling water and place in refrigerator for at least 2 hours, preferably overnight, to ripen. Add sparkling water and ice just before serving.

"Too good for any but fishermen or very honest men." Izaak Walton.

LORD BOTETOURT'S PUNCH

4 bottles Burgundy or Claret
1 bottle brandy
4 bottles sparkling water
3 oranges, peeled and sliced
1 small pineapple, thinly sliced
sugar

Mix wine and brandy, add orange and pineapple slices, and let stand for 30 minutes. Add sugar to taste and sparkling water just before serving. Pour over block of ice in punch bowl. Serves 25.

LEMON SHERRY BOWL

rind of 6 lemons
4 cups water
¼ cup lemon juice
1 cup rum
4 cups Sherry
1 cup brandy
4 cups sugar
2 cups scalded milk

Simmer lemon rind in 1 cup water 30 minutes. Strain, add all other ingredients, and chill for at least 4 hours. Serves 30.

MT. VERNON PUNCH

juice of 6 lemons
juice of 6 oranges
1 bottle Sauterne or Claret
2 ounces apricot or peach brandy
1 pint sparkling water

Strain fruit juices, and mix with wine and brandy. Add sparkling water and ice just before serving. Serves about 10.

JAMAICA PUNCH

2 quarts green tea
3 oranges, unpeeled, sliced very thin
juice of 3 lemons
1 quart Jamaica rum
1 pint brandy
2 quarts Chablis

Have tea boiling, pour over sliced oranges, and allow to stand 1 hour. Add other ingredients and serve with block of ice in bowl. Approximately 5½ quarts.

HALLOWEEN APPLEJACK PUNCH

1 quart applejack
1 quart Sauterne
½ cup pineapple juice
½ cup lemon juice
4 baked apples, cored
sugar or honey to taste

Pour over large piece of ice in punch bowl and serve with apples floating. Best if made several hours ahead and apples, pricked with a fork, allowed to soak up the punch. Serves 20.

MAY WINE BOWL

2 dozen (approximately) sprigs woodruff, fresh or dried
5 bottles very dry white wine
1 quart strawberries, halved
¼ cup sugar

Tie woodruff loosely in muslin bag. Add wine and let stand 1 hour. Remove bag and squeeze well. Add strawberries, which have been soaking in sugar. Chill thoroughly and serve over large block of ice. Approximately 6 quarts.

STRAWBERRY BOWL

1 quart strawberries
2 cups sugar
½ cup water
3 bottles very dry white wine, iced

Put berries in bowl, cover with sugar and water, and stir until well mixed. Cover and put in refrigerator for at least 8 hours. Add well-chilled wine, but no ice, just before serving. Serves 12.

GLUGG (SWEDISH)

1½ cups dry red wine
1 quart brandy
6 whole cloves
3 cardamom seeds
1 2-inch piece stick cinnamon
⅓ cup seeded or seedless raisins
¾ cup sugar
10-12 blanched almonds

Put all ingredients into uncovered saucepan and bring to a boil. Lower heat, ignite, and immediately sprinkle in about ½ teaspoon sugar. Allow to blaze 15 seconds and extinguish with cover. Serve very hot in 2-ounce glasses with a few raisins and almonds in each. Serves 25 to 30.

CHRISTMAS WASSAIL

1 teaspoon ground ginger
½ teaspoon mace or nutmeg
1 teaspoon allspice
2 teaspoons cinnamon
¼ teaspoon ground cloves
¼ cup water
4 bottles dry red or white wine
4 cups sugar
14 eggs, separated
14 baked apples

Stir spices in water, bring to a boil, and simmer ½ minute. Add to wine and heat not quite to simmering; add sugar and stir until dissolved. Beat egg yolks and whites separately. Fold yolks into whites and put in punch bowl. Pour in heated wine and whip until frothy. Float apples, hot from the oven, on top.

MULLED CLARET

¼ cup sugar
½ cup water
grated rind of 2 lemons
4 inches stick cinnamon, broken up
6 whole cloves
2 bottles Claret
4 tablespoons brandy

Simmer sugar, lemon rind, and spices in water 15-20 minutes. Strain, add Claret, and reheat but do not allow to simmer. Add brandy and serve hot. Serves 6 to 8.

SHERRY NOG

1 egg
1 teaspoon powdered sugar
3 jiggers Sherry
2 jiggers cream

Shake well in cocktail shaker. Strain into a 10-ounce goblet.

SPANISH TISANE

(from Gretchen Green—The Whole World & Co.)

Simmer for 1 hour 3 heaping tablespoons of very bitter orange marmalade with 1 sauterne glass of Malaga wine and 4 cups boiling water. The shreds of marmalade should entirely disappear. If too sweet add juice of a lemon or lime. Serve hot in the place of after-dinner coffee.

THE ARCHBISHOP

1 medium-sized orange
24 whole cloves
4 cups Claret
sugar

Stick cloves in orange and bake in a moderate oven (350-375°) until a rich brown. Quarter, remove seeds, and simmer in wine for 15 minutes. Add sugar to taste, strain, and serve hot. Serves 4.

PORT NEGUS

1 cube sugar
lemon
½ cup Port
½ cup boiling water
nutmeg

Rub cube of sugar on lemon until it is well impregnated with the oil. Dissolve in boiling water, add Port, and sprinkle nutmeg on top. Serves 1.

If a quantity is desired, the best grade of lemon extract may be substituted for the lemon-rubbed sugar. For 20 persons use 1 tablespoon lemon extract.

POPE'S POSSET

¾ pound almonds
1 cup water
2 cups Sherry
3 tablespoons sugar

Blanch almonds and crush in a mortar with a little water to prevent the oil from separating. Test between fingers—it must be as smooth as butter. Mix thoroughly with water, bring to a boil, and simmer 2 minutes. In another pan bring the Sherry and sugar just to a boil. Mix with the almond liquid and serve at once. Serves 4.

SACK POSSET

(Credited to Sir Walter Raleigh)

1 cup ale
1 cup Sherry
4 cups boiling milk or cream
½ teaspoon nutmeg
1 cup sugar
2 egg yolks

Heat ale and Sherry to simmering, and add milk or cream, nutmeg and sugar. Simmer very slowly ½ hour. Just before serving, beat in egg yolks. Serve hot. Serves 8.

MULLED WINE

1½ cups boiling water
½ cup sugar (approximately)
rind of ½ lemon, cut up
1 2-inch stick cinnamon
10 cloves
1 quart dry red wine or Port
nutmeg

Simmer all ingredients except wine and nutmeg together for 15 minutes. Heat wine separately not quite to simmering. Strain first mixture, add wine, and serve very hot, flecked with nutmeg. Serves 4 to 6.

HOT PUNCH OR CHILL KILL

½ cup sugar
2 cups boiling water
juice and grated rind of 1 lemon
¼ cup brandy
½ cup rum
1 cup Sherry
¼ cup Stout or Porter

Add ingredients in order, stir until foamy, and serve at once in tumblers. Serves 4.

ICED CHOCOLATE WITH SHERRY

2 squares unsweetened chocolate
¾ cup boiling water
4 tablespoons sugar
¼ teaspoon salt
3 cups milk
¼ cup Sherry

Melt chocolate in double boiler, add boiling water, sugar, and salt, and boil 5 minutes, stirring constantly. Stir in milk and heat thoroughly, add Sherry, and beat 3 minutes. Chill and pour over cracked ice. Serves 4 to 6.

ORANGE LIQUEUR

3 medium-sized oranges
4 cups Sauterne
½ cup brandy
2 cups sugar

Extract juice from oranges, add to wine, brandy, and sugar, and stir until sugar is dissolved. Remove pulp from peels and put them in hot oven (400-450°) for 5 minutes. Cut up and add to sirup in 2-quart fruit jar or similar container. Keep in warm place for a week or 10 days, shaking morning and evening. Strain and bottle. Approximately 6 cups.

CANAPÉ FOUNDATION

Toast squares or rounds of bread in oven until brown and crisp. Dip in Sherry and fry in smoking-hot vegetable shortening. Drain on absorbent paper.

CANAPÉS WITH SHERRY NO. I

¼ cup butter
¼ cup ground Smithfield ham *or* Smithfield ham spread
1 dozen shredded wheat wafers
½ cup Sherry
¼ pound Swiss cheese

Blend ham and butter, spread on wafers, dip quickly in Sherry, top with ⅛-inch slices of cheese cut to fit wafers, and put under broiler until cheese is lightly browned. 12 canapés.

CANAPÉS WITH SHERRY NO. II

1 package cream cheese
2 tablespoons cream
2 tablespoons Sherry
salt
paprika
12 2-inch toast rounds
12 chopped stuffed olives

Cream together cheese, cream, and Sherry; season and spread on toast rounds. Top with chopped olives. Chill very thoroughly. 12 canapés.

MUSHROOM-CUCUMBER CANAPÉS

12 medium-sized mushrooms
¼ cup butter
12 2-inch rounds of bread
12 thin slices of cucumber
3 tablespoons thick sour cream
1 tablespoon Sherry

Take a thin slice from the top of each mushroom cap so they will stand without rolling. Sauté in butter, then sauté bread rounds in same butter. Place cucumber slice and mushroom on each slice of bread and fill with sour cream and Sherry well mixed. 12 canapés.

CRAB MEAT CANAPÉ NO. I

1 can condensed cream of mushroom soup
1 cup cooked crab meat, coarsely cut up
1 tablespoon finely chopped green peppers
1 tablespoon finely chopped pimiento
salt
cayenne
3 tablespoons dry Sherry
3 tablespoons grated cheese, not too sharp
3 tablespoons butter
24 small patty cases

Heat undiluted soup in double boiler. Parboil peppers in boiling water, drain, and add together with pimiento and crab meat. Do not over-season as mushroom soup is apt to be quite salty. Bring to a simmer, add Sherry, and fill patty cases; sprinkle with grated cheese and dot with butter. Brown under boiler. Serves 24.

CRAB MEAT CANAPÉ NO. II

4 tablespoons butter
2½ tablespoons flour
2 tablespoons chopped onion
½ clove garlic, crushed and minced
1 teaspoon sugar
½ cup condensed consommé
4 cups flaked crab meat
½ cup dry white wine
½ cup cream
buttered toast squares
½ cup grated cheese

Simmer onion and garlic gently in 2 tablespoons butter until onion is tender; add flour and mix well. Season, add sugar and consommé, and cook until smooth. Add crab meat, wine, and cream and simmer very slowly, stirring constantly, for 10 minutes. Spread on small squares of buttered toast, sprinkle with grated cheese, dot with rest of butter, and brown under broiler. Serves 20.

CREAM ROQUEFORT CHEESE

2 packages cream cheese
¼ pound Roquefort cheese
2 tablespoons very dry white wine

Beat cream cheese until soft and smooth. Add Roquefort cheese which has been broken into tiny pieces. Add the wine drop by drop. Continue to beat until a rich smooth consistency. This is a delicious spread to use with crackers and serve with wines.

CHEESE SAVORY

½ cup grated Parmesan cheese
½ cup grated American cheese
Sherry
salt
24 rounds toast or sautéed bread

Make a paste of cheeses and Sherry. Season and spread on half of the toast or bread rounds. Cover with rest of rounds and put in hot oven (425-450°) until cheese is melted. 12 canapés.

AVOCADO CANAPÉS

1 cup mashed avocado
1 tablespoon Sherry
1 teaspoon brandy
salt
24 2-inch rounds toast or sautéed bread
paprika

Mash together avocado pulp, Sherry, brandy, and salt. Spread on toast or bread rounds, dust with paprika, and serve very cold. 24 canapés.

MUSHROOM CANAPÉS

12 medium-sized mushrooms
¼ cup butter
12 2-inch rounds of bread
Sherry

Take a thin slice from top of each mushroom cap so they will stand without rolling. Sauté in butter. Sauté bread rounds in same butter. Place mushroom on each slice of bread and fill about ⅔ full of Sherry, which has been heated just to simmering. 12 canapés.

PRUNE APPETIZERS

¼ pound dried prunes
¾ cup Sherry
2-ounce package processed Swiss cheese

Soak prunes in Sherry for 24 hours, adding more wine if necessary (if prunes are very dry more will be absorbed). Remove pits, keeping shape of prunes as far as possible. Stuff with cheese. Serve as an appetizer or with salads or as a garnish for roast veal or ham.

Variations: Stuff with cream cheese, nuts, ham spread, or fresh-grated coconut. Or roll in grated bitter chocolate.

GLOSSARY

Bisque—a cream soup, usually of fish or shellfish; rich ice cream containing nuts, or macaroon or cake crumbs.

Blanch—to pour boiling water over nuts or fruit, then plunging into cold water and slipping off skins.

Beurre Manié—butter and flour kneaded together for thickening sauces and soups.

Croutons—cubes or small pieces of bread, fried or toasted.

Filé—a powder made from sassafras used to thicken as well as to flavor gumbos and similar dishes.

Filet—boneless strip cut from fish or meat.

Fines Herbes—a loosely used term; it may be any combination of the milder herbs.

Glacé de Viande—beef extract.

Julienne—vegetables in thin, matchlike strips.

Marinate—to allow food to remain in a solution containing wine or vinegar or both, usually with water, oil, and seasonings.

Marinade—a liquid used for marinating.

Mirepoix—a mixture of chopped vegetables.

Purée—to press through a sieve or mash to a smooth consistency.

Reduce—to lessen quantity of a liquid by boiling.

Roux—a smooth mixture of starch and fat, cooked or uncooked, used for thickening.

INDEX

A CATALOGUE OF SELECTED DOVER BOOKS IN ALL FIELDS OF INTEREST

A CATALOGUE OF SELECTED DOVER BOOKS IN ALL FIELDS OF INTEREST

AMERICA'S OLD MASTERS, James T. Flexner. Four men emerged unexpectedly from provincial 18th century America to leadership in European art: Benjamin West, J. S. Copley, C. R. Peale, Gilbert Stuart. Brilliant coverage of lives and contributions. Revised, 1967 edition. 69 plates. 365pp. of text.
21806-6 Paperbound $3.00

FIRST FLOWERS OF OUR WILDERNESS: AMERICAN PAINTING, THE COLONIAL PERIOD, James T. Flexner. Painters, and regional painting traditions from earliest Colonial times up to the emergence of Copley, West and Peale Sr., Foster, Gustavus Hesselius, Feke, John Smibert and many anonymous painters in the primitive manner. Engaging presentation, with 162 illustrations. xxii + 368pp.
22180-6 Paperbound $3.50

THE LIGHT OF DISTANT SKIES: AMERICAN PAINTING, 1760-1835, James T. Flexner. The great generation of early American painters goes to Europe to learn and to teach: West, Copley, Gilbert Stuart and others. Allston, Trumbull, Morse; also contemporary American painters—primitives, derivatives, academics—who remained in America. 102 illustrations. xiii + 306pp. 22179-2 Paperbound $3.00

A HISTORY OF THE RISE AND PROGRESS OF THE ARTS OF DESIGN IN THE UNITED STATES, William Dunlap. Much the richest mine of information on early American painters, sculptors, architects, engravers, miniaturists, etc. The only source of information for scores of artists, the major primary source for many others. Unabridged reprint of rare original 1834 edition, with new introduction by James T. Flexner, and 394 new illustrations. Edited by Rita Weiss. 6⅝ x 9⅝.
21695-0, 21696-9, 21697-7 Three volumes, Paperbound $13.50

EPOCHS OF CHINESE AND JAPANESE ART, Ernest F. Fenollosa. From primitive Chinese art to the 20th century, thorough history, explanation of every important art period and form, including Japanese woodcuts; main stress on China and Japan, but Tibet, Korea also included. Still unexcelled for its detailed, rich coverage of cultural background, aesthetic elements, diffusion studies, particularly of the historical period. 2nd, 1913 edition. 242 illustrations. lii + 439pp. of text.
20364-6, 20365-4 Two volumes, Paperbound $6.00

THE GENTLE ART OF MAKING ENEMIES, James A. M. Whistler. Greatest wit of his day deflates Oscar Wilde, Ruskin, Swinburne; strikes back at inane critics, exhibitions, art journalism; aesthetics of impressionist revolution in most striking form. Highly readable classic by great painter. Reproduction of edition designed by Whistler. Introduction by Alfred Werner. xxxvi + 334pp.
21875-9 Paperbound $2.50

VISUAL ILLUSIONS: THEIR CAUSES, CHARACTERISTICS, AND APPLICATIONS, Matthew Luckiesh. Thorough description and discussion of optical illusion, geometric and perspective, particularly; size and shape distortions, illusions of color, of motion; natural illusions; use of illusion in art and magic, industry, etc. Most useful today with op art, also for classical art. Scores of effects illustrated. Introduction by William H. Ittleson. 100 illustrations. xxi + 252pp.
21530-X Paperbound $2.00

A HANDBOOK OF ANATOMY FOR ART STUDENTS, Arthur Thomson. Thorough, virtually exhaustive coverage of skeletal structure, musculature, etc. Full text, supplemented by anatomical diagrams and drawings and by photographs of undraped figures. Unique in its comparison of male and female forms, pointing out differences of contour, texture, form. 211 figures, 40 drawings, 86 photographs. xx + 459pp. 5⅜ x 8⅜. 21163-0 Paperbound $3.50

150 MASTERPIECES OF DRAWING, Selected by Anthony Toney. Full page reproductions of drawings from the early 16th to the end of the 18th century, all beautifully reproduced: Rembrandt, Michelangelo, Dürer, Fragonard, Urs, Graf, Wouwerman, many others. First-rate browsing book, model book for artists. xviii + 150pp. 8⅜ x 11¼. 21032-4 Paperbound $2.50

THE LATER WORK OF AUBREY BEARDSLEY, Aubrey Beardsley. Exotic, erotic, ironic masterpieces in full maturity: Comedy Ballet, Venus and Tannhauser, Pierrot, Lysistrata, Rape of the Lock, Savoy material, Ali Baba, Volpone, etc. This material revolutionized the art world, and is still powerful, fresh, brilliant. With *The Early Work,* all Beardsley's finest work. 174 plates, 2 in color. xiv + 176pp. 8⅛ x 11.
21817-1 Paperbound $3.00

DRAWINGS OF REMBRANDT, Rembrandt van Rijn. Complete reproduction of fabulously rare edition by Lippmann and Hofstede de Groot, completely reedited, updated, improved by Prof. Seymour Slive, Fogg Museum. Portraits, Biblical sketches, landscapes, Oriental types, nudes, episodes from classical mythology—All Rembrandt's fertile genius. Also selection of drawings by his pupils and followers. "Stunning volumes," *Saturday Review.* 550 illustrations. lxxviii + 552pp. 9⅛ x 12¼. 21485-0, 21486-9 Two volumes, Paperbound $10.00

THE DISASTERS OF WAR, Francisco Goya. One of the masterpieces of Western civilization—83 etchings that record Goya's shattering, bitter reaction to the Napoleonic war that swept through Spain after the insurrection of 1808 and to war in general. Reprint of the first edition, with three additional plates from Boston's Museum of Fine Arts. All plates facsimile size. Introduction by Philip Hofer, Fogg Museum. v + 97pp. 9⅜ x 8¼. 21872-4 Paperbound $2.00

GRAPHIC WORKS OF ODILON REDON. Largest collection of Redon's graphic works ever assembled: 172 lithographs, 28 etchings and engravings, 9 drawings. These include some of his most famous works. All the plates from *Odilon Redon: oeuvre graphique complet,* plus additional plates. New introduction and caption translations by Alfred Werner. 209 illustrations. xxvii + 209pp. 9⅛ x 12¼.
21966-8 Paperbound $4.00

DESIGN BY ACCIDENT; A BOOK OF "ACCIDENTAL EFFECTS" FOR ARTISTS AND DESIGNERS, James F. O'Brien. Create your own unique, striking, imaginative effects by "controlled accident" interaction of materials: paints and lacquers, oil and water based paints, splatter, crackling materials, shatter, similar items. Everything you do will be different; first book on this limitless art, so useful to both fine artist and commercial artist. Full instructions. 192 plates showing "accidents," 8 in color. viii + 215pp. 8⅜ x 11¼. 21942-9 Paperbound $3.50

THE BOOK OF SIGNS, Rudolf Koch. Famed German type designer draws 493 beautiful symbols: religious, mystical, alchemical, imperial, property marks, runes, etc. Remarkable fusion of traditional and modern. Good for suggestions of timelessness, smartness, modernity. Text. vi + 104pp. 6⅛ x 9¼.
20162-7 Paperbound $1.25

HISTORY OF INDIAN AND INDONESIAN ART, Ananda K. Coomaraswamy. An unabridged republication of one of the finest books by a great scholar in Eastern art. Rich in descriptive material, history, social backgrounds; Sunga reliefs, Rajput paintings, Gupta temples, Burmese frescoes, textiles, jewelry, sculpture, etc. 400 photos. viii + 423pp. 6⅜ x 9¾. 21436-2 Paperbound $4.00

PRIMITIVE ART, Franz Boas. America's foremost anthropologist surveys textiles, ceramics, woodcarving, basketry, metalwork, etc.; patterns, technology, creation of symbols, style origins. All areas of world, but very full on Northwest Coast Indians. More than 350 illustrations of baskets, boxes, totem poles, weapons, etc. 378 pp.
20025-6 Paperbound $3.00

THE GENTLEMAN AND CABINET MAKER'S DIRECTOR, Thomas Chippendale. Full reprint (third edition, 1762) of most influential furniture book of all time, by master cabinetmaker. 200 plates, illustrating chairs, sofas, mirrors, tables, cabinets, plus 24 photographs of surviving pieces. Biographical introduction by N. Bienenstock. vi + 249pp. 9⅞ x 12¾. 21601-2 Paperbound $4.00

AMERICAN ANTIQUE FURNITURE, Edgar G. Miller, Jr. The basic coverage of all American furniture before 1840. Individual chapters cover type of furniture—clocks, tables, sideboards, etc.—chronologically, with inexhaustible wealth of data. More than 2100 photographs, all identified, commented on. Essential to all early American collectors. Introduction by H. E. Keyes. vi + 1106pp. 7⅞ x 10¾.
21599-7, 21600-4 Two volumes, Paperbound $11.00

PENNSYLVANIA DUTCH AMERICAN FOLK ART, Henry J. Kauffman. 279 photos, 28 drawings of tulipware, Fraktur script, painted tinware, toys, flowered furniture, quilts, samplers, hex signs, house interiors, etc. Full descriptive text. Excellent for tourist, rewarding for designer, collector. Map. 146pp. 7⅞ x 10¾.
21205-X Paperbound $2.50

EARLY NEW ENGLAND GRAVESTONE RUBBINGS, Edmund V. Gillon, Jr. 43 photographs, 226 carefully reproduced rubbings show heavily symbolic, sometimes macabre early gravestones, up to early 19th century. Remarkable early American primitive art, occasionally strikingly beautiful; always powerful. Text. xxvi + 207pp. 8⅜ x 11¼. 21380-3 Paperbound $3.50

ALPHABETS AND ORNAMENTS, Ernst Lehner. Well-known pictorial source for decorative alphabets, script examples, cartouches, frames, decorative title pages, calligraphic initials, borders, similar material. 14th to 19th century, mostly European. Useful in almost any graphic arts designing, varied styles. 750 illustrations. 256pp. 7 x 10. 21905-4 Paperbound $4.00

PAINTING: A CREATIVE APPROACH, Norman Colquhoun. For the beginner simple guide provides an instructive approach to painting: major stumbling blocks for beginner; overcoming them, technical points; paints and pigments; oil painting; watercolor and other media and color. New section on "plastic" paints. Glossary. Formerly *Paint Your Own Pictures*. 221pp. 22000-1 Paperbound $1.75

THE ENJOYMENT AND USE OF COLOR, Walter Sargent. Explanation of the relations between colors themselves and between colors in nature and art, including hundreds of little-known facts about color values, intensities, effects of high and low illumination, complementary colors. Many practical hints for painters, references to great masters. 7 color plates, 29 illustrations. x + 274pp.
20944-X Paperbound $2.75

THE NOTEBOOKS OF LEONARDO DA VINCI, compiled and edited by Jean Paul Richter. 1566 extracts from original manuscripts reveal the full range of Leonardo's versatile genius: all his writings on painting, sculpture, architecture, anatomy, astronomy, geography, topography, physiology, mining, music, etc., in both Italian and English, with 186 plates of manuscript pages and more than 500 additional drawings. Includes studies for the Last Supper, the lost Sforza monument, and other works. Total of xlvii + 866pp. 7⅞ x 10¾.
22572-0, 22573-9 Two volumes, Paperbound $10.00

MONTGOMERY WARD CATALOGUE OF 1895. Tea gowns, yards of flannel and pillow-case lace, stereoscopes, books of gospel hymns, the New Improved Singer Sewing Machine, side saddles, milk skimmers, straight-edged razors, high-button shoes, spittoons, and on and on . . . listing some 25,000 items, practically all illustrated. Essential to the shoppers of the 1890's, it is our truest record of the spirit of the period. Unaltered reprint of Issue No. 57, Spring and Summer 1895. Introduction by Boris Emmet. Innumerable illustrations. xiii + 624pp. 8½ x 11⅝.
22377-9 Paperbound $6.95

THE CRYSTAL PALACE EXHIBITION ILLUSTRATED CATALOGUE (LONDON, 1851). One of the wonders of the modern world—the Crystal Palace Exhibition in which all the nations of the civilized world exhibited their achievements in the arts and sciences—presented in an equally important illustrated catalogue. More than 1700 items pictured with accompanying text—ceramics, textiles, cast-iron work, carpets, pianos, sleds, razors, wall-papers, billiard tables, beehives, silverware and hundreds of other artifacts—represent the focal point of Victorian culture in the Western World. Probably the largest collection of Victorian decorative art ever assembled—indispensable for antiquarians and designers. Unabridged republication of the Art-Journal Catalogue of the Great Exhibition of 1851, with all terminal essays. New introduction by John Gloag, F.S.A. xxxiv + 426pp. 9 x 12.
22503-8 Paperbound $4.50

A HISTORY OF COSTUME, Carl Köhler. Definitive history, based on surviving pieces of clothing primarily, and paintings, statues, etc. secondarily. Highly readable text, supplemented by 594 illustrations of costumes of the ancient Mediterranean peoples, Greece and Rome, the Teutonic prehistoric period; costumes of the Middle Ages, Renaissance, Baroque, 18th and 19th centuries. Clear, measured patterns are provided for many clothing articles. Approach is practical throughout. Enlarged by Emma von Sichart. 464pp. 21030-8 Paperbound $3.50

ORIENTAL RUGS, ANTIQUE AND MODERN, Walter A. Hawley. A complete and authoritative treatise on the Oriental rug—where they are made, by whom and how, designs and symbols, characteristics in detail of the six major groups, how to distinguish them and how to buy them. Detailed technical data is provided on periods, weaves, warps, wefts, textures, sides, ends and knots, although no technical background is required for an understanding. 11 color plates, 80 halftones, 4 maps. vi + 320pp. 6⅛ x 9⅛. 22366-3 Paperbound $5.00

TEN BOOKS ON ARCHITECTURE, Vitruvius. By any standards the most important book on architecture ever written. Early Roman discussion of aesthetics of building, construction methods, orders, sites, and every other aspect of architecture has inspired, instructed architecture for about 2,000 years. Stands behind Palladio, Michelangelo, Bramante, Wren, countless others. Definitive Morris H. Morgan translation. 68 illustrations. xii + 331pp. 20645-9 Paperbound $3.50

THE FOUR BOOKS OF ARCHITECTURE, Andrea Palladio. Translated into every major Western European language in the two centuries following its publication in 1570, this has been one of the most influential books in the history of architecture. Complete reprint of the 1738 Isaac Ware edition. New introduction by Adolf Placzek, Columbia Univ. 216 plates. xxii + 110pp. of text. 9½ x 12¾. 21308-0 Clothbound $10.00

STICKS AND STONES: A STUDY OF AMERICAN ARCHITECTURE AND CIVILIZATION, Lewis Mumford.One of the great classics of American cultural history. American architecture from the medieval-inspired earliest forms to the early 20th century; evolution of structure and style, and reciprocal influences on environment. 21 photographic illustrations. 238pp. 20202-X Paperbound $2.00

THE AMERICAN BUILDER'S COMPANION, Asher Benjamin. The most widely used early 19th century architectural style and source book, for colonial up into Greek Revival periods. Extensive development of geometry of carpentering, construction of sashes, frames, doors, stairs; plans and elevations of domestic and other buildings. Hundreds of thousands of houses were built according to this book, now invaluable to historians, architects, restorers, etc. 1827 edition. 59 plates. 114pp. 7⅞ x 10¾. 22236-5 Paperbound $3.50

DUTCH HOUSES IN THE HUDSON VALLEY BEFORE 1776, Helen Wilkinson Reynolds. The standard survey of the Dutch colonial house and outbuildings, with constructional features, decoration, and local history associated with individual homesteads. Introduction by Franklin D. Roosevelt. Map. 150 illustrations. 469pp. 6⅝ x 9¼. 21469-9 Paperbound $4.00

THE ARCHITECTURE OF COUNTRY HOUSES, Andrew J. Downing. Together with Vaux's *Villas and Cottages* this is the basic book for Hudson River Gothic architecture of the middle Victorian period. Full, sound discussions of general aspects of housing, architecture, style, decoration, furnishing, together with scores of detailed house plans, illustrations of specific buildings, accompanied by full text. Perhaps the most influential single American architectural book. 1850 edition. Introduction by J. Stewart Johnson. 321 figures, 34 architectural designs. xvi + 560pp.
22003-6 Paperbound $4.00

LOST EXAMPLES OF COLONIAL ARCHITECTURE, John Mead Howells. Full-page photographs of buildings that have disappeared or been so altered as to be denatured, including many designed by major early American architects. 245 plates. xvii + 248pp. 7⅞ x 10¾. 21143-6 Paperbound $3.50

DOMESTIC ARCHITECTURE OF THE AMERICAN COLONIES AND OF THE EARLY REPUBLIC, Fiske Kimball. Foremost architect and restorer of Williamsburg and Monticello covers nearly 200 homes between 1620-1825. Architectural details, construction, style features, special fixtures, floor plans, etc. Generally considered finest work in its area. 219 illustrations of houses, doorways, windows, capital mantels. xx + 314pp. 7⅞ x 10¾. 21743-4 Paperbound $4.00

EARLY AMERICAN ROOMS: 1650-1858, edited by Russell Hawes Kettell. Tour of 12 rooms, each representative of a different era in American history and each furnished, decorated, designed and occupied in the style of the era. 72 plans and elevations, 8-page color section, etc., show fabrics, wall papers, arrangements, etc. Full descriptive text. xvii + 200pp. of text. 8⅜ x 11¼.
21633-0 Paperbound $5.00

THE FITZWILLIAM VIRGINAL BOOK, edited by J. Fuller Maitland and W. B. Squire. Full modern printing of famous early 17th-century ms. volume of 300 works by Morley, Byrd, Bull, Gibbons, etc. For piano or other modern keyboard instrument; easy to read format. xxxvi + 938pp. 8⅜ x 11.
21068-5, 21069-3 Two volumes, Paperbound $10.00

KEYBOARD MUSIC, Johann Sebastian Bach. Bach Gesellschaft edition. A rich selection of Bach's masterpieces for the harpsichord: the six English Suites, six French Suites, the six Partitas (Clavierübung part I), the Goldberg Variations (Clavierübung part IV), the fifteen Two-Part Inventions and the fifteen Three-Part Sinfonias. Clearly reproduced on large sheets with ample margins; eminently playable. vi + 312pp. 8⅛ x 11. 22360-4 Paperbound $5.00

THE MUSIC OF BACH: AN INTRODUCTION, Charles Sanford Terry. A fine, nontechnical introduction to Bach's music, both instrumental and vocal. Covers organ music, chamber music, passion music, other types. Analyzes themes, developments, innovations. x + 114pp. 21075-8 Paperbound $1.25

BEETHOVEN AND HIS NINE SYMPHONIES, Sir George Grove. Noted British musicologist provides best history, analysis, commentary on symphonies. Very thorough, rigorously accurate; necessary to both advanced student and amateur music lover. 436 musical passages. vii + 407 pp. 20334-4 Paperbound $2.75

JOHANN SEBASTIAN BACH, Philipp Spitta. One of the great classics of musicology, this definitive analysis of Bach's music (and life) has never been surpassed. Lucid, nontechnical analyses of hundreds of pieces (30 pages devoted to St. Matthew Passion, 26 to B Minor Mass). Also includes major analysis of 18th-century music. 450 musical examples. 40-page musical supplement. Total of xx + 1799pp.
(EUK) 22278-0, 22279-9 Two volumes, Clothbound $17.50

MOZART AND HIS PIANO CONCERTOS, Cuthbert Girdlestone. The only full-length study of an important area of Mozart's creativity. Provides detailed analyses of all 23 concertos, traces inspirational sources. 417 musical examples. Second edition. 509pp.
(USO) 21271-8 Paperbound $3.50

THE PERFECT WAGNERITE: A COMMENTARY ON THE NIBLUNG'S RING, George Bernard Shaw. Brilliant and still relevant criticism in remarkable essays on Wagner's Ring cycle, Shaw's ideas on political and social ideology behind the plots, role of Leitmotifs, vocal requisites, etc. Prefaces. xxi + 136pp.
21707-8 Paperbound $1.50

DON GIOVANNI, W. A. Mozart. Complete libretto, modern English translation; biographies of composer and librettist; accounts of early performances and critical reaction. Lavishly illustrated. All the material you need to understand and appreciate this great work. Dover Opera Guide and Libretto Series; translated and introduced by Ellen Bleiler. 92 illustrations. 209pp.
21134-7 Paperbound $2.00

HIGH FIDELITY SYSTEMS: A LAYMAN'S GUIDE, Roy F. Allison. All the basic information you need for setting up your own audio system: high fidelity and stereo record players, tape records, F.M. Connections, adjusting tone arm, cartridge, checking needle alignment, positioning speakers, phasing speakers, adjusting hums, trouble-shooting, maintenance, and similar topics. Enlarged 1965 edition. More than 50 charts, diagrams, photos. iv + 91pp. 21514-8 Paperbound $1.25

REPRODUCTION OF SOUND, Edgar Villchur. Thorough coverage for laymen of high fidelity systems, reproducing systems in general, needles, amplifiers, preamps, loudspeakers, feedback, explaining physical background. "A rare talent for making technicalities vividly comprehensible," R. Darrell, *High Fidelity.* 69 figures. iv + 92pp.
21515-6 Paperbound $1.25

HEAR ME TALKIN' TO YA: THE STORY OF JAZZ AS TOLD BY THE MEN WHO MADE IT, Nat Shapiro and Nat Hentoff. Louis Armstrong, Fats Waller, Jo Jones, Clarence Williams, Billy Holiday, Duke Ellington, Jelly Roll Morton and dozens of other jazz greats tell how it was in Chicago's South Side, New Orleans, depression Harlem and the modern West Coast as jazz was born and grew. xvi + 429pp.
21726-4 Paperbound $2.50

FABLES OF AESOP, translated by Sir Roger L'Estrange. A reproduction of the very rare 1931 Paris edition; a selection of the most interesting fables, together with 50 imaginative drawings by Alexander Calder. v + 128pp. 6½x9¼.
21780-9 Paperbound $1.50

AGAINST THE GRAIN (A REBOURS), Joris K. Huysmans. Filled with weird images, evidences of a bizarre imagination, exotic experiments with hallucinatory drugs, rich tastes and smells and the diversions of its sybarite hero Duc Jean des Esseintes, this classic novel pushed 19th-century literary decadence to its limits. Full unabridged edition. Do not confuse this with abridged editions generally sold. Introduction by Havelock Ellis. xlix + 206pp. 22190-3 Paperbound $2.00

VARIORUM SHAKESPEARE: HAMLET. Edited by Horace H. Furness; a landmark of American scholarship. Exhaustive footnotes and appendices treat all doubtful words and phrases, as well as suggested critical emendations throughout the play's history. First volume contains editor's own text, collated with all Quartos and Folios. Second volume contains full first Quarto, translations of Shakespeare's sources (Belleforest, and Saxo Grammaticus), Der Bestrafte Brudermord, and many essays on critical and historical points of interest by major authorities of past and present. Includes details of staging and costuming over the years. By far the best edition available for serious students of Shakespeare. Total of xx + 905pp.
21004-9, 21005-7, 2 volumes, Paperbound $7.00

A LIFE OF WILLIAM SHAKESPEARE, Sir Sidney Lee. This is the standard life of Shakespeare, summarizing everything known about Shakespeare and his plays. Incredibly rich in material, broad in coverage, clear and judicious, it has served thousands as the best introduction to Shakespeare. 1931 edition. 9 plates. xxix + 792pp. (USO) 21967-4 Paperbound $3.75

MASTERS OF THE DRAMA, John Gassner. Most comprehensive history of the drama in print, covering every tradition from Greeks to modern Europe and America, including India, Far East, etc. Covers more than 800 dramatists, 2000 plays, with biographical material, plot summaries, theatre history, criticism, etc. "Best of its kind in English," *New Republic*. 77 illustrations. xxii + 890pp.
20100-7 Clothbound $8.50

THE EVOLUTION OF THE ENGLISH LANGUAGE, George McKnight. The growth of English, from the 14th century to the present. Unusual, non-technical account presents basic information in very interesting form: sound shifts, change in grammar and syntax, vocabulary growth, similar topics. Abundantly illustrated with quotations. Formerly *Modern English in the Making*. xii + 590pp.
21932-1 Paperbound $3.50

AN ETYMOLOGICAL DICTIONARY OF MODERN ENGLISH, Ernest Weekley. Fullest, richest work of its sort, by foremost British lexicographer. Detailed word histories, including many colloquial and archaic words; extensive quotations. Do not confuse this with the Concise Etymological Dictionary, which is much abridged. Total of xxvii + 830pp. 6½ x 9¼.
21873-2, 21874-0 Two volumes, Paperbound $6.00

FLATLAND: A ROMANCE OF MANY DIMENSIONS, E. A. Abbott. Classic of science-fiction explores ramifications of life in a two-dimensional world, and what happens when a three-dimensional being intrudes. Amusing reading, but also useful as introduction to thought about hyperspace. Introduction by Banesh Hoffmann. 16 illustrations. xx + 103pp. 20001-9 Paperbound $1.00

POEMS OF ANNE BRADSTREET, edited with an introduction by Robert Hutchinson. A new selection of poems by America's first poet and perhaps the first significant woman poet in the English language. 48 poems display her development in works of considerable variety—love poems, domestic poems, religious meditations, formal elegies, "quaternions," etc. Notes, bibliography. viii + 222pp.
22160-1 Paperbound $2.00

THREE GOTHIC NOVELS: THE CASTLE OF OTRANTO BY HORACE WALPOLE; VATHEK BY WILLIAM BECKFORD; THE VAMPYRE BY JOHN POLIDORI, WITH FRAGMENT OF A NOVEL BY LORD BYRON, edited by E. F. Bleiler. The first Gothic novel, by Walpole; the finest Oriental tale in English, by Beckford; powerful Romantic supernatural story in versions by Polidori and Byron. All extremely important in history of literature; all still exciting, packed with supernatural thrills, ghosts, haunted castles, magic, etc. xl + 291pp.
21232-7 Paperbound $2.50

THE BEST TALES OF HOFFMANN, E. T. A. Hoffmann. 10 of Hoffmann's most important stories, in modern re-editings of standard translations: Nutcracker and the King of Mice, Signor Formica, Automata, The Sandman, Rath Krespel, The Golden Flowerpot, Master Martin the Cooper, The Mines of Falun, The King's Betrothed, A New Year's Eve Adventure. 7 illustrations by Hoffmann. Edited by E. F. Bleiler. xxxix + 419pp. 21793-0 Paperbound $3.00

GHOST AND HORROR STORIES OF AMBROSE BIERCE, Ambrose Bierce. 23 strikingly modern stories of the horrors latent in the human mind: The Eyes of the Panther, The Damned Thing, An Occurrence at Owl Creek Bridge, An Inhabitant of Carcosa, etc., plus the dream-essay, Visions of the Night. Edited by E. F. Bleiler. xxii + 199pp. 20767-6 Paperbound $1.50

BEST GHOST STORIES OF J. S. LEFANU, J. Sheridan LeFanu. Finest stories by Victorian master often considered greatest supernatural writer of all. Carmilla, Green Tea, The Haunted Baronet, The Familiar, and 12 others. Most never before available in the U. S. A. Edited by E. F. Bleiler. 8 illustrations from Victorian publications. xvii + 467pp. 20415-4 Paperbound $3.00

MATHEMATICAL FOUNDATIONS OF INFORMATION THEORY, A. I. Khinchin. Comprehensive introduction to work of Shannon, McMillan, Feinstein and Khinchin, placing these investigations on a rigorous mathematical basis. Covers entropy concept in probability theory, uniqueness theorem, Shannon's inequality, ergodic sources, the E property, martingale concept, noise, Feinstein's fundamental lemma, Shanon's first and second theorems. Translated by R. A. Silverman and M. D. Friedman. iii + 120pp. 60434-9 Paperbound $1.75

SEVEN SCIENCE FICTION NOVELS, H. G. Wells. The standard collection of the great novels. Complete, unabridged. *First Men in the Moon, Island of Dr. Moreau, War of the Worlds, Food of the Gods, Invisible Man, Time Machine, In the Days of the Comet.* Not only science fiction fans, but every educated person owes it to himself to read these novels. 1015pp. 20264-X Clothbound $5.00

LAST AND FIRST MEN AND STAR MAKER, TWO SCIENCE FICTION NOVELS, Olaf Stapledon. Greatest future histories in science fiction. In the first, human intelligence is the "hero," through strange paths of evolution, interplanetary invasions, incredible technologies, near extinctions and reemergences. Star Maker describes the quest of a band of star rovers for intelligence itself, through time and space: weird inhuman civilizations, crustacean minds, symbiotic worlds, etc. Complete, unabridged. v + 438pp. 21962-3 Paperbound $2.50

THREE PROPHETIC NOVELS, H. G. WELLS. Stages of a consistently planned future for mankind. *When the Sleeper Wakes,* and *A Story of the Days to Come,* anticipate *Brave New World* and *1984,* in the 21st Century; *The Time Machine,* only complete version in print, shows farther future and the end of mankind. All show Wells's greatest gifts as storyteller and novelist. Edited by E. F. Bleiler. x + 335pp. (USO) 20605-X Paperbound $2.50

THE DEVIL'S DICTIONARY, Ambrose Bierce. America's own Oscar Wilde—Ambrose Bierce—offers his barbed iconoclastic wisdom in over 1,000 definitions hailed by H. L. Mencken as "some of the most gorgeous witticisms in the English language." 145pp. 20487-1 Paperbound $1.25

MAX AND MORITZ, Wilhelm Busch. Great children's classic, father of comic strip, of two bad boys, Max and Moritz. Also Ker and Plunk (Plisch und Plumm), Cat and Mouse, Deceitful Henry, Ice-Peter, The Boy and the Pipe, and five other pieces. Original German, with English translation. Edited by H. Arthur Klein; translations by various hands and H. Arthur Klein. vi + 216pp.
20181-3 Paperbound $2.00

PIGS IS PIGS AND OTHER FAVORITES, Ellis Parker Butler. The title story is one of the best humor short stories, as Mike Flannery obfuscates biology and English. Also included, That Pup of Murchison's, The Great American Pie Company, and Perkins of Portland. 14 illustrations. v + 109pp. 21532-6 Paperbound $1.25

THE PETERKIN PAPERS, Lucretia P. Hale. It takes genius to be as stupidly mad as the Peterkins, as they decide to become wise, celebrate the "Fourth," keep a cow, and otherwise strain the resources of the Lady from Philadelphia. Basic book of American humor. 153 illustrations. 219pp. 20794-3 Paperbound $1.50

PERRAULT'S FAIRY TALES, translated by A. E. Johnson and S. R. Littlewood, with 34 full-page illustrations by Gustave Doré. All the original Perrault stories—Cinderella, Sleeping Beauty, Bluebeard, Little Red Riding Hood, Puss in Boots, Tom Thumb, etc.—with their witty verse morals and the magnificent illustrations of Doré. One of the five or six great books of European fairy tales. viii + 117pp. 8⅛ x 11. 22311-6 Paperbound $2.00

OLD HUNGARIAN FAIRY TALES, Baroness Orczy. Favorites translated and adapted by author of the *Scarlet Pimpernel.* Eight fairy tales include "The Suitors of Princess Fire-Fly," "The Twin Hunchbacks," "Mr. Cuttlefish's Love Story," and "The Enchanted Cat." This little volume of magic and adventure will captivate children as it has for generations. 90 drawings by Montagu Barstow. 96pp.
(USO) 22293-4 Paperbound $1.95

THE RED FAIRY BOOK, Andrew Lang. Lang's color fairy books have long been children's favorites. This volume includes Rapunzel, Jack and the Bean-stalk and 35 other stories, familiar and unfamiliar. 4 plates, 93 illustrations x + 367pp.
21673-X Paperbound $2.50

THE BLUE FAIRY BOOK, Andrew Lang. Lang's tales come from all countries and all times. Here are 37 tales from Grimm, the Arabian Nights, Greek Mythology, and other fascinating sources. 8 plates, 130 illustrations. xi + 390pp.
21437-0 Paperbound $2.50

HOUSEHOLD STORIES BY THE BROTHERS GRIMM. Classic English-language edition of the well-known tales — Rumpelstiltskin, Snow White, Hansel and Gretel, The Twelve Brothers, Faithful John, Rapunzel, Tom Thumb (52 stories in all). Translated into simple, straightforward English by Lucy Crane. Ornamented with headpieces, vignettes, elaborate decorative initials and a dozen full-page illustrations by Walter Crane. x + 269pp. 21080-4 Paperbound $2.50

THE MERRY ADVENTURES OF ROBIN HOOD, Howard Pyle. The finest modern versions of the traditional ballads and tales about the great English outlaw. Howard Pyle's complete prose version, with every word, every illustration of the first edition. Do not confuse this facsimile of the original (1883) with modern editions that change text or illustrations. 23 plates plus many page decorations. xxii + 296pp.
22043-5 Paperbound $2.50

THE STORY OF KING ARTHUR AND HIS KNIGHTS, Howard Pyle. The finest children's version of the life of King Arthur; brilliantly retold by Pyle, with 48 of his most imaginative illustrations. xviii + 313pp. $6\frac{1}{8}$ x $9\frac{1}{4}$.
21445-1 Paperbound $2.50

THE WONDERFUL WIZARD OF OZ, L. Frank Baum. America's finest children's book in facsimile of first edition with all Denslow illustrations in full color. The edition a child should have. Introduction by Martin Gardner. 23 color plates, scores of drawings. iv + 267pp. 20691-2 Paperbound $2.50

THE MARVELOUS LAND OF OZ, L. Frank Baum. The second Oz book, every bit as imaginative as the Wizard. The hero is a boy named Tip, but the Scarecrow and the Tin Woodman are back, as is the Oz magic. 16 color plates, 120 drawings by John R. Neill. 287pp. 20692-0 Paperbound $2.50

THE MAGICAL MONARCH OF MO, L. Frank Baum. Remarkable adventures in a land even stranger than Oz. The best of Baum's books not in the Oz series. 15 color plates and dozens of drawings by Frank Verbeck. xviii + 237pp.
21892-9 Paperbound $2.25

THE BAD CHILD'S BOOK OF BEASTS, MORE BEASTS FOR WORSE CHILDREN, A MORAL ALPHABET, Hilaire Belloc. Three complete humor classics in one volume. Be kind to the frog, and do not call him names . . . and 28 other whimsical animals. Familiar favorites and some not so well known. Illustrated by Basil Blackwell. 156pp. (USO) 20749-8 Paperbound $1.50

EAST O' THE SUN AND WEST O' THE MOON, George W. Dasent. Considered the best of all translations of these Norwegian folk tales, this collection has been enjoyed by generations of children (and folklorists too). Includes True and Untrue, Why the Sea is Salt, East O' the Sun and West O' the Moon, Why the Bear is Stumpy-Tailed, Boots and the Troll, The Cock and the Hen, Rich Peter the Pedlar, and 52 more. The only edition with all 59 tales. 77 illustrations by Erik Werenskiold and Theodor Kittelsen. xv + 418pp. 22521-6 Paperbound $3.50

GOOPS AND HOW TO BE THEM, Gelett Burgess. Classic of tongue-in-cheek humor, masquerading as etiquette book. 87 verses, twice as many cartoons, show mischievous Goops as they demonstrate to children virtues of table manners, neatness, courtesy, etc. Favorite for generations. viii + 88pp. 6½ x 9¼.
22233-0 Paperbound $1.25

ALICE'S ADVENTURES UNDER GROUND, Lewis Carroll. The first version, quite different from the final *Alice in Wonderland,* printed out by Carroll himself with his own illustrations. Complete facsimile of the "million dollar" manuscript Carroll gave to Alice Liddell in 1864. Introduction by Martin Gardner. viii + 96pp. Title and dedication pages in color. 21482-6 Paperbound $1.25

THE BROWNIES, THEIR BOOK, Palmer Cox. Small as mice, cunning as foxes, exuberant and full of mischief, the Brownies go to the zoo, toy shop, seashore, circus, etc., in 24 verse adventures and 266 illustrations. Long a favorite, since their first appearance in St. Nicholas Magazine. xi + 144pp. 6⅝ x 9¼.
21265-3 Paperbound $1.75

SONGS OF CHILDHOOD, Walter De La Mare. Published (under the pseudonym Walter Ramal) when De La Mare was only 29, this charming collection has long been a favorite children's book. A facsimile of the first edition in paper, the 47 poems capture the simplicity of the nursery rhyme and the ballad, including such lyrics as I Met Eve, Tartary, The Silver Penny. vii + 106pp. 21972-0 Paperbound $1.25

THE COMPLETE NONSENSE OF EDWARD LEAR, Edward Lear. The finest 19th-century humorist-cartoonist in full: all nonsense limericks, zany alphabets, Owl and Pussycat, songs, nonsense botany, and more than 500 illustrations by Lear himself. Edited by Holbrook Jackson. xxix + 287pp. (USO) 20167-8 Paperbound $2.00

BILLY WHISKERS: THE AUTOBIOGRAPHY OF A GOAT, Frances Trego Montgomery. A favorite of children since the early 20th century, here are the escapades of that rambunctious, irresistible and mischievous goat—Billy Whiskers. Much in the spirit of *Peck's Bad Boy,* this is a book that children never tire of reading or hearing. All the original familiar illustrations by W. H. Fry are included: 6 color plates, 18 black and white drawings. 159pp. 22345-0 Paperbound $2.00

MOTHER GOOSE MELODIES. Faithful republication of the fabulously rare Munroe and Francis "copyright 1833" Boston edition—the most important Mother Goose collection, usually referred to as the "original." Familiar rhymes plus many rare ones, with wonderful old woodcut illustrations. Edited by E. F. Bleiler. 128pp. 4½ x 6⅜. 22577-1 Paperbound $1.25

TWO LITTLE SAVAGES; BEING THE ADVENTURES OF TWO BOYS WHO LIVED AS INDIANS AND WHAT THEY LEARNED, Ernest Thompson Seton. Great classic of nature and boyhood provides a vast range of woodlore in most palatable form, a genuinely entertaining story. Two farm boys build a teepee in woods and live in it for a month, working out Indian solutions to living problems, star lore, birds and animals, plants, etc. 293 illustrations. vii + 286pp.
20985-7 Paperbound $2.50

PETER PIPER'S PRACTICAL PRINCIPLES OF PLAIN & PERFECT PRONUNCIATION. Alliterative jingles and tongue-twisters of surprising charm, that made their first appearance in America about 1830. Republished in full with the spirited woodcut illustrations from this earliest American edition. 32pp. 4½ x 6⅜.
22560-7 Paperbound $1.00

SCIENCE EXPERIMENTS AND AMUSEMENTS FOR CHILDREN, Charles Vivian. 73 easy experiments, requiring only materials found at home or easily available, such as candles, coins, steel wool, etc.; illustrate basic phenomena like vacuum, simple chemical reaction, etc. All safe. Modern, well-planned. Formerly *Science Games for Children*. 102 photos, numerous drawings. 96pp. 6⅛ x 9¼.
21856-2 Paperbound $1.25

AN INTRODUCTION TO CHESS MOVES AND TACTICS SIMPLY EXPLAINED, Leonard Barden. Informal intermediate introduction, quite strong in explaining reasons for moves. Covers basic material, tactics, important openings, traps, positional play in middle game, end game. Attempts to isolate patterns and recurrent configurations. Formerly *Chess*. 58 figures. 102pp. (USO) 21210-6 Paperbound $1.25

LASKER'S MANUAL OF CHESS, Dr. Emanuel Lasker. Lasker was not only one of the five great World Champions, he was also one of the ablest expositors, theorists, and analysts. In many ways, his Manual, permeated with his philosophy of battle, filled with keen insights, is one of the greatest works ever written on chess. Filled with analyzed games by the great players. A single-volume library that will profit almost any chess player, beginner or master. 308 diagrams. xli x 349pp.
20640-8 Paperbound $2.75

THE MASTER BOOK OF MATHEMATICAL RECREATIONS, Fred Schuh. In opinion of many the finest work ever prepared on mathematical puzzles, stunts, recreations; exhaustively thorough explanations of mathematics involved, analysis of effects, citation of puzzles and games. Mathematics involved is elementary. Translated by F. Göbel. 194 figures. xxiv + 430pp. 22134-2 Paperbound $3.00

MATHEMATICS, MAGIC AND MYSTERY, Martin Gardner. Puzzle editor for Scientific American explains mathematics behind various mystifying tricks: card tricks, stage "mind reading," coin and match tricks, counting out games, geometric dissections, etc. Probability sets, theory of numbers clearly explained. Also provides more than 400 tricks, guaranteed to work, that you can do. 135 illustrations. xii + 176pp.
20338-2 Paperbound $1.50

CATALOGUE OF DOVER BOOKS

MATHEMATICAL PUZZLES FOR BEGINNERS AND ENTHUSIASTS, [illegible]. 189 puzzles from easy to difficult [illegible] mathematical principles behind the puzzles. 135 illustrations. [illegible] Paperbound [illegible]

PAPER FOLDING FOR BEGINNERS, [illegible] 10 projects [illegible] Paperbound [illegible]

TRICKS AND GAMES ON THE POOL TABLE, [illegible] 19 figures. [illegible] Paperbound [illegible]

HAND SHADOWS [illegible] AMUSING FIGURES [illegible] Paperbound [illegible]

WHITTLING AND WOODCARVING, E. J. Tangerman. [illegible] Paperbound [illegible]

HISTORY OF PHILOSOPHY, [illegible] Europe. [illegible] xviii + 505pp. [illegible] Paperbound [illegible]

YOGA: A SCIENTIFIC EVALUATION, [illegible] Paperbound [illegible]

Prices subject to change without notice.
Available at your book dealer or write for free catalogue to [illegible] Dover Publications, Inc., 180 Varick St., N.Y., N.Y. 10014. [illegible] 150 books each year on science, elementary and advanced mathematics, [illegible] literary history, social sciences and other areas.